Moments to Remember with Peter and Mary

Our Life in Show Business from Vaudeville to Video

**Peter Lind Hayes
and Mary Healy**

VANTAGE PRESS
New York

FIRST EDITION

All rights reserved, including the right of
reproduction in whole or in part in any form.

Copyright © 2004 by Peter Lind Hayes and Mary Healy

Published by Vantage Press, Inc.
419 Park Ave. South, New York, NY 10016

Manufactured in the United States of America
ISBN: 0-533-14922-3

Library of Congress Catalog Card No.: 2004092811

0 9 8 7 6 5 4 3 2 1

Contents

Acknowledgment   v
Preface   vii

One	"I Can't Give You Anything But Love, Baby"	1
Two	"Way Down Yonder in New Orleans"	11
Three	"Charley, My Boy"	27
Four	"Lilac Chiffon"	40
Five	"My Ideal"	52
Six	"California, Here I Come"	68
Seven	"Home Sweet Home"	80
Eight	"Hooray for Hollywood"	91
Nine	"Star Dust"	102
Ten	"Jam Jumpin'"	119
Eleven	"Why Do They Call a Private a Private?"	143
Twelve	"Once in Love with Mary"	165
Thirteen	"Around the World"	188
Fourteen	"There's No Business Like Show Business"	203
Fifteen	"Getting to Know You"	223
Sixteen	"Many Questions Have No Answers"	258
Seventeen	"Moments to Remember"	275

Acknowledgment

Peter and I want to thank Jan Seagrave for her continuous support and encouragement in writing this book.

Preface

Peter and Mary:

Looking back on our life together, it seemed like a kaleidoscope of exciting times in every facet of show business. We were called "stars of stage, screen, radio and television," and we almost always worked together. It was good for our marriage, careers and later, for our family.

We met many talented and fascinating people along the way. Some of them seemed larger than life—actors, singers, writers, composers, artists, presidents. Their talents, their style and the media through which the audience met them contributed to their images. But we were fortunate to know some of them as "real" not "reel" people—the Seven Little Foys, Frank Sinatra, Judy Garland, Lucille Ball and Desi Arnaz, Ronald Reagan, Orson Welles, Cole Porter and so many more.

One of our neighbors, Phyllis McGinley, the Pulitzer Prize winning poet, wrote "On The Fifties" in her book *Times Three:*

A pretty pair I like to praise
Are Peter Lind and Mary Hayes.
Excuse it, please, what I mean really
Is Linda Hayes and Peter Healy.
No, No, I'm coming all unpinned
It's Healy Hayes and Mary Lind.
Or anyhow some close relation.

Mary:

Peter and I first met in his mother's famous Grace Hayes Lodge in North Hollywood in 1939. Peter's mother was a former vaudeville star who had opened a wildly popular saloon where the movie stars all loved to go after work to relax and be entertained. I had just appeared in my first movie, *Second Fiddle,* starring Tyrone Power. I don't remember falling in love with Peter at first sight, but I certainly do remember admiring his comedic and singing talents, perfected over the years on the road with his famous mother. Which takes us back to the beginning of our journey.

Turn on the spotlight and bring up the curtain! We'll share some of our favorite Moments to Remember.

One
"I Can't Give You Anything But Love, Baby"

I can't give you anything but love, baby
That's the only thing I've plenty of, baby.

—*Music by Jimmy McHugh,*
  Lyrics by Dorothy Fields

Peter:

When I first met my mother we were both disappointed.

A beautiful willowy blonde from San Francisco, Grace Hayes sang her heart out nightly for tips in a Chicago saloon called Colosimo's Café. Big Jim Colosimo was the lord of the Chicago underworld. He was shot in a phone booth in 1920 at his club, rumor had it, by his 26-year-old bodyguard Al Capone.

I was born in 1915. My father Joseph Lind was already a semi-invalid, so my mother had to keep singing to pay the bills. Being a woman of action, she bought three tickets for a train trip to a little town in southern Illinois called Cairo, nine miles out of Chicago. She got off only long enough to leave my father and me with his family, then went right back to Colosimo's.

Vaudeville star Grace Hayes, mother of Peter Lind Hayes

Hazy's decision was made—her reasons were her own. She moved in with Dale Winters, who later became Big Jim's wife. Hazy and Dale danced and shilled for the stuttering dancer-comedian J-J-Joe F-F-Frisco, starting the nickels, dimes, and quarters rolling on the dance floor. Maybe you never heard of him, but Frisco was a show business legend. He later played a big part in the story of Hazy's life and in mine.

My father and I took up residence with the Lind family at 409 Eleventh Street. My father was a gambler so no one was surprised when he took the wrong end of a 100-to-1 shot and died on the operating table.

Grace Hayes spent the next two years paying doctor bills and sending money home to take care of "Junior," who had by now developed a terrific crush on his Grandmother Lind and wasn't even grateful to the "nice mother" who kept showering him with glittering toys sent from Marshall Field's. After all, who wanted a big red firetruck when Uncle Charles had just made him a wonderful "king stick" with a real steel point on the end of it!

Hazy at this point in our lives decided that I was not returning the devotion she expected from an only child, so she sent for me. We moved into an apartment on the south side of Chicago we shared with a woman named Emma Epstein and her blind daughter "Pearly." Pearly was very kind to me and we became fast friends. I used to spend hours describing taxicabs, fruit wagons and hauling trucks for her as they rumbled by our apartment window.

Hazy decided that I was a little frail and needed some exercise. One glorious morning, I became the proud possessor of a shiny new tricycle. I vaguely remember skipping lunch that day—riding the tricycle from seven in the morning until six in the evening. It was a tired little boy that climbed the backstairs of that typical Chicago apartment house. I asked Aunt Emma if I could take a nap before dinner. She agreed and I plopped down on the living room couch. I fell into a deep slumber, which was to last three days. When I awoke, I was in Children's Hospital with spinal meningitis and well on my way to becoming a famous case in the hands of Doctor Jampolis and Doctor Apt.

After two days of not responding to treatment, seemingly hopeless, they tried two spinal punctures as a last resort. The nurse reported to my mother that I had died, whereupon Hazy ran hysterically into the chill night air and caught pneumonia.

Now the punch line of this should be "The baby ate the tickets, we're on the wrong train and you're going to make trouble for me!" However, one of these two brilliant doctors decided to use a Pulmotor on me and back to life I came. Hazy recovered, but Junior had to spend a year in the hospital. The only thing I remember about the convalescence was a tremendous affection for a tall Norwegian nurse who won my love by sneaking me a piece of burned toast every so often.

When the day arrived for Hazy to take me home, I cried bitterly and clung to the side of the bed. I would not leave until the nurse promised to visit me twice a week. She promised and I waited every day at the window for two months. She never came and from that day to this I haven't even trusted a male nurse.

Mother and son eventually regained their health, but the combined sicknesses had emptied the family pocketbook, so back to Cairo I went. The plan was a simple one—nine months a year with grandmother for school, and three months a year traveling the vaudeville circuits with my mother.

I was never very pleased with the prospect of joining Hazy for those three months. After all, it was the beginning of the summer and I was going to miss out on all the fun with my school pals. Furthermore, I didn't care for those loud "show people" that my mother associated with and, to top it all, she insisted on dressing me like a sissy.

One year I rebelled so violently that I absolutely refused to leave Cairo without my bulldog "Foy." Grandmother finally consented, so I boarded the train for the long trip to New York City. I was told the dog was in the baggage car and would change trains the same as I would in Chicago. Early the next morning, as the train came to a stop under those big dark sheds in the old Chicago station, I ran eagerly back to the baggage car. "Foy" wasn't there. The baggage man wasn't much interested in my plight, but finally volunteered the information that the dog might be on the next train. That made sense to me so I set up light housekeeping in the waiting room. For a day and a half I met every train that came into that station. At the same time, Hazy was meeting every train that came into New York's Grand Central Station.

Finally, with tears streaming down my face I explained my predicament to a kindly old conductor. He fixed up the ticket situation and I was once more on my way to New York, crying all the way. You see, Grandmother had never fibbed to me before. I was eight years old but even now I remember the slap I got when my mother flew at me in Grand Central Station.

That summer I spent most of my time scribbling letters to a wonderful girl back home. Her name was Ruth Crabtree and she lived directly in back of us. I had plans to marry her and I would have but she ruined it all by hanging silk curtains in our "gang house."

Life is very odd and I grow misty-eyed when suddenly I recall tiny things that meant so much then and so little now. For instance, whatever happened to that plan that my pals and I had to go our separate ways, make our fortunes, return to Cairo on our 25th birthdays and build a mighty castle on the Mississippi. There's a signed document to that effect buried in a cave under the Old Soldiers' Hospital out at the end of Eleventh Street.

When I was visiting my mother in her New York apartment, the first thing she did was junk all the Cairo clothes and put me into my "Little Lord Fauntleroy" suit. However, it did not stop me from my pursuit of coins that had been dropped down subway gratings. I very carefully stuck a piece of chewing gum on the end of a string and fished for my just rewards. This drew a lot of attention from passersby who started dropping coins in the grating to see if I could retrieve them.

By the time I got home, filthy from my "fishing" trip, my mother glared at me and shouted, "Look at you. Dirty hands, dirty face." Grant Clark, a songwriter friend who was visiting, sat down at the piano and composed the traditional song, "Dirty Hands, Dirty Face." Although I was only six or seven years old, Hazy put me in her act and sang the song to me as I stood in the corner of the stage dressed like Jackie Coogan in *The Kid*. Judy Garland sang the song often and Al Jolson sang it in the first all-singing, all-talking motion picture, *The Jazz Singer* in 1927.

During the Twenties, my mother was recording songs that are still around today: "Sunny Side of the Street," "Can't Help Lovin' That Man of Mine," "I Can't Give You Anything But Love, Baby," "Three O'Clock in the Morning." The big recording stars of the day at RCA Victor then were Grace Hayes and Ruth Etting (played by Doris Day in the movie *Love Me or Leave Me*).

Peter Lind Hayes with *Dirty Hands, Dirty Face*

Grace Hayes and young Peter

My life from age 8 to 15 was pretty much the same pattern—the school year with Grandmother Lind and summers traveling the vaudeville circuits with "Grace Hayes, star of stage, screen and radio." Later on when she took me into her act, she changed my name from Joseph Lind to Lind Hayes because some old ladies in her audience thought she was robbing the cradle.

On my tenth birthday, we were on a tour of the state of Texas arranged by our press representative, Lela Rogers, mother of Ginger Rogers. Ginger and her mother helped me celebrate the big day and gave me a pair of custom-made children's cowboy boots (which were unheard of then). I must have made quite a spectacle, strutting up and down the aisle of the train with my pant legs pulled up to show them off. Ginger encouraged me to do the Charleston in the aisle.

By the time I was 15, I had won practically every Charleston contest in Southern Illinois. I was such a sharp young man that I decided to dress the part. The suit I ordered from Sears & Roebuck was typical of the "Harold Teen" era and I was exhilarated when the tailor finished the alterations in time for my annual train trip east.

That particular suit, with its bell-bottom trousers, heavily padded shoulders and belt in the back proved my undoing. Hazy took one look at her only child and in a steel blue voice said, "No more Cairo for you!" Come to think of it, my nasal twang and "Dutch" haircut probably had a little to do with her decision.

I was beginning to feel I needed a more understanding woman in my life. That's what I finally found in my wife, Mary Healy Hayes. We've been married more than 50 years and counting. And my mother said, "It will never last."

I was going to tell you all about "Baby Healy" now, but on second thought, I think I better let her tell you herself. Mary . . .

Two
"Way Down Yonder in New Orleans"

Way down yonder in New Orleans
In the land of dreamy dreams....

—*Words and Music by Henry Creamer and J. Turner Layton*

M:

The person I would spend more than 50 years of my life with was growing up on the Mississippi River, just like I was. I often think God had a plan that Peter and I would meet, because there were several twists of fate that seemed to lead us to each other. Little did I dream when I became Miss New Orleans that my life would be changed forever.

Someone once said that you can't see your destiny on the first step of your journey. My journey began way down yonder in New Orleans. Even though it was many years ago, I can still remember the Gulf Coast, the Mississippi River, the Vieux Carre, magnolia blossoms, night-blooming jasmine, the moss hanging from giant old oak trees. When I close my eyes, I can recall the aroma of crayfish, shrimp, oysters, okra and a great variety of spe-

The Healy children in New Orleans

cial herbs used by Creole cooks. New Orleans, it's not unlike a bouillabaisse—well seasoned with the spice of life.

I loved Mardi Gras time with all kinds of people in costumes coming together to have fun. I remember New Orleans music, especially all that jazz. One of my earliest memories was of Uncle Lloyd handing me what looked like a cigar box with earphones, which he gently placed on my ears. I could hear the one and only Louis Armstrong playing from the Forrest Club, two miles away. He held that high note on his trumpet—wow! The magic of radio brought him to me out of "thin air." That was about 1922. I didn't know it then but music and radio would one day be a big part of my own destiny.

Uncle Lloyd took a special interest in me and my brothers and sister because we were the four little children of his widowed sister Viola. She was only 25 when her husband John died at 27 in the great flu epidemic at the end of World War I. This dreadful disease took millions of lives all over the world with no medication (penicillin) to stop it.

The flu virus was brought back from Europe after the war by returning servicemen. Married men with young children had not been taken into the service but ironically, my father died, just as surely as if he had gone off to war. I was only six months old. I once asked my French grandmother—Ma Mere we called her—if she remembered her son ever actually saying one word about me. She told me that the night he was so sick and dying, my mother was trying to comfort me, but I kept crying. He said, "Viola, can't you keep the baby from crying?" How could she possibly do that?

In my scrapbook, I have a letter he wrote in 1918, the last year of his life. It was to his brother Elmo, handwritten on stationery from his office at a steamship company.

I also have a picture of him as a teenager and a later one as a young husband proudly holding my brother John on his lap. He looked like a very happy and handsome man. I've always had a strong feeling about his presence in my life and I've always missed him.

I went to St. Mary's School in the Irish Channel. I remember there was a little stone grotto next to the church where I visited often. The trickling water echoed in the dark and the rows of lighted candles made the statue of the Virgin Mary flicker and glow. When I would kneel in front of her statue and say, "Our Father, who art in heaven," I would be thinking of my own father in heaven, John Joseph George Healy. Somehow I knew she would tell him what was in my heart and mind.

He was of French and Irish descent. Ma Mere told me his great uncle was George Peter Alexander Healy, who painted portraits of so many U.S. presidents, including the famous one of Lincoln in the White House.

My father's mother lived in the French Quarter near the Cabildo, where family records about ancestors were kept. It was built in 1796 when the Spanish ruled New Orleans. Ma Mere lived in a grand house on Esplanade Avenue near the Vieux Carre. It had beautiful hardwood floors, crystal chandeliers and antique furniture. I used to love to visit my French grandmother. I also loved it when she would come to visit us. When we were sick, she'd sit by our bed and take care of us. She would make delicious flan custard and vanilla wafers that made me feel a lot better.

My mother's maiden name was Viola Armbruster. She was of German and Irish descent and very pretty. Ma Mere told me my mother had the best-looking legs of anybody she ever saw in her life. Though she had chances, my mom never remarried. Only the good Lord knows how she survived and I've no doubt He had a lot to do with it. It was quite miraculous how she made our clothes, fed this little family and sent us through school. There was John, my oldest brother and our protector, then Edward, Viola my sister, and me, Mary. I was the youngest, so they called me "Baby" even long after I stopped being one.

In the schoolyard, my brother John always seemed to be battling his way through recess. To this day, I can't stand fighting. I would always get in the middle and try to stop them. A tow-headed tomboy, I'd get banged up pretty good trying to protect my family.

Mama was eager to fatten up my younger brother Edward. When he wore the knickers of his school uniform, his little legs in the black lisle stockings looked like sticks. My sister Viola was the honor student—she got all A's in her classes, but I could never quite make the grade. There was about a year and a half age difference between each of the Healy children, so we were all very close growing up, despite the skirmishes.

I'd hear Mama getting up at dawn, washing our clothes on a washboard out in a shed behind our house. Then we'd hear the sounds and enjoy the smells from the kitchen that let us know she was fixing our breakfast. She also had to prepare for the night's supper before she left for work. On Tuesday we would have red beans and rice, which I loved. Mama would put them on a low, low gas fire first thing in the morning. They have to cook forever. She'd rush out of the house to catch that eight o'clock Jackson Avenue streetcar. It cost five cents to take her to her job downtown at the New Orleans Public Service, which also happened to run the city's streetcars. The last thing she would say as she sent us off to school was, "Don't forget to turn off the stove when you get home."

That meant at three o'clock I'd better turn those beans off or they'd burn the house down.

I'd eagerly wait for that streetcar to bring her home at five in the evening. She'd prepare supper while giving us each duties to perform. She'd usually send me to the corner store for a bottle of milk for seven cents or a loaf of freshly baked French bread. It smelled mighty good.

Her salary was less than $20 a week and with that, she had to pay the rent, feed us, pay our school tuition and make clothes for us on her sewing machine.

I'm sure she must have found her life overwhelming at times. She was strict with us and ruled with an iron hand and we had great respect for her. (We'd better, or else!) I remember how I loved the times I would be sitting on her lap in that old rocking chair by the wood-burning fireplace. She'd hold me in her arms and sing, "Rock-a-bye Baby." I wonder what she was thinking then. Probably how to pay the rent and that she was missing her husband.

Viola, John, Edward and I learned to be resourceful too. We wanted to earn money to add to the widow's mite. Sometimes I'd go on Saturday morning to the Horseshoe Pickle Works where they gave me a penny or two for each empty bottle I found. I can still hear my little red wagon full of empty pickle jars rattling along the brick sidewalks.

About that time my brother Edward had a successful Liberty Magazine route. He soon moved up in the world and got a job at the Glidden Paint Company so I took over his job and inherited his customers. Liberty Magazine cost a nickel but the customers sometimes gave me a dime tip or a "lagniappe." The word "lagniappe" was frequently used in New Orleans. It means "something beyond what is expected." I remember going to the butcher shop in the market with my mother (a scary place for me) and the butcher, meaning to be kind, giving me a hot dog for lagniappe when my mother purchased meats. But I couldn't appreciate his gift. I was too sick from seeing dead rabbits hanging on a hook!

Another extra source of income was the brown coupons Liberty Magazine gave us as a bonus. We could earn bikes and roller skates by selling more of their magazines. I loved to roller-skate and ride my hard-earned bike. I later skated many times to the public library at Robert E. Lee Circle—around and around that brave general on his marble horse. I rested in the library, my favorite place. Even back then, I was hooked on mysteries. I'd skate back home loaded down with books by S.S. Van Dyne. We all loved to read and Mom was often heard calling to us, late in the night, to turn out the lights! I would beg, "Just let me finish this chapter." There was no television in those days.

The Depression didn't bother me. I remember very well in 1929 when the stock market crashed. The *Times Picayune* reported people were jumping out of windows. I just couldn't figure out why! The paper said it was because they lost all their money but money for me was a nickel for lunch or a dime here and there and that was it.

Our school picnics were the high point. We'd pile into trucks that had been rented for the occasion and, with our lunch in baskets, sing our way to the Audubon Park. One day at a school picnic, the carousel music was playing nearby but I had already spent the allowance Mom had given me and was unhappily walking around a little swimming pool. Looking down to the bottom, I saw something shining and silver. There it was—the coin for another ride on the merry-go-round! I think throughout my life I was always looking for something good and, usually, I found it.

Today they say the world is a "global village." Back during the Twenties my "village" was the Irish Channel of New Orleans. Miegs O. Frost of the *Times Picayune* described it as "that vaguely boundaried section where they've produced fighting men and beautiful women for generations, out of little cottages with scoured white doorsteps that come straight down to the sidewalk; the doorsteps where folks sit in the cool of the evening and chat, neighborly, with the folks next door or the ones who stroll past."

We lived in a little house on Laurel Street near Josephine. It was the center of my universe. On that corner there were two streetlights and after Mom gave us our supper we played games there until it got dark. The streets were dirt roads with very little traffic to disturb our games like "kick the stick." We would gather and sit on the breadbox at the corner grocery store. The Italian family that owned it sold lunch to the children at the nearby school. Mr. Tony and his wife sometimes had me help out when my school friends stormed the place at noon for five-cent sandwiches. A big bottle of Nehi root beer was another five cents. When I helped out at noontime I often got a free lunch, another "lagniappe." On hot nights we'd ride the ice truck for half a block till the ice was placed next to the big breadbox.

The houses on Josephine were fronted with little look-alike wooden steps where we would gather. In one, a scary old lady had a shop with a bell that would ting-a-ling when you entered so she knew she had a customer. She sold very little but she had a box of "penny" chocolate covered candies. Some had white centers and some pink. If you got one with a pink center you won a five-cent candy bar so I used to lean on them a little to see inside. I guess all the children did so that they could win the prize! Our house was next door to an old firehouse that was no longer in operation. The best part about it was the poles! We must have slid down them a thousand times, just like the firemen who answered cries for help so long ago. That was our fun world—near enough to home so we could hear Mama when she called us to get inside and do our homework or go to bed.

Mama saw to it that I sang at the eight o'clock mass every morning in St. Mary's church choir. Mass was in Latin, which was Greek to me! I remember I had a crush on a beautiful blond-haired altar boy named Herbie who sang and looked like an angel. The choir was one of the few places boys and girls in the Catholic schools were brought together and that was on special occasions. Herbie never noticed me, but other people did, which later led to my singing on the radio, then on stage and in the movies. But I'm getting ahead of my story.

There were two churches in the heart of the "Irish Channel." The early German and Irish settlers each built their own, and in the same neighborhood. I don't know why or what happened to the Germans, but they built beautiful churches in those days. Our house was near St. Mary's Church and I could hear the chimes of the church bells as they marked the hour. The chimes were music to my ears—but music that meant it was time for school, or eight o'clock Mass, or sometimes even a funeral. When they rang at seven o'clock in the evening, it was time for "Angelus"—time to get home and make sure my homework was done for the next day. The Pastor was a friend and on occasion I got to visit the priest house next to the church and watch them pull the ropes for the chimes. I even got to hold onto the ropes myself and swing up and down, but not often. St. Mary's Church has been designated a landmark in New Orleans. It's a beautiful work of art.

Our family only had to walk about a block and a half to get to our schools. My sister and I went to St. Mary's School for girls, built in the 1850s. It's now a New Orleans landmark too. My brothers went to St. Alphonsus School for boys. Naturally, we had to wear uniforms—this was traditional for Catholic schools. Girls wore a navy skirt, white midi blouse and black tie. Keeping our blouses washed and ironed in those days before electric irons was another chore for poor overworked Mama. I'd watch till the steam came off the flat-top iron, heated by the gas stove. I liked the smell of steam coming from our starched shirts.

Some people say how stern the nuns in Catholic schools were, but I had the Notre Dame nuns all through grade school and looking back, I think they were dedicated and devoted women. After school, we'd see them walking back to their convent in their black habits. I'm grateful to them for many things, especially the love of reading that they instilled in me.

Oh yes, I used to get poked in the back sometimes if I failed to kneel or stand up straight or didn't do my homework! When we had our scrambles and fusses at home, Mama, almost driven to tears, would say, "I don't know what I'm going to do with you children. If you don't behave yourselves, I'm going to put you in a convent." Now that was supposed to be a threat, but the convent was a lovely place and I thought I wouldn't have minded.

I remember one day at recess, a little girl came up to me and said, "Are you rich?" I thought, "I wonder what that means?" People talk a lot about being rich or poor. I suppose there's something to be said for both. Being poor made me become independent and self-sufficient. I was never afraid to try new things.

The only thing I remember being frightened of was the terrible Gulf of Mexico storms and the threat that the Mississippi River might overflow the levee—or that the levee might even break—and carry us away. When I was home alone, I used to light blessed candles and hide under the bed, as if that would have helped.

I loved to sit on our front steps and watch my brother Ed and his pals tinkering with a homemade auto of some kind, trying to crank it to a start. When it finally went chugging down the dirt street, the whole gang of boys would run after it with great shouts of joy. But it would always sputter and come to a dead stop on the corner of Jackson Avenue. Then the group happily helped Ed push it back to 2123 Laurel Street.

I liked that word *laurel* and I looked it up in the dictionary once. It's not only the leaves they crowned people with in ancient Greece. It's also the honors you win in life—and what you must never be content to rest upon!

Laurel Street was only a few blocks from the Mississippi River banks on Jackson Avenue, where sometimes on Saturday, Uncle Lloyd would take us to catch a ferryboat ride over to Gretna. It cost 10 cents and was a big treat. The ferryboat bell clanged as we took off across the river, with the paddlewheel churning up the muddy, greenish waters of the Mississippi. We'd watch the big sailing ships coming in to port. Many people were loading and unloading boats from all over the world coming and going, sailors in uniforms of foreign countries, happy to be getting leave to visit New Orleans. Only New York City had a bigger port.

Later on, we moved uptown where we were fortunate to live near the Audubon Park, which I believe was built for the World Cotton Exhibition in the late 1800s. It was named for the artist, so well known for his paintings of wildlife, especially birds. The park had elephants, peacocks, zebras and many other exotic animals. The zoo was next to the aquarium, which was near the Mississippi River. We walked to the park for entertainment and when we got tired, my sister Viola and I would sit in the grass and make necklaces out of the clover. Those great old trees draped with hanging moss (they're still standing) shaded us from the humid summer heat. The heavy atmosphere accentuated the variety of scents, from the sweet magnolias to the many different odors from the animals in the zoo.

No, we certainly weren't rich in material wealth, but looking back I still think I had a very rich childhood, with the excitement of living in New Orleans and having the support of a loving family.

My aunts and uncles on both sides of the family seemed to take a special interest in us. We were the four babies of a widowed mother. My mother's brother, Lloyd, the one who let me hear Louis Armstrong on the radio, moved in with us when his wife died of tuberculosis. He also helped Mama pay the rent.

Uncle Lloyd gave me the gift of my first puppy. I'd been bedded with some childhood malady and he presented me with a baby Spitz! I fell in love immediately and named him Lucky. Who could have imagined this little bit of white fluff would become so vicious! Lucky hated the color black, which was the color the priests and nuns always wore back then. Since we lived near the priest house and convent, I chased after that dog so many times, indeed, he was often "lucky" to be alive!

My father's brother Elmo often showed up at Christmas with his arms full of toys and baskets of fruits and candy. He worked at the bank and was a self-taught Sunday painter. Watching my uncle paint—was that the beginning of my own love for art?

One Christmas I was given a big, beautiful doll who sang. It came from the Kingsley House, which did so much for the poor children in our neighborhood. The doll had long blonde hair and a blue dress. She was not the kind of doll you'd love and hug, but remarkable to me because she sang "Mary Had A Little Lamb" in a soft scratchy voice. The sound came from a hole in her back that held a small disk, a record, but I remember that the hole disturbed me.

It was also at the Kingsley House I learned to cook. The baked apple was my first culinary accomplishment. However, while carrying it home for Mama, like Eve in the garden, I was tempted. One little taste, then another. I ended up handing my dear, puzzled mother a few raisins and the core!

On Sundays we'd be bathed, hair washed, rinsed with vinegar and water after a good soaping, dressed in our best, and taken for a ride in the public streetcar to visit relatives after Mass. Four little ones on those trips made quite a handful for Mama—especially since my sister almost always got carsick and had to have the window seat so that she could lean out and not get sick all over us in our Sunday best.

My father's sister Ollie was a tall, handsome woman who lived with her little girl in Ma Mere's great house. Though she never had a sewing lesson, Aunt Ollie somehow became an outstanding clothes designer for the debutantes and the very rich in New Orleans who sought her out when they became the kings and queens of the Mardi Gras balls. They would arrive in their limousines at Ma Mere's house, where Aunt Ollie also had her studio. She often took trips to New York and bought her fabrics and pattern designs straight from Paris. The ladies all came to her because they had to have the best and she was the best. Their photographs often appeared on the society pages of the *Times Picayune,* but they treated my Aunt Ollie with great respect because she was an artist!

Aunt Ollie took a special interest in me because I was the daughter of her baby brother, who died so young. After a long day spent making beautiful clothes for the wealthy ladies, she would take her daughter "Little Ollie" and me for a drive in the city park nearby. I would get to sit on her lap while she let me drive by holding the steering wheel on the road.

It was then that I was becoming aware that people were separated by many differences and into many different classes. Some of my playmates were black children who lived in our neighborhood on Laurel Street. When we rode on the streetcar in those days, they had to ride in the back. I didn't understand why then and I still don't!

When I visited Ma Mere's house, I used to play with Aunt Ollie's daughter "Little Ollie" in her studio. We'd sit for hours on the floor making costumes for our dolls with scraps of material. I remember listening to Aunt Ollie's sewing machine in the background, surrounded by these beautiful fabrics of shining silver and gold, rich velvets, and ermine from Europe. We created costumes with the scraps for our very own little Mardi Gras king and queen dolls.

Over the years, I grew taller, but Little Ollie never did. It was a long time before I understood the medical reasons why, but even as a child I knew the look in my Aunt Ollie's eyes was sadness. She tried desperately to find out everything she could about her little girl and although I was puzzled and a little disturbed, I realized

Aunt Ollie was doing her utmost for Little Ollie. She found that the child had a medical problem that was unknown in New Orleans or anywhere else for that matter. I was too young to know but later realized that she was very involved (which was rare for a woman at that time) in founding the Magnolia School for Retarded Children. Little Ollie became blind, but she outlived her mother by two years, dying at age 70. Aunt Ollie lived to a ripe old age and made her most beautiful "comus" queen's costume for Mardi Gras the year before she died.

Aunt Ollie used to make clothes for me too. I'll always remember a little red velvet jacket with gold buttons she made for me one Christmas. Looking back, I'm sure the clothes Aunt Ollie made were the reason the little girl on the playground thought I was rich. Little did I dream then that I would wear beautiful gowns myself one day, on the stage, in the movies, and on television—gowns created for me by some of the most talented designers in the world, including Jan Louis, Norman Norell, Count Sarmi (Elizabeth Arden), Irene Sharaff, Mainebocher and so many others. So thank you Aunt Ollie for adding to the richness of my childhood and for teaching me respect for the artistry of designing clothes.

Another source of my childhood fantasies was the movies. When I baby-sat for neighbors, I'd earn ten cents! That's how much I needed for the movie at the Happy Hour Theater on nearby Magazine Street. If the movies scared me, I'd put my hands up to my face with my fingers spread so I could still see it, but I'd know it wasn't real.

One of my mother's youngest sisters, Aunt Mary, was married to a German butcher. He had lots of money and my aunt would take me with her to the Orpheum Theater to see a movie and five vaudeville acts. Looking back, I now think my pretty aunt had a crush on the saxophone player in the house band. Now how would a youngster know that?

I believe I saw Grace Hayes perform in vaudeville at the Orpheum Theater. Of course I never dreamed that the beautiful lady in a grand dress was the mother of my future husband, Peter Lind Hayes. She appeared many times on the same bill with Eddie Foy, Sr., and the Seven Little Foys, who played an important role in Peter's childhood.

Three
"Charley, My Boy"

Charley, my boy, oh Charley, my boy
You thrill me, you kill me with shivers of joy

—Words and Music by Gus Kahn and Ted Florito

P:

My mother Hazy had been married for about 10 years to the famous theatrical Foy family. Actually, she was only married to Charlie Foy, but when you marry one Foy, you marry them all. The Foy family's house in New Rochelle, New York, was a sort of halfway house for any actor, punch-drunk prizefighter or midget that happened to be motoring toward Boston. When James Cagney reprised his Oscar-winning role of that Yankee Doodle Dandy George M. Cohan in the film *The Seven Little Foys,* he did it for free in tribute to Eddie Foy, Sr. Cagney was one of the struggling young actors old man Foy had helped.

The nuns that I was involved with back in Cairo, Illinois, were from the order of Notre Dame. (Some of them were hunch-backed.) Sister Roberta was a towering woman (we called her "Big Bertha" behind her back). Sister Alphonso was two inches taller than a midget, but she knew just how to hold your palm back by the fingers while she slit the inside of your hand with the sharp edge of a ruler. I do believe a lot of nuns were frustrated by their calling and many of them regretted having taken up the habit (pun intended).

In retrospect, I feel that Sister Norina had a crush on me. I was cute as hell at 11 and one day she suggested that I accompany her to the attic in search of a long-lost book. We browsed through the cobwebs for a while and when I looked up, she was crying. Actually she was sobbing—and I thought she just had a bad cold! Of course the modern nuns have done away with those habits and hurrah for them. I always thought those heavy dark robes with the rosary dangling from the side were sinister and forbidding. They presented a mystery to me. I often wondered what they were hiding and why.

As an altar boy, I also wondered why the priests consumed so much sacristy wine. I accepted the drinking of the wine with the giving out of Holy Communion, but after Mass, I would see Father Dempsey rush to the cupboard and guzzle what was left of the wine. Celibacy is not all that it's cracked up to be and I have never approved of fooling around with Mother Nature. The human spirit is weak at its best and I never could understand why priests and nuns were deprived of what comes naturally. Perhaps that is why so many members of the cloth are in institutions.

It was decided that I should live in the Foy house and attend Iona Prep. This was all decided against my better judgment. You see, I wanted to go back to Cairo, Illinois, Ruth Crabtree and the nuns who understood me. I had reached the third year of high school by being personable, smiling a lot and never taking a book home at night.

Now the Irish Christian Brothers who taught at Iona were a different set of dudes entirely. Most of them weren't even Irish. As I look back, I think of them as "Hitler's Children." They didn't think I was personable. They hit me with a piece of chalk when I smiled and had never even heard of Ruth Crabtree.

The Foys were a race unto themselves. Eddie Foy and the seven little Foys were immortalized on film by Bob Hope and still the legend goes on. Old Mr. Foy was born Edward Fitzgerald and the mother's name was Morando. This combination gives you the volatile cross breeding of Irish and Italian. Eddie Foy was considered America's greatest comedian in the early 1900s and his fame finally reached its peak when he bravely tried to calm a berserk audience during the tragic fire at the old Iroquois Theater in Chicago. Hundreds of people died and hundreds more would have perished had he not led them over the footlights to the safety of the asbestos curtain.

The Seven Little Foys who helped to raise me were Brynie, Charlie, Dickie, Mary, Madeline, Eddie and Irving.

The fabled house in New Rochelle also had in residence an ancient housekeeper. Old Lady Bradley was quite senile and only left her attic bedroom once a week. I used to check her out occasionally to find out if she was still alive. Mrs. Foy's elder sister, Aunt Clara, a very gaunt and ashen woman, was also seen floating from one room to another.

Aunt Clara's prized possession was a very old and cranky parrot. It seems the parrot had mastered the names of six of the little Foys, but for some reason he would never say "Dickie." Dickie was very sensitive about this but more on that later.

The last, but certainly not the least member of the

menagerie was Richy, the butler. He was a short black man who had fancied himself as a prizefighter. About 20 of his opponents had decided he was not a prizefighter and set about giving Richy an addled brain. He had a way of breathing heavily and jumping at things I never could see.

Sunday was always Richy's big day. When the Foys and Hazy were not on tour, I always looked to Sunday too. It was never lonely, at least 20 or 30 people would show up for a big community Italian dinner. Usually around mid-afternoon Richy would slip upstairs with a .45-caliber pistol and a bottle of ketchup. Suddenly the big house would shudder from the boom of the .45 and we would all rush upstairs to find Richy slumped on the floor with blood (red ketchup) oozing from the side of his head. Some women fainted and others giggled a lot, but then Richy would jump to his feet with his toothless grin. His club date was over for another week.

One evening I returned home quite late from a high school prom. The house was pitch dark except for a light in the kitchen. I heard voices so I tiptoed to the kitchen. Dickie was seated in front of the parrot's cage. He was in his shirtsleeves and the right sleeve had been rolled up past his elbow. The door to the cage was open and Dickie was intensely suggesting that the parrot say "Dickie . . . Dickie . . . Dickie." At this point the parrot would rattle off, "Hello Brynie, hello Eddie, hello Irving, hello Madeline, hello Mary, hello Charlie!" But no Dickie.

Dickie would study the parrot for a moment and then cautiously stick his arm into the cage to fondle the parrot. The parrot wasn't buying this and would simply take another beakful out of Dickie's arm. I gathered by the amount of blood that this had been going on for quite some time. I bandaged Dickie as best I could and led him off to bed. He had been drinking a lot but the last thing he said was, "He won't say Dickie."

After tucking Dickie in, I thought I was bedded down for the night, but around 4:00 A.M., a tremendous row emanated from the kitchen. The parrot was screaming hysterically. Eddie Foy, Jr., and an actor friend, Eddie Pardo, had returned from a big blast of a party in Manhattan. They were hungry and had turned violent when they discovered that the only thing in the icebox was a half can of Pet milk. They had decided to cook the parrot and had it half way to the oven when "Aunt Clara" made her entrance. Eddie Pardo took one look at the tall slender ghost and said, "Let's cook her!"

Aunt Clara finally wrestled her prize possession from the two clowns and the two "birds" flew up the stairs to safety.

Old Man Foy was constantly running afoul of the child labor laws. On one occasion, Irving, age seven, was making an appearance in court to substantiate his claim that Irving had the IQ of a boy twice his age. The judge was a kindly old gentleman who urged Irving not to be frightened during the questioning.

"Now Irving, what is the capital of New York?"

"Albany, your honor."

"And what is the capital of California?"

"Sacramento, your honor."

"What about Illinois?"

"Springfield, your honor."

"What is the capital of North Dakota?"

"I don't know sir, we never played there."

Old Man Foy was proud of his home in New Rochelle and had prevailed upon a very famous English author to motor up-country with him. At that time, Mr. Foy was driving an open Stutz Bearcat. The trip from the Lamb's

Club usually took 45 minutes back then. As George M. Cohan once said, "Forty-five minutes from Broadway."

All was going well and Mr. Foy was explaining the various points of interest to the English author. Finally he turned into the driveway, pulled the Stutz to a stop and said, "Well, this is it!" Unfortunately, the author wasn't in the car. He had fallen out a mile back and didn't show up for more than an hour. When he did show up, a lot of broad "A's" were dropped and the old man agreed to buy him a new suit.

In spite of a comedic appearance and a fine spray that emitted from his mouth every time he spoke, Eddie Foy, Sr. longed to do Shakespeare. He was well-versed in the Bard's immortal words and had committed to memory pages and pages of his favorite speeches. His eyesight and hearing were failing fast, so the kids never had to worry about being caught in their revelry. By the time they heard the Bearcat churning up the gravel driveway, they had plenty of time to douse the lights, jump into bed, pull up the covers and feign sleep. The old man always stormed through the front door cursing at the top of his lungs. He always sensed something was wrong but could never prove it. Nevertheless, he always made a cursory bed check just to be sure.

This particular night he was full of the grape and in no mood to retire. After the bed check, he roared into the master bedroom and removed his clothes down to his long johns. I always thought his long johns would stand in the corner unassisted but I think he fancied them because they looked something like Shakespearean tights, and as I mentioned, he loved Shakespeare.

His bedroom was lined with wall-to-wall mirrors, which he used for rehearsals. Tonight it was going to be

Shakespeare, and Shakespeare it was. "To be or not to be, that is the question. . . ."

Now the question down the hall was, "How long is he going to keep this up?" Charlie was having trouble getting to sleep, so he crept to the bathroom, soaked a large bath towel in ice cold water, stood on a chair, leaned through the transom and hit the "Melancholy Dane" flush in the face with the towel. He barely made it back to bed before the thunder hit the hallway, "Awright you sons-of-bitches, who's the smart-ass, who did that?" No answer was forthcoming so he rumbled around for a while and then went back to the Bard.

"How often would you and I, upon faint primrose bed were wont to lie, emptying our bosoms of their council sweet, there my Lysander and myself were wont to meet. . . ." WHAP! Another cold towel. This time he took the door right off the hinges, frantically turned mattresses upside down, sent midgets, punch-drunk prizefighters and actors scurrying in every direction for safety. Finally he wearied of the task and fell into a deep sleep.

Next morning several of the Little Foys were sipping coffee around the big kitchen table. In spite of a blistering hangover, the old man always made a great pretense at cheerfulness in the morning. He strolled into the kitchen, light and bubbly, and said, "Good morning children. I had the God-damnedest nightmare last night!" Several of the "children" spewed their coffee all over themselves and took turns ducking the old man's wild swings as well as cups and saucers and anything else he could lay a hand to. One by one they made their exits and went into hiding for several days.

Mr. Foy naturally thought of himself as the comedy king of Broadway. It alarmed him one bright sunny day to see "his" street aglow with advertising announcing the arrival of England's greatest comedian, Raymond Hitchcock. He paused momentarily at a window to read a placard extolling the talents of Mr. Hitchcock. After reading the accolade, he turned to a complete stranger.

"You ever see this fellow Hitchcock?"

"Yes I did, and he's magnificent."

"Is he really funny?"

"Oh yes, indeed, he's the funniest man alive."

"Funnier than Eddie Foy?"

"You can't be serious. Foy couldn't carry Mr. Hitchcock's makeup kit."

"That's too bad."

"Oh really, why?"

"I'm Eddie Foy."

"I know you are. I'm Raymond Hitchcock!"

While Brynie was still one of the Seven Little Foys, they did a command performance for President Woodrow Wilson. At the finish of the act, the kids all stood at attention while the old man paraded in front of them and sang "Charley, My Boy." At the end of the song they received an ovation, and suddenly the President stood up in his box. He waved for silence and proceeded to make a speech praising this fine American family. "What a joy to behold the talents molded from the great tradition of the American theater, to think that such a lovely couple could give birth to seven beautiful children and that they too would inherit such wonderful and sparkling talent." In the middle of the speech Brynie turned to Charlie and whispered out of the side of his mouth, "Little does the President know, I've got the clap."

It is true that by the time the five boys had reached the age of reason, they saw no reason why they shouldn't dilly-dally with girls. The Italian side of the Foys controlled their taste buds and in every city the first thing they looked for was the best Italian restaurant. They were lucky in one instance because the restaurant was just down the alley from the stage door.

The five boys patronized the place three nights in a row, which prompted the owner to invite them to have dinner on the house on Friday, their closing night. The old Italian retired to the kitchen to personally supervise their dinner. Suddenly a vision they had not seen before appeared.

The owner's daughter strolled in from the kitchen and she was the most voluptuous teenager you can imagine. She made Dolly Parton look like a boy. They immediately started teasing her and eventually tried to get her dress off. Naturally she began to scream and naturally Daddy came rushing out of the kitchen with a meat ax.

One by one the Foy boys ducked the lethal swing of the ax, and one by one they reached the back door exit and hastily departed. The last one through the door was Charlie and as he sped through the door he looked back and yelled, "Does this kill it for Friday?"

One afternoon at the old Foy house, two famous guests showed up. Gallagher and Sheehan were a very successful Vaudeville team. Later in the afternoon Brynie sat down and in ten minutes wrote their theme song, "Oh! Mr. Gallagher. Oh! Mr. Sheehan."

Incidentally, Brynie was the first to leave the Seven Little Foys. He migrated to Hollywood to investigate the flowering motion picture business and became a "B" producer at Warner Brothers Studios. Things were not going well for the Brothers Warner, and all the brothers took off for New York to raise money for their foundering studio. Before leaving they had given Brynie a check for $2,500 to finish a "short" he was working on.

As soon as they were out of earshot, Brynie forged the

check into $25,000 and made the first all talking movie, *The Lights of New York*, starring Cullen Landis. The year was 1926. When the Warner brothers returned and found out what Brynie had done, they had him arrested and put in jail. The next day they decided to screen the film the son-of-a-bitch had made with the forged check. After screening the film, they took Brynie out of jail and made him the head of the studio. He eventually lost that position to Daryl F. Zanuck, but *The Lights of New York* is in the Smithsonian Institute as the first all-talking motion picture ever made.

Brynie became an independent producer. He conjured up an idea to make a movie about a nudist camp. No self-respecting actor would accept the lead in such a film. Brynie's casting director was a burly man named Red Mecham. Brynie called him in to his office one day and said, "Red, take off your pants!" Red was confused but followed orders.

"Now, take off your underwear!" Red followed orders.

When Brynie saw how well endowed Red was, he shouted, "You've got the lead in *Valley of the Nudes*." If the censors hadn't banned the film, Brynie would have become a billionaire. It packed the West Coast theaters but could never get past the Rockies.

I had been toying with the idea of an act for my mother and myself. I hit Hazy with the idea, and in scanning my record as a scholar, she decided to chance it. I like to think of this as my "bloody" debut or "Who's Afraid of the Big Bad Palace." I was 16 at the time and, after a three-day break-in at the RKO Fordham, I was on the threshold of the ultimate aim of every performer. Egad! The Palace.

When one is fresh out of high school (and I was very fresh at the time), it takes a bit of doing to be impressed.

Peter Lind Hayes and Grace Hayes playing the Palace

Hazy was terribly nervous about my debut and also about my apparent lack of interest. When the spirit moved her, she called me terribly unflattering names that actually reflected on her. But zero hour finally arrived, and there we were, standing in the wings waiting to go on.

The year was 1932 and the act we were to follow was "on" and "killing" the audience. It was a brother and sister comedy team named Fritz and Jean Hubert. Down toward the finish Fritz did a knock-about comedy fall that propelled his body with great speed the full width of the stage. To break his fall he hurled himself headlong into the main curtain.

The stagehands had pushed our piano a little too far downstage, and as Fritz threw himself into the curtain, there was a resounding whack and suddenly a completely unconscious comic crumpled to the floor. Blood started spouting from a deep gash in his forehead. At the first sign of blood, his sister tore off her male wig and frantically screamed, "My brother, my brother, you've killed my brother!"

Stepping gingerly into the spotlight, the stagehands grabbed poor Fritz by the heels and dragged him off stage. At this moment several things started happening. The audience started mumbling and the sister started threatening the theater staff in a high screeching voice. Hazy, anxiously watching from the wings, started parading on the stage in all her grandeur singing the hit song of that year, "Lovable."

The gown she was wearing was a full-length, white organdy appliquéd with forget-me-nots, at least it was until she had paraded across the stage twice. By that time, it had turned blood red to the knees. At long last the audience settled down and decided to watch the rest of our act. By this time we had arrived at my entrance. I was hidden behind a big papier mâché dummy that was meant to represent the spirit of radio. I controlled the operation of the dummy's mouth by means of a sharp cord, which I had wrapped securely around my index finger.

At the finish of the dummy bit, I ran for the first entrance in one, to take my bow. In the excitement I forgot to unwind the sharp cord, so at the end of my slack, it cut my finger to the bone.

My mother had warned me not to be late for my bow, so I removed the cord, doubled up my fist and stuck my injured hand into my coat pocket. By now Hazy was trumpeting a warm introduction of her new partner. (The agent said it would hurt her professionally if she acknowledged that she had a teenage son.) Then she announced that I would do my impression of Cab Calloway.

As I started "trucking" to the microphone—uh huh, more blood, mine!—was splashing happily all over my beautiful white suit from Abercrombie & Fitch.

In spite of all this we were a big hit, and as we stepped down to make a thank you speech, Lynne Cantor, one of my mother's close girlfriends, stood up in that little box at the Palace and with mascara streaming down her face and shrieked, "I knew you'd do it! I knew you'd do it!" and promptly fell out of the box. As they carried her from the theater, we retired to our dressing room and started a partnership that was destined to have many a rough row to hoe.

But meanwhile, way down yonder in New Orleans . . .

Four
"Lilac Chiffon"

The gown I had on it was lilac chiffon
I remember, I remember

—*Music by Bobby Allen,*
 Lyrics by Peter Lind Hayes

M:

Peter had a very theatrical childhood, but in a way, so did I. New Orleans is a very theatrical and musical city, especially during the Carnival season, with so many parades, balls and galas and fantastic costumes.

One of my earliest Mardi Gras memories was of Mama sewing far into the night on our costumes. I always wanted to be a fairy princess or a ballerina. My dress was usually blue tarlatan trimmed with silver stars, with a wand and a mask to match. I recall my brother Edward was a pirate, John was a cowboy and Viola was a gypsy. She was the actress in the family then and her costumes were usually dramatic.

When we were youngsters, the social life in New Orleans was taken very seriously. The well-to-do would give many coming-out parties for the debutante daughters

Mary Healy, the future Miss New Orleans?

and the pace was in high gear by the time the queens were selected to take part in the different parades.

Our family gathered on St. Charles Avenue to review the magical festivities, as so many other families did and still do. The parade route passed St. Charles Avenue and Jackson Avenue, where we did our viewing, and on down past Robert E. Lee Circle, then to the Vieux Carre. There were many vendors with their wagons of hot dogs and bags of warm peanuts, which kept us well occupied while we waited for the parades. Mama tried to keep us together so we would not disappear into the dangerously crowded street. Uncle Lloyd helped out in this task and I recall many times when the parade finally came by our street corner, he would hoist me up on his shoulders.

"Throw me something Mister," I'd call out. The masked men on the floats would reach into their sacks and throw beads to the crowd. There were times when John, Ed, Viola and Baby Healy were dejected because we did not catch a single souvenir—not one. Mama came to the rescue with some trinkets she'd secretly bought at Woolworth's earlier. "Look what I caught," she'd say. Oh, she was a wonderful woman.

On the great day, we would be up early, running around with our costumes and masks in place and trying to have anybody guess who we were. Then we'd run on to other friends or neighbors, all of whom would greet us in the spirit of "Guess who I am?" We loved the mystery of it all.

Then the family would take that long walk—eight blocks—to watch the parade on St. Charles Avenue. By the time the Mardi Gras parade of the King Rex came into sight in the distance, the crowds on either side of the street had closed in so that it would have been impossible for the floats to come by. The path was cleared by very,

very angry-sounding motorcycles and horses with policemen scaring us and forcing us back to the sidewalk.

Then city officials got us settled down for the big event. School bands marched proudly by in bright uniforms, playing their shiny instruments. They followed each other so closely that the fading music of one and the coming music of the next created a cacophony of sounds to accompany the magnificent papier-mâché floats painted in gold and silver leaf and so many colors!

Each of the parades had a theme, often taken from Greek mythology—King Neptune and his sea nymphs, or Bacchus, the god of song, dance and wine. I have been told that the very day after the parades are over, the work begins immediately on the next year's floats.

The King with his court of masked men dressed in colorful costumes waved his wand majestically to the throng. The horse-drawn floats, each more and more dazzling, were lighted by flaming kerosene lamps carried by black men, who marched alongside in rhythm. The black marching hands were the best, because they would improvise music from their heart and the jazz would just flow! That's where jazz came from I guess—people playing the music they felt. I can remember the crowds dancing in the streets with total abandon.

By the time these parades moved on downtown to the French Quarter, widow Healy gathered her clan and took us back to Laurel Street. The winding down of Mardi Gras began. Meantime King Rex, his Queen and court would gather at the convention hall for dining and dancing till midnight when masks were removed. Fat Tuesday was over and Ash Wednesday ushered in the holy season of Lent.

What a thrilling experience it was for me as a teenager to receive an invitation to the balls. It was magic to hear your name called out by a handsome young man wearing white tie and tails. Then his white-gloved hand presented you, wearing your best formal, to the King and his Court of Knights. Some member of the court with costume and mask, who had earlier been tossing gifts to the people from a float, would take you in his arms for a dance. After that, this stranger would present you with a special gift. I wondered who this Knight might be behind the mask. It probably was some old inebriated fellow whom you'd never want to see again but at 16 the mystery of it was very romantic as we danced *At the Mardi Gras,* a lovely old waltz.

I grew up to be a dreamer and a believer in fate. I believe it was preordained for me to be a singer and go to Hollywood. Becoming Miss New Orleans was the first step on my journey.

I sang in church all the time and became well known in the Irish Channel as "the daughter of the Widow Healy," taking part in local events and taking voice lessons from Joseph Schramm's music school. It was very difficult for my mother to pay for them. She must have known how much I loved to sing and she made many sacrifices raising four little children on her limited salary. I'll never know but have often thought that Joseph Schramm gave us special consideration because my mother was a widow earning too little to make ends meet.

Dr. Schramm's pupils would be presented on radio station WWL on Sundays. The program was broadcast from the elegant Roosevelt Hotel, a place that later had a big part in my destiny. The first song I ever sang on the radio—maybe I was 12 or 13—was "East of the Sun, West of the Moon." It was written by Brooks Bowman for a Princeton Triangle Club Production. He was killed in an auto accident soon after, but his song is still being played.

At that time songs were published weekly in the Green Song Book, very popular in my neighborhood. The Green Song Book (all the pages were green) was not more than a few pages with small print that contained just the lyrics, not the music, of the popular songs. We couldn't wait for its arrival in the stores. It cost five cents. Sometimes there was a line missing in the lyrics, but if you liked the song you'd find out what was missing by listening to the radio singers, usually to Ruth Etting, the famous radio and recording star of the Roaring Twenties.

After graduating from St. Mary's School, I then went to a secretarial school on Jackson Avenue. I practiced my shorthand by listening to the radio, jotting down the lyrics of the songs in those neat little Gregg lines and circles—then typing the lyrics by Cole Porter, Irving Berlin, and the other composers of the day. I never dreamed that one day in the not-too-distant future, these and other greats like Jule Styne, Frank Loesser, Kurt Weill, Teddy Wilson, Robert Allen, Noel Coward and Richard Rodgers would play for little-old-me while I sang their songs.

But back in 1935 I needed a job and started pounding the pavement in New Orleans.

"What experience do you have?"

What a silly question. How could I have experience if no one gave me a job? I finally landed a secretarial job in the Lionel Favret Construction office. My salary was about $17.50 per week.

About that time a new beer was being launched at the Jackson Avenue brewery, 4 X Beer. The owner, Mr. Burke, was from the Irish Channel. He and his wife Audrey heard me sing and asked my mother if I could enter the beauty contest for Miss New Orleans at Ponchartrain Beach. It would also promote their new beer! Well, of course, my mother was horrified!

"My daughter in a bathing suit? In front of all those people? *4 X Beer!*"

At that time the decision to appear in public in a bathing suit, to launch a beer at that—was frowned upon and not taken lightly in my family. After all, I was the youngest of the four children Mother had raised all by herself. Mr. Burke kept assuring her that nothing awful would happen to her baby girl and to my surprise, she finally agreed. The next thing was to take me shopping. Audrey Burke of the beer company took me in hand and we went to all the expensive stores on Canal Street to find the "winning" bathing suit. It turned out to be a white silk jersey with a little skirt to please Mama. Audrey added a red, white, and blue sash around my waist to match my hand-painted patriotic sandals. She also thought I should get in better shape and jogged with me daily on the beach. I gained weight, but my trainer lost!

The big event was held at Lake Ponchartrain beach. My mother had made a beautiful lilac chiffon dress for me to wear. I was only 16, so it was somewhat like going to my first prom but in front of 20,000 people! One day my dear husband Peter would write a song about a first prom dress, and name it "Lilac Chiffon."

No formal gown I'll ever own
Compares with the one I hold alone in memory.
It may not have been stylish or smart
Ah, but it won my schoolgirl heart.
Just a dress made by my Mom that I wore to my very
    first prom.
Oh the gown I had on, it was lilac chiffon. I remember, I
    remember.
And the orchid I wore, he pinned on at the door of the
    high school, his and my school.

Then we swept through the crowd on a cloud while the
   orchestra played on and on.
We stayed out past eleven, and I was in heaven
When I wore my lilac chiffon.

There were many pretty girls in the contest, but somehow I won. My old scrapbook, full of scraps of my past, includes telegrams, cards, pressed flowers and newspaper articles about the contest. There are pictures of me sitting at my desk behind a typewriter with a loving-cup trophy. (Years later, my husband said it was "the first thing that turned green in the spring!") Several newspaper articles described me as a bathing beauty, five-feet-four inches, 125 pounds. ("A healthy and rounded figure," they said, which meant chubby? Fat?)

My prize was a trip to Atlantic City and to San Diego. It turned out I was too young to enter the Miss America pageant, but they gave me the trip to San Diego and Los Angeles. Mama took a leave of absence from her job at Public Service and off we went. It was our first trip to California! At the train station when we left for San Diego, there were many well-wishers and friends, old and new, and even a brass band. My arms were full of red roses, the article said, and I was interviewed by the reporters.

Would I try to get into the movies?

"I think I would be scared to death of the movies—not that I wouldn't like it," I answered. "But I'd rather sing over the radio."

As the train pulled away, the crowd began singing to me, "So long, Mary."

"We hope fate is kind to you Mary!" someone called from the crowd.

Fate was kind. Kind enough not to let me be discovered the first time I went to California, when I was only

16. That's what happened to Linda Darnell, the beautiful dark-eyed teenager who shared a train ride with me three years later when we both went for our Hollywood screen tests. But I keep getting ahead of my story. It's easy to do—does anyone remember life in a chronological order?

The articles say I met Cary Grant in California, though believe it or not, I don't remember the details. I do remember sitting next to him many years later on a private jet that was taking Frank Sinatra's party to Caesars Palace in Las Vegas. I fell asleep on Cary Grant's arm and he was charming. Some time later, when I was sure he'd forgotten the event, we met again. He gave me one of those wonderful sophisticated looks and asked, "Been on any planes lately?"

But back to 1935 and my first trip to California. In Hollywood, I met Gail Patrick, who was a Paramount star from Birmingham, Alabama. She was very kind, showing me around the studio. We two Southerners had our picture taken together and I still have it. Ben Piazza, Paramount's talent scout, was also very helpful and wrote several encouraging letters (advising me to lose a few pounds!). Those letters are in my scrapbook too.

I was offered a singing job in a club in California, but I wanted to go home.

I loved my hometown. Besides, I had a couple of boyfriends I missed. It was certainly no letdown to be back in New Orleans. Far from it. Life was very exciting for me then. The 4 X Beer company presented me with a 1935 cream-colored Ford to go tooting around town. I tried to cover the beer sign on the door, but no luck.

Luck was working in my favor, however. I got a secretarial job at Gaumont British Pictures, which meant I had a desk, typewriter and chair in an office that boasted one salesman. He traveled through the Cajun country to book films for $10 (plus $2 for the soundtrack). Can you imagine what an experience it was for those people in the country who spoke almost no English, to see movies from Britain! Stewart Granger was just starting out with his "veddy" British accent, that will give you an idea of how long ago it was, and Jesse Matthews was the big musical comedy star.

What a fortunate teenager I was to see all the "first-run" movies the minute they came to New Orleans absolutely free! My office was in the corner of Twentieth Century-Fox Film Exchange, which was internationally associated with Gaumont British. Their building was in an area of town called film row because it boasted of MGM, Paramount, Universal, and all the well-known film companies that booked the films in the region.

I was still singing on Sunday afternoon on the WWL radio shows broadcasting from the Roosevelt Hotel. Seymour Weiss, who owned the hotel, offered me a job singing in the hotel's famous Fountain Room. It would be hard work to hold two jobs, but it was an offer I couldn't refuse. My sumptuous salaries were $20 a week at the office and $75 a week at the hotel. I worked in the office from 8 in the morning until 4 P.M. Then I walked from work to the Roosevelt, changed into the beautiful evening dresses Mama made for me and sang with the fabulous Fountain Room orchestra from 6 until 9 at night. Sitting at a corner table between sets, I watched all the famous people of New Orleans—the mayor, governor, even Huey Long the "Kingfish," no less. Most of them ended up in jail! When the violinist/orchestra leader Albert Kirsch gave me the nod, I'd walk up to the bandstand, step on the platform with the musicians, take the microphone, and sing my heart out. I loved it.

Politicians weren't the only important people to come

to the Roosevelt Hotel's Fountain Room. One fateful night, Twentieth Century-Fox's number one talent scout, Ivan Kahn, was in the audience.

This was 1938, when David O. Selznick was searching the South for Scarlett O'Hara. Fox was also anxious to build up its "stable of stars" as they put it, and sent Ivan Kahn, a punch-drunk ex-prizefighter and a wonderful man, to several cities in the South, including New Orleans. Whenever the word got around he was coming to town, hopefuls came out of the woodwork. After interviewing 200 prospects, he decided to test four young people. One of them was me—Baby Healy, "Miss New Orleans of 1935." Ivan Kahn heard me sing at the Roosevelt Hotel, then he saw me the next day typing away at the Twentieth Century-Fox office. Coincidence?

If this is all beginning to sound like the plot of a Hollywood musical, maybe it's because Ivan's wife, Jesse Malo, a writer, later turned my real life story into a screenplay for the movie *Star Dust*. I appeared in the movie and sang *Star Dust,* but it starred Linda Darnell—that's Hollywood!

It was a very special moment when we boarded the train for Hollywood, accompanied by yet another brass band playing "When the Saints Go Marching In" and all that jazz. If there's one thing New Orleans has plenty of, it's brass bands. I was wearing a huge corsage of orchids from my chin to my knees, according to the memories of Dorris Bowden, another Hollywood-bound hopeful from the South who would become my lifelong friend.

There was a handsome football star on the train with us, Arvine Henry, who was tall and looked a little too much like Gary Cooper for his own good. It seems I remember his saying something gallant while standing between Dorris and me about never wanting that train ride to end! He wasn't given a contract so I don't know what his final destiny was—but it wasn't Hollywood.

However, the beautiful little girl who got on our train in Texas was destined to become a major star, Linda Darnell, or as we knew her then, Monetta Eloyse Darnell. Dorris thought I was a spectacle getting on the train with my orchids and Dixieland band, but Monetta's entrance was stranger yet. She climbed on the train, wearing her mother's old-fashioned veiled hat, perhaps to look older than her 15 years. (So pretty, I thought, but rather sad.) She got on with her hatchet-faced mother and her pet chicken named Weedie, who later actually lived in Hollywood with Linda and her family.

I've often wondered what dear Ivan thought when our menagerie got off the train, four Hollywood hopefuls: Dorris the student, Arvine the pretty boy, I was still gaining weight, and then came Linda with her mother and her chicken!

On that train ride, Dorris had little time for Linda or me. A petite doll, she was a very serious actress, who had just completed her drama degree at Louisiana State University. She was madly in love with another student and reluctant to leave him. What she didn't know was that she was taking a train ride to her future husband, the brilliant movie screenwriter and producer, Nunnally Johnson. And I was taking a train ride to my future husband too.

Five

"My Ideal"

Will I ever find the girl on my mind
The one who is my ideal?

—*Words by Leo Robin*
 Music by Newell Chase and Richard Whiting

P:

Hazy and I were determined to get work. She decided the first thing we needed was a good pianist. Through a visiting brother-in-law, she finally met one, Newell Chase, who henceforth shall be known as "Noodle Pie."

Noodle Pie had spent two years at Harvard and also wrote the music to the song "My Ideal" with Richard Whiting. After two rehearsals, he took to calling Hazey "Mommy." Hazy was impressed by this tall, handsome "Mommy's" boy, especially the fact that he'd spent two years at "Hahvahd." I was impressed with the knowledge that his nose had been broken in a football game and that after three drinks he had extreme difficulty in breathing. This last bit of information was to give me many a valuable clue in the years to come.

Noodle Pie was a devout alcoholic. His drinking hab-

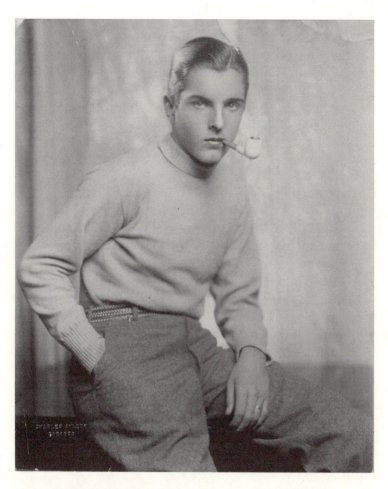

Peter Lind Hayes tries to make it in show business

its were soft-pedaled in the first six or seven months of our association and it was only after Hazy and he were married in a blimp over Las Vegas that he started to drink in earnest.

The most reasonable "good address" we could find was the old Devon Hotel on west 55th Street in the heart of Manhattan. Vaudeville was fading, but live entertainment was making a valiant effort to survive through a new form called "presentation." A presentation meant a big name band appeared in a movie theater with a sprinkling of "name acts" to fill out the bill. We played several movie theaters in and around New York and for a while it looked as though we were on our way to the full life. Noodle Pie was full of life every day by noon and we were finding it almost impossible to get him to stagger to the piano at the right time for five shows a day. He was a composer at heart and resented the low station of being Grace Hayes' pianist.

Hard times were at our door again and so was the manager of the Devon Hotel. He loved us dearly but would we please "pay up or get out by Friday!" Noodle Pie had been missing since early morning so it was no surprise to see him weave past the manager, wild-eyed and breathing heavily through that broken nose. All this we expected, but the shocking thing was his next move. Suddenly, he stood very tall, plunged both hands into the pockets of his camel hair overcoat (the one Hazy had bought him at De Pina's two weeks earlier) and emitted a shrill little "Ah ha!" and threw $1,350 in cash all over the living room floor.

After Hazy had secured the cash, the logical question was answered quite simply. The money was for songs that he had written years before. The amazing thing, of course, was his goodness in bringing it home to mother and son. Hazy decided this stroke of luck was a good omen and she also decided that New Rochelle, New York, would be a wonderful place to spend Christmas. We rented a small, furnished house on Beechmont Place for $90 a month. She also reasoned that Noodle Pie might cut down on his drinking if those Sixth Avenue saloons were not so convenient.

While driving to our new home, we had a lengthy discussion about this in our 1934 Ford sedan. Noodle Pie, suffering from an open-pore hangover, swore off the sauce for the 11th time. This kind of ritual always prompted my mother to stop at the nearest candy store and stock up on rich creamy chocolates. When a man is departing from John Barleycorn, a little sugar goes a long way in staying his thirst. I've seen Noodle Pie eat a whole box of chocolate covered cherries at one sitting. Of course, he always threw up, but that's beside the point.

Hazy always felt guilty that she had allowed me to neglect my education. As a matter of fact, I think she even envied Noodle Pie his two years at Harvard. As we made our first entrance into our new home, she mentioned how nice she thought those birds looked in the two frames hanging over the piano. Noodle Pie, with a fleeting glance said, "Oh yes, Audubon prints!" My mother, with a kindly and patronizing look, turned to me and whispered, "You see?"

That particular Christmas is one I shall long remember. Hazy was behaving like the proverbial mother hen. Here we were in our own little nest and her contented clucking could be heard from every roost in that six-room coop. Noodle Pie and I had our own rooms and Madame Queen had the large bedroom running across the front of the second floor. A bitter cold winter had closed in on us three blithe spirits, but the radiant warmth from within made our frosty window panes sparkle like gems from Cartier.

Hazy, realizing that the kitchen was the nerve center of any happy home, had stuffed the refrigerator with pickles, cole slaw, potato salad and a tremendous variety of cold cuts. Also, for tapering off purposes, there were a half a dozen bottles of beer being chilled to perfection. Noodle Pie was the only heavy drinker I have ever known who was also a glutton. To further show her confidence in Noodle Pie's latest promise, Hazy showed him two gallons of gin, a bottle of scotch and a bottle of bourbon.

"You see, dear. It isn't as though it wasn't here. It *is* here, but we are all grown people. If we would only think in terms of moderation what a happy Christmas we could all have. Besides, if friends drop in, I can fix them a little toddy to help celebrate the holidays!"

My mother always spoke in deathly prose, but Noodle Pie agreed that we were all indeed "grown people" and after carefully noting where the gin was stashed, announced that he was going down to the kitchen to fix a little snack. Mother and son retired to their separate rooms and smiled a Christmas smile as we listened to Noodle Pie humming "Silent Night" while he built his sandwich.

"Silent Night" suddenly came to an abrupt halt with a horrendous crash—apparently Noodle Pie had decided to eat his sandwich in bed and, with a bottle of beer in each pocket of his bathrobe, had obviously opened the wrong door and fallen down the cellar steps. Noodle Pie was a large, heavy man and both bottles exploded under the impact of his weight. When we finally got the lights back on, two bulging, dark and apologetic eyes were peering up at us. All else was foam. He looked like Frosty the Snowman and the above-mentioned pickles, cole slaw, potato salad, salami, chicken and roast beef were splattered all over the basement. We finally reassembled him and after a few harsh words Noodle Pie was put to bed without his supper.

The day before Christmas and all through the house not a creature was stirring, not even our souse. I was the first one to stir and before checking on Hazy, I peeked into Noodle Pie's room. There he was, snoring loudly and propped up almost to a sitting position by four pillows. One of the gallon jugs of gin was half empty and his arm was draped over the nightstand with only the ashes of a completely burned cigarette between his fingers. As I recall this pathetic scene, I utter a silent prayer for the poor soul that was lying there suspended somewhere between heaven and hell. I had grown fond of Noodle Pie. He had a wild sense of humor and a compulsion for forced gaiety. He always laughed a little too loud at simple jokes but his eyes were tightly closed and one could never determine whether he was really laughing or perhaps crying over some ancient wound that hadn't quite healed.

Duty bound, I moved on to my mother's room and awakened her with, "Come see what I've found." Hazy sensed it was Noodle Pie and was up like a shot. I helped her into a checkered flannel robe and stealthily Mother and son tip-toed into Noodle's bedroom.

Hazy studied the situation for a long moment and then suddenly struck Noodle Pie on the side of the face as hard as she could. He awoke with a start, belched once, and through half-closed eyes said, "Now Mommy . . ."

Mommy, in the meantime, had grabbed the half-empty jug of gin and was pouring it all over the top of Noodle Pie's head, "Here, you son-of-a-bitch, if it's gin you want, take it all," she shrieked. By now the gin was cascading down and around that broken nose and believe it or not, Noodle Pie was laughing and actually licking his alcoholic baptismal. When the gin had spent itself, Noodle Pie received the order of the day.

"Get up, change the bed clothing, brush your teeth, get dressed and come down to breakfast!"

Hazy and I descended the stairs to prepare a "sobering" breakfast for our gastronomic, gin-filled gourmet. The pancakes were perfect and the bacon was crisp when she sent me to fetch the naughty boy.

"Noodle Pie!" I bellowed, but there was no answer. Perhaps he's fallen asleep, I figured. But no, his camel hair coat was gone and so was he. Well, there it was Christmas Day, and once again mother and son were faced with a staring contest because once again there was no one else to stare at. We exchanged foolish little presents and sat back trying to figure out where to look for him. His footprints in the snow gave us a clue until they reached the cleared sidewalks and then he was gone.

That December 25th was a long, lonely day, and for that matter so were the 26th and 27th, but on the 28th, the telephone rang and as I turned off a radio version of "The Music Goes Round and Round" my mother picked up the phone. With all the dignity she could muster, she said, "Yes?"

The voice on the other end of the phone was a frantic, small-time agent, eagerly explaining that an act had canceled out at the last moment and, if we were available, we could play three days in Hershey, Scranton and Wilkes-Barre, Pennsylvania. For our trouble we were to receive $1,250 for the nine days.

Would we do it? Why, of course we would do it. The 28th fell on a Friday that year and, if we wanted that money, we had to open on the following Tuesday. My mother grabbed her tweezers and plucked a few stray hairs out of her chin. Presently she turned to me and said, "You've got to go find him!"

"Sure," I said, "Where are the keys?"

Forty-five minutes later I was prowling up Sixth Avenue, "dropping in" on every empty bar between 45th and 57th Streets. The camel hair coat was nowhere in sight. Several bartenders acknowledged that they had seen the "big drunk with the broken nose" but they had no idea where he'd gone after they had thrown him out. At that time Third Avenue still had the El train zigzagging its noisy way up and down the slender island of Manhattan. For some strange reason, the cacophonous sound of steel banging against steel had not thwarted a little cluster of saloons around 56th Street that boasted music as one of their main attractions.

Noodle Pie was never allowed pocket money and, actually, I was completely baffled as to how he got to New York in the first place. But knowing the slyness of a drunk, I deduced that if Sixth Avenue was too rich for his blood, Third Avenue, with its honky-tonks, would be the logical place to run to. I was right. The second saloon I entered was ablaze with frivolity. I stood at the bar just long enough to have a drunk with plaid eyeballs turn to me and whisper secretly: "I told my wife she could keep the Buick and the furniture!" I agreed with him half-heartily and then walked over to collect the only thing that stood between us and $1,250.

Noodle Pie was banging the piano and singing and crying and drinking all at the same time. I got his ear just long enough to explain the job we had been offered and he decided to come with me. We left amid the jeers of a half a dozen Christmas carolers who accused me of being a spoilsport. The drive home was uneventful. He slept and for a change I cried. I was 18 at the time.

When we arrived back at Beechmont Place, there were many more tears. My mother was given to emotional outbursts. First Hazy promised and then he promised. Then she cried and then he cried. Then we all hugged each other and we all cried.

Monday we left for Hershey, Pennsylvania. I'm sure you've heard the expression "bringing coals to Newcastle." Well, here were three nuts going to a chocolate bar. Mr. Hershey is or was a well-known philanthropist. He not only sent all of the children of his employees through school but he built the townspeople a most beautiful theater. For the actors that would grace this theater, he constructed exquisite dressing rooms—a billiard parlor, a private kitchen, a playroom with ping pong tables and a completely furnished gymnasium. Let's face it. Mr. Hershey just didn't know actors.

Within three weeks after he had opened this spectacular contribution to culture, everything from ping pong balls to barbells had been stolen. One thing I have learned about actors: they live for today, they really don't trust tomorrow. If the barbells are here today, take them. You may need them tomorrow.

We arrived in Hershey just in time to inhale the aroma of chocolate cooking and, incidentally, just in time to sweat out a cranky rehearsal with the local conductor who was also the local barber. He conducted with a scratchy fiddle from under a homburg hat. Both the hat and the fiddle needed a shave.

The next night was New Year's Eve and we opened to a gala crowd that had decided to secede from the union. During some of our more delicate humor, chants were heard like "Hershey for President" or "We want Hershey." I decided to quell this unruly mob with a plea to their sensibilities. Through my off stage microphone, I squeaked,

"Ladies and gentlemen, this lady is a star of motion pictures, the legitimate theater and the National Broadcasting Company."

Something I said apparently unhinged the entire mob because, at this point, a man stood up in the balcony and, holding one end of a roll of toilet paper, threw the other end at my mother like a streamer in a ticker tape parade.

I made the fatal mistake of opening my big mouth again and through the microphone I said these immortal words, "Please, ladies and gentlemen, this is America!" Sure it was America and one of my American friends shot my mother in the ass with a staple. This was the crowning insult that even a star of motion pictures, the legitimate theater and the National Broadcasting Company couldn't tolerate, so the curtain was lowered and we slipped silently off into the night. The rest of the engagement was uneventful in Hershey simply because no one came to the theater. Three days later we moved on to Scranton and then to Wilkes-Barre.

Now, unless you're a miner, I don't advise you to play Wilkes-Barre, Pennsylvania. The subtle humor we were so proud of completely eluded each and every resident of Wilkes-Barre, regardless of how powerful the lamp on his mining hat happened to be.

To coin a phrase, "They couldn't see us for coal dust!" Noodle Pie had been strangely silent and abjectly obedient, but the lack of response in Wilkes-Barre was just what he needed for an excuse to jump at the grape again. Hazy had sensed this, so once more he became my roommate. Noodle Pie and I had twin beds. There was a connecting bathroom and Hazy (who needed her rest) was on the other side of the bathroom in a big double bed. This particular night I was trying desperately to sleep but Noodle Pie was badgering me for a loan.

Our conversation was carried on in hushed tones so as not to disturb the boss. He knew that I always had some pinball money hidden away. To get some sleep, I finally dug down deep in my shoe and handed him a five-dollar bill. He blew me a kiss and ran for the elevator. Later that morning I was awakened by the sound of running water.

I vaguely remembered that I had forgotten to close the window, so in a semi-comatose condition I reached over and turned on the bed lamp. As the light shattered the darkness of the room, I saw the reason for the sound of running water. Noodle Pie, camel hair coat and all, was urinating in the center of my bed. I wouldn't say it was deliberate because his eyes were closed and he was humming softly. Nevertheless, I thought this was a hell of a way to repay a friend who had just loaned him five dollars' worth of pinball money. I added a few dirty names and threw the bed lamp at him. The bed lamp made a tremendous noise as it crashed to the floor and suddenly the light went on in the bathroom.

We both turned and there, framed in the bathroom door, was my mother. Her hair was in curlers, she was wearing a long flowing nightgown and her face glistened with an overabundance of white skin lotion. The bathroom bulb, swaying to and fro on its cord, gave her the shimmering appearance of Jacob Marley's ghost. Suddenly, in her best Ethel Barrymore voice, she asked, "What is the meaning of this?"

"Oh, it's nothing," I said. "This jerk was peeing in the middle of my bed." My mother fixed Noodle Pie with her steel blue eyes and, speaking very slowly, she said, "It isn't enough that you shit on me but now you piss on my son!"

With this dramatic summation, she slammed the door and went back to bed. Noodle Pie turned back to me with a bewildered look and at once we were both convulsed with silent laughter.

Next morning we received an offer of one week in St. Louis if we could drive the back-breaking jaunt in time to open the following Tuesday. The money was good enough to convince us that our backs needed breaking. We closed in Wilkes-Barre at eleven that night and drove straight through to St. Louis, stopping only for gas and hamburgers.

St. Louis in the dead of winter is dead enough, but in the year 1934 it became the setting for a scene that would have made Madame X run for cover. Noodle Pie, stiff as a billy goat, was threatening not to play the supper show unless some pocket money was immediately forthcoming. Hazy in the meantime was expounding at great length on the theory that "The show must go on! I'll call the musicians union! You can't do this to me! That's loyalty for you!"

The mention of "loyalty" registered with Noodle Pie and with a slight shove from me the great man finally stumbled to the piano and gave the downbeat for the opening of our act. After a couple of warm-up tunes, my mother gingerly directed the spotlight to the popular young composer at the piano and announced triumphantly that he would now play a medley of his hits. By this time, the popular young composer was breathing heavily and glaring indignantly at the unsuspecting audience. Suddenly, and without warning, he bellowed a "Haw! Haw!" at them, then placed a fixed stare in the general direction of Miss Hayes, encircled his puckered lips with his thumb and index finger and emitted a shrill and soul-shaking razz.

Miss Hayes, severely shaken by this ad-lib, retired to the wings and eagerly awaited the last bow the "popular young composer" would ever take with us. As Noodle Pie stepped from the blinding spotlight into the dark recesses of the velvet curtain, I'm quite sure he never knew what hit him. It seems Hazy had borrowed a stage-brace from an innocent stage hand and anyone will tell you that a stage-brace in the hands of a panic-stricken star of motion pictures, the legitimate theater and the National Broadcasting Company can be a most formidable weapon. She laid him low with one well-placed blow and then went on to improvise the finish of our act.

After the show quite an argument took place regarding an advance in salary as well as a heated discussion about the low punch in the wings. We thought we had escaped our giddy friend. Mother and son were scurrying past the front of the theater just as the audience was wandering aimlessly back into the cold, cold night when several charitable people recognized us and stopped briefly to tell us they had enjoyed the show. They added, "It was gratifying to see mother and son doing so nicely."

And then it happened. A voice rang out on the crisp night air and, as we turned, there was Noodle Pie, stripped from the waist up and looking like a wounded sea lion. He struck a dramatic pose and screamed at the top of his lungs, "Well for Christ's sake, can't Grace Hayes' piano player even have a nickel for a cup of coffee?" Unfortunately, the manager of the theater was standing in the lobby at the time. We were paid off promptly for three days work and canceled.

It was a long difficult drive back to New Rochelle and, needless to say, a sullen atmosphere of hostility prevailed. For three dreary days we sat around that little house on Beechmont Place and listened to the quiet.

Noodle Pie was getting the silent treatment from Madame Queen and he didn't like it. He finally devised an ingenious plan. He started playing the piano on a house-to-house basis. He would shuffle from one house to another, introduce himself as a new neighbor and follow quickly with, "Oh, I see you have a piano." As far as free drinks were concerned, he had it made.

One afternoon while Noodle Pie was out foraging, my mother drove up in front of the house in a brand new 1935 Ford four-door sedan, with, of all things, a trunk trailer hooked on the back. The old Ford was still in the garage so naturally I was completely baffled.

"My God! What have you done?" I asked.

"Shut up," she explained. (We both loved Ring Lardner.)

I was told to pack my trunk, shove it onto the trailer and then do the same with her trunk. Two broken fingernails, seven bruises and a twisted ankle later, I accomplished my mission.

Hazy in the meantime had prepared my reward—a hamburger, baked beans and a Coca-Cola. As I finished my Coke, she placed a steaming cup of black coffee in front of me.

"I don't like coffee," I said.

"Drink it. You'll need it. We're driving to California tonight."

"But what about the other car?"

"He can have it," she said. "It's the only thing I'm leaving him outside of another month's rent that we've already paid."

At this point, "him" staggered through the front door and wanted to know who owned the new car and trailer in front of our house. Once again my mother's sense of drama flew out of bounds. She arched her back and with eyes blazing hissed, "How long do you think I'd put up with a drunken bum like you? My son and I are motoring to California tonight."

Now, the secret word in that speech is "motoring." One just doesn't "motor" in a 1935 Ford sedan with a trailer on the back. Noodle Pie knew this and started to laugh. The more he laughed the more strident my mother's voice became. The little house was fairly rocking with harsh insults and hysterical laughter. Just about the time my mother was running out of invectives, Noodle Pie developed the hiccups. This gave Hazy the opportunity to be heard . . . while he held his breath, she threw a $20 bill at him and said, "Here, that's all you're worth."

This "coup de grace" set him off in another paroxysm of hysteria and with his laughter ringing in our ears, mother and son dashed for the 1935 Ford with the trailer on the back to start our "motor" trip west.

When my mother said we were driving to California that night, I had no idea she meant to drive straight through, but that's what she meant. As we gassed up and asked for road maps, she explained that we could not afford to stop on the way. Furthermore, the most important thing was to get to California as quickly and as cheaply as possible.

Eventually my mother and Noodle Pie were divorced. I was always curious about what happened to our Amadeus. I did a little research and found that after the divorce, Noodle Pie had married a Russian ballerina. He could play the piano, but he sure couldn't dance. They found him in a drunken stupor in a gutter on Eighth Avenue. He died in Bellevue Hospital.

How similar his death was to America's great composer, Stephen Foster. Foster also was found in a gutter on Eighth Avenue and he too died in Bellevue Hospital. When they found Foster, he had thirty-five cents in his pocket and a scribbled title, "Dear Hearts and Gentle People." Victor Herbert and Jerome Kern were having dinner at Luchow's in the village. When they heard the tragic news, they put their heads together and started to form ASCAP (American Society of Composers, Authors and Publishers), an organization to protect derelict writers.

Six
"California, Here I Come"

California, here I come
Right back where I started from

—*Words and Music by Al Jolson, B.G. De Sylva,*
 Joseph Meyer

P:

As we drove to Hollywood, I was treated to a lengthy lecture on the evils of alcohol. The only things that punctuated these tirades were occasional stops for gas or hamburgers and coffee to keep "Junior" awake. About midnight Hazy fell into a tearful sleep and, to ward off the boredom of following that damn white line in the center of the road I began to think about my childhood in Cairo, Illinois.

I had been exposed to demon alcohol long before I met Noodle Pie. Grandmother Lind was always in a panic about Grandfather's drinking. I think women are so frightened of men drinking because alcohol strips a man of his innate inhibitions. It also gives him enough phony courage to face life in general and level with himself in particular. A female has a strong advantage over a sober male, but the moment a male distorts the "mother image" with alcohol, the advantage disappears and so does the female.

Grandfather Lind would be case in point. Monday through Friday he was the calmest, most reserved man you could hope to meet. But let me tell you about Saturday. "Poppa" was not my Poppa. (He was actually my grandfather, but everyone in the household at 409 Eleventh Street called him "Poppa" so I just naturally followed suit.)

Poppa was the type of German that had two faces—one on the back of his neck. He was very proud of his Kaiser mustache and was obsessed with the idea that he could whip Jack Dempsey. He was devoted to his eldest son, my Uncle Harry. Harry was the breadwinner of the family and Poppa loved bread, especially dunked in gravy. Every Saturday Uncle Harry would give Poppa $3 and Poppa would trip the light fantastic to Pope's barroom to play cards.

As he staggered from Pope's, the kids in Cairo, Illinois, would take up the chant, "Mr. Lind's drunk again!" This meant only one thing. Poppa methodically converted his winnings into pennies and, to the delighted squeals of the children, would march boldly through Eighth Street tossing pennies to the eager small fry.

At about 6 P.M. he would arrive home for a session with his favorite radio show. A man from the south named W. K. Henderson was waging a relentless battle against the evils of the monopolistic characteristics of the Great Atlantic and Pacific Tea Company. Poppa agreed with him entirely and would sit with his ear cupped quietly for an hour—occasionally he would strike the radio with his fist to try to make it louder. Poppa was deaf.

At 7 P.M. he would eat dinner with the rest of the family, borrow another $3 from Uncle Harry and, with a mumbled promise to "come home early," stalk off toward a frivolous Saturday night. I could never figure out how a man could get so drunk on $3, but around midnight the Cairo police would pull up in front of our house and dump "Mr. Lind" in the front yard.

The front of our house was identical to the house next door which belonged to a childless couple named Mr. and Mrs. Whipple. For some strange reason Poppa invariably mounted the wrong steps and after a brief but rowdy discussion with poor Mr. Whipple would literally throw him off his own front porch with the admonition to "get out and stay out of my house!"

At this point Grandmother and I would usually go down, help Mr. Whipple to his feet and plead with Poppa to come to "our house." This took quite a bit of doing, but eventually Poppa would follow us.

Upon reaching the familiar surroundings of his own living room, he would immediately start to destroy every piece of furniture that would break. Grandmother and I then would retire to the cellar steps and hide. We would wait there until Uncle Charles would come home from the Bell Telephone dance. Uncle Charles was Poppa's youngest son and consequently was outweighed in the tussle that followed. He usually sparred around a bit, anxiously awaiting the arrival of Uncle Albert.

Between Charles and Albert they could often trip the old man and hold him down merely by sitting on the upper and lower parts of his powerful body. At this point Grandmother and I would emerge from the cellar and, while she chided him vocally, I would beat the bottoms of his shoes with my drumsticks. This comic charade always lasted until the welcome footsteps of Uncle Harry resounded on the front stairs.

At this point the entire action stopped as though we were posing for a tintype. The front door would open, Uncle Harry would wipe off his glasses, clear his throat and say, "Poppa, go to bed!" Albert and Charles would promptly get off of Poppa. Grandmother would stop talking. I would stop hitting his feet. And Poppa would struggle to an upright position, curse a little and go up to bed.

This was indeed a strange pattern, but it happened almost every Saturday night for 14 years. Even Mr. and Mrs. Whipple didn't seem to mind!

Look homeward angel in your flight. By now we were about 400 miles west of Chicago and outside of stopping a number of times for gas and hamburgers, there was little or no communication between Hazy and me. She wept and slept and I drove and drove and remembered my father's family.

I mentioned Uncle Albert as one of the participants in the weekly struggles to tame Poppa. After my father's death, Albert became second in command, being the third oldest son. He always resented the "Big brother stuff" from Uncle Harry, but as he was happily married, he played his part rather stoically. At least he did until one tragic afternoon in the latter part of the year 1925.

Uncle Albert was nervously pacing the floor at 409 Eleventh Street and complaining bitterly to Grandmother that Dr. Madra had no right to go off to St. Louis for the World Series. Albert's wife, Ruth, had given birth to twins two days before and one had been born with a twisted foot. Dr. Madra had said he was sorry but assured everyone that in time the foot could be healed. He also predicted that Ruth would recover rapidly and, so saying, he boarded the Illinois Central for St. Louis and the World Series.

Uncle Albert was 37, and I was 10. He was the most

intense man I've ever known. His hair was jet black and always too short. There was usually an inch and a half of wrinkled skin between the tips of his ears and the beginning of his straight black hair. His eyes were dark brown and separated only by the narrow bridge of his long hooked nose, which sort of pointed at a chin that just wasn't. His mouth was small and tight and even a broad smile revealed only two very large front teeth. The rest of his body was slender except for a little pot belly, which made his trousers grip him around the waist as though they would never let go.

Grandmother was asking Albert to "sit a spell" and "stop fussing." Like Dr. Madra had said, Ruth would recover rapidly. Ruth was not recovering, though, and Albert had just returned from St. Mary's Hospital after a gloomy discussion with a nun. The nun had asked him not to disturb his wife for another day or so.

At this point, the telephone rang and Grandmother answered it. She spoke softly for a moment, returned to the parlor, looked at Albert and said, "Ruth died 10 minutes ago!"

Albert lurched forward in his chair, emitted a heartbreaking scream and, with tears streaming down his face, threw open the front door, stumbled and fell down the porch steps, struggled to his feet and ran 16 blocks to St. Mary's.

He arrived just as a male nurse was placing Ruth's body in a basket. The sight of her tiny gray face renewed his madness and, with another tortured scream, he punched and kicked the male nurse to the floor, grabbed Ruth's body from the basket and disappeared through the back entrance of the hospital.

When they found him, he was sitting in the middle of the streetcar tracks on Walnut Avenue. He had apparently fallen with Ruth's body and was now holding her in his lap. He was rocking to and fro and repeating over and over again, "There, there, honey, everything will be all right." Several children were standing around pointing and giggling when the ambulance drove up and took them both away.

Uncle Albert was much too sick to attend Ruth's funeral and all he kept saying was, "Dr. Madra said she would be all right."

Days went by and suddenly an ominous calm settled upon Albert. He spoke little and ate less. Ruth's mother was caring for the twins, which he had not seen since their birth. He gave up his scrap iron business and spent most of his time hanging around the Illinois Central Railroad yard on Eighth Street. He explained to Grandmother that he liked to watch the Ohio River, which ran parallel to the I.C. tracks. He said it was peaceful there and he wanted to be peaceful.

It finally happened. Grandmother was called to the telephone. There had been an accident. Albert had been struck by a train. Well not exactly struck.

Tiny Watson, the fellow who ran the Blue Front Restaurant, had seen the whole thing. He thought that Albert had "sorta walked right into that train." Anyway, the belt on Albert's overcoat had caught on to something protruding from the coal car of a switch engine. The engine was only going about 15 miles an hour and Albert had been dragged 200 to 300 yards. Charlie Seifert, the yard boss, was relaying all of this to Grandmother. He didn't think Albert had been hurt much but as a precaution they had taken him to St. Mary's.

Uncle Charles borrowed the Elk's Cleaning and Dyeing Co.'s delivery truck and drove Grandmother and me to the hospital. Albert was conscious and seemed in pretty good shape, except for a few cuts and bruises.

Dr. Brewer was attending him and explaining that his injuries were superficial and that he should be out of the hospital in two or three days. Albert looked at the doctor for a long time, and then suddenly he smiled, "No, doctor, you're wrong," he said. "In two or three days I will die."

Dr. Brewer laughed and, with an aimless gesture of his hands, said, "Albert, it isn't that easy. There has to be something wrong with you to die." But in two or three days Uncle Albert did die—deliberately!

Oh yes, a social note from the *Cairo Evening Citizen:* "Dr. Thomas Madra returned from St. Louis last week and said it sure had been a wonderful series."

After Albert's death a whale of a court battle was in the offing. Ruth's parents had already taken their daughter, Mary Ann. Grandmother Lind was determined to keep the twins and Ruth's parents, (the Tholmans) were just as determined to capture the two boys. Uncle Harry was still a bachelor and in no mood to add two more mouths to feed to that already crowded house at 409 Eleventh Street.

At Grandmother's insistence he had half-heartedly hired a lawyer, and the trial made the front page of the *Cairo Evening Citizen* for many weeks to come.

Hazy was appearing in St. Louis in a vaudeville theater and, upon hearing news of the lawsuit, had decided to drive down to Cairo as a character witness for Grandmother Lind. Cairo had never seen a convertible Packard with six wire wheels and Cairo had never seen the "willowy blond" who was driving it. There was, however, a sign in the front yard of a boarding house on Eleventh Street which stated, "We Do Not Lease Rooms to Theatricals." She parked the Packard in front of the old courthouse and paraded up the steps, dragging her furs behind her.

Her scene in the witness chair would have sent shivers up and down Ethel Barrymore's spine. She wailed and whispered, shouted and laughed and wept, seemingly all at the same time. At the end of her performance, the attorney simply inquired, "What is your profession Madam?"

When Hazy answered, "I am an actress!" the lawyer smirked in the direction of the judge and said, "That is all your honor." This little innuendo enraged my mother. As she left the stand, she shouted, "You son-of-a-bitch, your fly is open!"

Cairo had never seen a drama like this, and as Hazy stepped back into her six wire wheels, one old codger sitting on the steps turned from his whittling long enough to spit out a mouthful of tobacco juice and comment, "Piss-pot millionaire!"

The Linds lost the case and I think Uncle Harry heaved a sigh of relief. Uncle Harry was in a sense the comptroller of 409 Eleventh Street. It was natural that his every wish was Grandmother Lind's desire. Our local newspaper, The *Cairo Evening Citizen,* was taboo, until after Uncle Harry had perused the stock market report carefully and fallen asleep gently humming the song "Marguita" in the key of R. As soon as he emitted the first snore, I knew it was safe to remove the second half of the *Citizen* from his forehead and squat Japanese-style on the living room floor to catch up with some serious reading—important things like "Andy Gump," "Gasoline Alley," "Out Our Way," "Who Tied the Can on the Old Dog's Tail?," "Toonerville Trolley" and the further adventures of that timid soul, "Caspar Milquetoast."

Uncle Harry actually resembled Caspar Milquetoast physically, but there the resemblance ended. Because he was the second oldest son, he had dutifully taken on the role of breadwinner after my father's death. Grandmother Lind adored Harry. He was the only one "forgiven" for occasionally missing Mass on Sunday. After all, "he worked so hard and the good Lord was never one to damn the dutiful."

Uncle Harry was always served first, always given the preferred cut of meat, the choice dessert and always left the table first, leaving the rest of us to watch Poppa spear the bread with the fork, wallow it around in the gravy and slop it into his walrus mouth.

Uncle Harry was an enigma to me. He apparently was a long-suffering silent man. Yet when he would speak, I can remember a wry sense of humor and a tremendous accuracy, whether the subject was money, marbles or chalk.

He was definitely the subtle leader of the "in" group in Cairo, Illinois, and the older members of the Elks Club were often heard quoting Harry's dry observations. He admired Will Rogers warmly and might have conceded Rogers' wit to be superior to his own—on occasion.

Harry derived most of his income from a big soybean and cotton warehouse in Mound City, Illinois. Uncle Charles and I used to work there on Saturdays checking out empty freight cars. The big thrill to me, of course, was not only the adventurous 15-mile drive to Mound City, but the anticipation of blustering into the local drug store at lunch time and drooling over a steaming bowl of hot tamales floating in a sea of chili con carne and topped off with a double Coke with lots of ice.

Those were exciting days for me in spite of the fact that Uncle Charles and I lived in awe of Uncle Harry. Uncle Charles was only 12 years older than I so we formed a sort of conspiracy to outsmart the rest of the Lind family. We were buddies.

In thinking back, it has ever been thus. Whoever holds the purse strings is under constant attack by the unqualified peasants who suffer his rule. Both Charles and Albert always secretly resented Harry, the noble. Harry tolerated all this with an agreeable weariness and confounded their envy by a complete lack of communication.

Harry, it turns out, was also the "Playboy of the Mid-Western World." Imagine the embarrassment of the Linds when Uncle Charles revealed that Uncle Harry was maintaining a luxurious apartment on Commercial Street overlooking the Ohio River, a rendezvous for the "in" crowd, a garish hideaway where extraordinary poker games and, occasionally, an orgy or two took place.

By this time I had managed to push that little Ford straight from New Rochelle, New York, to the outskirts of El Paso, Texas. The first indication that Hazy was beginning to crack from the strain occurred when she suddenly sat bolt upright and shouted, "Look out for that apartment building!"

We were in the middle of the desert and the "apartment building" was a desert sentinel standing next to a yucca tree. We also had a vague feeling that we were lost. I pulled in to the next gas station and asked for directions. The attendant was more than polite and gave me every detail of where I had gone wrong. I followed his instructions to the best of my ability and one hour and 45 minutes later we were back in his station.

He took one look at my bulging eyes and suggested to my mother that I looked terribly tired. She agreed and asked for "simple" directions to the nearest motel. The motel was called the Red Mill and I'm sure that, if I ever see Heaven, it will look like the Red Mill.

Whoever created the phrase "the cool kiss of clean white sheets" knew what he was talking about. I had developed a bad case of the whips and the jangles. Even the roar of the trailer trucks thundering by our room soon sounded like a lullaby to my exhausted brain. We had gone to bed at 4:15 A.M. and by 4:20 A.M. I was sleeping with clenched eyes. Hazy had left a wake-up call for 8:30 A.M., explaining that if Edison could survive on six hours we could certainly do it on four. I was too tired to argue and too anxious to get to sleep.

I forgot what the dream was, but I do recall Hazy yanking the covers off me and telling me in no uncertain terms to get up and get dressed quickly. "What's wrong?" I asked.

"Those bastards forgot to call us and we've slept the whole day through! Look!" she wailed. "The sun is going down."

I whispered a small thank you prayer for our benefactors and sat on the edge of the bed with one sock in my hand. I think I would have sat there for another hour but Hazy was storming around the room and telling me to hurry for a quick breakfast.

Over the bacon and eggs, I finally convinced her that we needed the rest and the whole thing was a blessing in disguise. After belting our breakfast, mother and son once more took to the open road. No longer were we the two quivering souls from the night before. Now we were carefree and exhilarated, two happy motorists singing along life's highway, songs like "San Francisco" and "California, Here We Come."

Oh, God, we were happy and God was happy too. He

was happy to see the dawn of a new day. For that is exactly what was happening. The sun was not going down. It was actually coming up. Not only had we wasted eight bucks, but the sum total of our restful sleep turned out to be a little less than one hour.

From the outskirts of El Paso, Texas, to the floor of Hollywood's Lookout Mountain is quite a few miles and, believe me, it seems farther with hot tears streaming down your face. We cried all the way.

Seven
"Home Sweet Home"

**Mid pleasures and palaces, though we may roam,
Be it ever so humble, there's no place like home.**

—*Music by Henry R. Bishop,
Lyrics by John H. Payne*

P:

We moved into a 14-room mansion my mother had purchased during her earlier halcyon days. The house hung on a cliff high atop Lookout Mountain in Hollywood. The inventory proved that we were worth about $2,200, which isn't a lot when you consider the upkeep of a 14-room house.

"This house is a shambles," Hazy said. "I will buy the paint and you will paint every one of these 14 rooms!"

I had just driven a Ford and trailer almost 2,600 miles and the thought of painter's colic didn't really appeal to me at that moment, but to avoid an argument I said something that sounded like "uh-huh." We locked the doors, turned off the telephones and slept for 48 hours. We would have slept longer but we got hungry.

When we finally awoke, it was one of those unusual

California days. Some clown had prayed for rain and the Lord had seen fit to answer his prayers. Not only was the mansion leaking, but the retaining wall, which gave one some minute feeling of security, was beginning to crumble. Hazy noticed this and very casually turned to me and said, "As soon as you finish painting the rooms, I want you to rebuild that retaining wall!"

I looked down the four stories at the retaining wall and said, "All righty. Swell. You bet. Uh-huh!" My mother was happy to hear that I had retained my voice. With a smile of deep satisfaction, she went to the telephone.

"Hello, Ted. This is Grace Hayes. I'm back in the big house on the hill and things are a little rough. Yes, my son is with me and I was wondering if there was anything you could do for him? What? Oh sure, he'd be glad to. Anything. Just as long as he can get into a studio and find out what makes the wheels go 'round. O.K. I'll send him over to see you at MGM tomorrow."

"Who was that?" I asked.

"That was one of the dearest friends I've ever had," she said. "That was Ted Healy, the famous comedian, and he assured me that he could get you the job of being his stand-in, if you were interested."

Ted Healy had long been an idol of mine and I had a lot of trouble getting to sleep that night wondering whether or not I would qualify for the job. The next day I started a warm friendship with the most outrageously funny man I have ever known. Had he lived, I would not have to take this moment to refresh our memory. Now people mostly remember him as the creator of the Three Stooges.

He was not related to my future wife, Mary Healy. His real name was Lee Nash. He was half Irish and half

Jewish. At times he was violently anti-Semitic and at other times, just as violently anti-Christian.

A few years before his tragic death, he left the Stooges behind and was well on his way to being mentioned in the same breath with Chaplin, Keaton, Fields or any of the other great screen artists that one might care to name. Hazy had worked with him in several Shubert musicals and he decided to try to help her offspring.

"Listen, kid, it doesn't pay much," he said, "about six and a quarter a day, but if you want the job, here's my letter of request which will get you a B classification in the Screen Actors Guild." I knew I had to join the newly formed union to be a stand-in so after borrowing the initiation fee from Ted, I rushed over to sign up.

For two frantic years, beginning in around 1936, I was Ted Healy's stand-in. I had bought a secondhand 1928 Dodge for $80 and to save money I once in a while carried a lengthy tube of hose for siphoning gasoline from whatever car had the misfortune to be next to mine in the parking lot. At the end of each day my salary was dutifully turned over to Hazy and, when Ted wasn't working, I was gainfully employed at painting another of those rooms or trying to figure out how to save the crumbling retaining wall.

My mother, in the meantime, had decided to take in boarders. This worked out for a while until the police started dropping in every other night wanting to know what all those cars were doing out front! We were living in a rather restricted, exclusive neighborhood so this sort of nonsense had to stop.

One night I came home and, as I walked into the dining room, I was shocked to see Hazy with a green eyeshade, dealing seven-card poker to seven of the weirdest people I have ever seen outside of Madame Toussaud's

Wax Museum. One was a professional gambler down on his luck. He had befriended Hazy many years before in Colosimo's back in Chicago. She felt sorry for him. He was not really a Lilliputian, but somewhere between a midget and a dwarf.

I was told that he had been gambling elsewhere for four days and that I should get him a sandwich. "Then take him down to your room and let him sleep in the twin bed."

His luck wasn't getting any better, so after the sandwich "Little Billy Kane" allowed me to steer him downstairs to my room. I didn't really feel strange about "Little Billy" because I had heard my mother speak of him often. As a matter of fact, at age 11, I had won a Southern Illinois Charleston contest in one of "Little Billy's" hand-me-down tuxedos. Hazy had sent it to me. All I had to do was let out the sleeves a little.

"Well, Billy, I'll bet you're tired," I said.

"Yes, Joe (he called me by my father's name), I sure am!"

"Well," I replied, "you just tuck yourself in and get a good night's sleep." Within two minutes "Little Billy" was snoring loudly. Now I don't mind snoring, but "Little Billy" had invented a very unique type of snoring. He would inhale quickly six or seven times and then hold his breath. When one is accustomed to the sound of breathing, one doesn't quite know what to do when the sound of breathing stops, especially when the breather is a four-foot-six dwarf with a size nine hat.

I raised myself up on one elbow and whispered softly, "Billy, are you all right?"

There was no answer. I can't tell you all of the thoughts that raced through my mind at that moment, but one that I do recall was, "How the hell is my mother going to explain a dead midget in her son's bedroom to the police?"

At this point "Little Billy" calmed my fears by exhaling with all the gusto of a bull that had just been stabbed by Manolette. Once again I asked, "Are you all right?"

"Of course, I'm all right," he rumbled. "I got a three king full. What you got?"

"I've got an earnest desire to get some sleep!" I said, but by this time he was already holding his breath again. At 5:15 A.M.—I clocked him—he held his breath for four minutes and 12 seconds. Now that may not be a world record, but it probably is for a midget.

At 7:15 A.M. Hazy shook me violently, "Ted Healy's waiting for you and you're late. He wants you to drive him to Pomona," she said. Even over the roar of "Little Billy's" exhaust I could hear Ted honking his horn impatiently. Hazy removed the green eyeshade wearily and with a hasty warning to "drive safely," trundled off to her bedroom with a big brown paper bag full of small change. The big brown paper bag contained her share of "cutting the poker pot," and she always "counted" and "stacked" the coins before lowering the curtain on those steel blue eyes.

Ted moved over and I took the wheel of his big 1936 Buick. In spite of my tardiness he was in a good mood. As we drove to Pomona for a week of "location shots," he started to reminisce about his early days with the Three Stooges. Ted, you may recall, was the boss and original "Big Slapper" of the group. When they lost him, Moe, Larry and Curly had to learn how to slap each other and apparently accomplished their art without any perceptible signs of getting "punch drunk."

As the car rolled on toward Pomona, Ted recounted an experience he had endured at the hands of a famous team of producers. The producers were brothers and were accustomed to eating two or three actors every day for lunch. Ted was telling the producer, Lee Shubert, what he thought of the producer J.J. Shubert and then, just for good measure, what he thought of all the Shuberts in general—and that he did not want the job in their new musical anyway and that, if money meant that much to them, they could do their new revue without him or the Stooges and, oh, yes, go to hell and good-bye.

The boys were disappointed to hear this, but, as Ted was the boss, they bowed to his judgment and were told to keep themselves available while he paid a casual visit to his old hometown of Kansas City.

Kansas City was not as happy to see Ted Healy as Ted Healy was to see Kansas City. When Ted was depressed, he drank. Apparently the argument with the Shuberts had depressed the hell out of him. He roared from one saloon to another and was dizzily engaged watching a small-time mind reading act when the Shuberts located him. They had decided to meet his demands, but the important thing was that he must open a week from Thursday in Philadelphia. He'd have two spots in the show, 12 minutes in the first half and 10 minutes in the second half, just before the finale. Could he do it?

"Why, of course, he could." Ted Healy could do anything! Isn't it wonderful how easy everything is when you are full of "flit?"

With the cold gray dawn, it suddenly occurred to him that he didn't have anything to do for that all-important second spot. "What about those mind readers last night? Suppose I send one of them into the audience while one stands behind the curtain and gives me the right answers?" What a brilliant idea! "Healy, the mind reader."

The mind readers were ecstatic when they heard the plan. "At last," they thought, "a chance at the big time, a

Shubert show, Philadelphia! Oh joy!" They kissed Ted's hand, borrowed the money for bus fare and agreed to meet him in Philadelphia for the big opening night. Ted immediately called the Stooges, told them the good news and hopped a train for the City of Brotherly Love.

The big day arrived but not the mind readers. Frantically, Ted called the saloon in Kansas City. Yes, they had left Kansas City for Philadelphia and that was all anyone knew!

Ted formed a posse with the Stooges and together they combed the city but to no avail. Apparently no small-time mind readers had checked into the theatrical hotels and apparently Mr. Healy was not going to be able to perform his mental gymnastics in that "down-next-to-closing-spot."

The show must go on and on it went. Ted and the Stooges were a big hit in the first half while Mr. Healy was eagerly describing the physical appearance of the mind readers to the stage manager. Suddenly they appeared, although appeared is not exactly the word. Let's say they staggered into view and appeared to be drunker than $1,100. Ted hissed a few undiluted words, banged their heads together and slammed them both against the electrician's board. While he was trying to force hot coffee down one, the other stepped blithely on the stage in the middle of a ballet and started to tell jokes.

He got as far as "A funny thing happened to me . . ." Sure enough, a funny thing did happen to him. The long arm of Ted Healy encircled his neck. Before he knew it, the impromptu comic was offstage again. He was terribly indignant at this sudden turn of events and when he finally managed to straighten himself up, he cocked one eye at Healy and asked, "What's the matter, Ted, are we too fast for you?"

Ted was in no mood to argue this point as he was now being introduced for that all-important "down-next-to-closing-spot." As he rushed for the wings, he hastily babbled some last second instructions to one of the Stooges, "Make sure that son-of-a-bitch stands in back of the center curtain and gives me the right answers for the mind reading act!"

The opening night mainliners greeted Ted Healy's second appearance with wild anticipation. He had already scored heavily and was now predicting an incredible feat of legerdemain. As he secured the blindfold, the number one accomplice half stumbled into the august presence of Philadelphia's first-nighters. He recovered just long enough to lift a gold watch from the vest of a stuffed shirt in the first row. Triumphantly he turned toward the stage and bawled, "What have I got in my hand, Teddy Boy?"

"Teddy Boy" echoed the question in the general direction of the number two accomplice, who, by this time, was singing softly from behind the curtain *"Dear old girl, the robin sings above you . . ."*

Ted put an end to the singing with a sharp elbow and repeated the question, "What has he got in his hand?" The number two drunk was shocked into blurting out, "He's got a watch in his hand!" Ted proudly repeated this knowledge to the astonished gathering, whereupon the number one drunk yelled "Bravo!" and continued, "Now tell me the inscription on the back of the watch, Teddy Boy?"

Valiantly Ted once again repeated the question, but, this time, the number two drunk was determined to finish his solo. *"The blinding tears are falling as I dream of my lost pearl. . . ."*

At this juncture Healy gave up mind reading completely and screamed for the Three Stooges. The boys bounded on to the stage and the four of them improvised some inane nonsense, which they did rather well. However, the number one drunk was not about to give up mind reading and for the rest of the evening, during a quiet dramatic scene or an impassioned love ballad from a frightened tenor, there could be heard a croaking "Teddy Boy! What have I got in my hand?"

Two ushers in sneakers finally captured the elusive mentalist in time to save the spectacular finale. Anyone who has ever seen a Shubert finale knows that they were really, really big and this one was no exception. The Shuberts had imported three Germans with a very unique invention—a large cannon was packed tightly with a tremendous wad of heavy brown paper. A fuse would glow for a brief second and, suddenly, an earth-shaking explosion would propel the wadding straight at the ceiling. Upon hitting the ceiling, the impact would break open the brown paper wad and hundreds of flags of all nations would come floating gently down on the heads of an entranced audience.

Unfortunately, the Shuberts had not advanced any money to the three Germans and the three Germans were very angry—so angry, in fact, that one of the Germans deliberately tilted the cannon down. The fuse glowed brightly, the earth-shaking explosion took place but instead of heading for the ceiling, the projectile flew straight at the first balcony!

It struck the railing of the balcony with a resounding "whoomp." A large piece of it also struck a man in tails full in the face. The force of the blow managed to split his forehead and with the blood spattering all over his white tie and shirt front, all he could managed to say was "Good God Almighty!"

He kept repeating this phrase to the thunderous applause of the audience who thought the whole thing was pretty damn good! No one stopped him and he deliriously staggered down the stairs and out into the night. As a matter of fact, he was two blocks away when a big Irish cop walked over to him and asked, "What's the matter, Johnny?"

"Officer, I was sitting in the first balcony of the Forrest Theater when three men came on the stage with a cannon and . . ."

"Now look laddie, why don't you just go home and sleep it off. Everything will be all right in the morning. . . ."

"But officer!"

By this time I was out of my skull with laughter and the only thing that brought me to my senses was the forlorn sound of a police siren. We were pulled over to the curb and given a ticket for driving 55 miles per hour, on the wrong wide of the street, through the business section of Pomona, California. Ted was so pleased with my response as an audience that he promptly accepted the entire responsibility for my misdemeanor and advised me not to worry about it.

Ted Healy's untimely death in 1937 was a great shock to a lot of people. Under Doctor's orders never to drink again, he was at the Trocadero celebrating the birth of his first child. He lined up an endless row of Old Fashioneds on the bar and proceeded to drink them. He was rushed to the hospital but it was too late. Everyone said, "Isn't it a shame that such a talented man in the prime of life should be taken from us?"

Ted Healy was a man who was dangling in the limbo of life somewhere between a genius and a lunatic. He had a tremendous capacity for alcohol, but a steady eye that defied any man to say he was drunk. I always knew he had been drinking when he started playing with matches. If anything bothered him, he always wanted to set it on fire.

Many times I saved Metro-Goldwyn-Mayer Studios by merely blowing out a match!

Eight
"Hooray for Hollywood"

Hooray for Hollywood
That screwy, ballyhooey Hollywood!

—Words by Johnny Mercer,
 Music by Richard Whiting

P:

The poker games were slimming down, and the mighty Hazy decided that something had to be done. Hugh Herbert, the famous "Woo! Woo!" comedian, had been badgering us to come down and look at a small saloon in the valley called the Log Cabin. It had been a "front" for a gambling joint that functioned whenever the local politicians felt it was safe for it to operate.

Election time was coming up and even we knew that election time is not a safe time to permit a gambling joint to operate in full view of the voters who had lost a great deal of money there recently. The Log Cabin was therefore closed and available for lease at $200 a month, including knives, forks, spoons, linen and kitchenware.

We were too low on funds to accept such a financial responsibility, but the "widow's might" would not be deterred. We mortgaged the house and hocked the car along with all available insurance policies. For six weeks I sanded and painted, sawed and hammered, butted and bolted, and ate and slept at the Log Cabin. The new name for our bistro was "The Grace Hayes Lodge," 11345 Ventura Boulevard, two shows nightly, the finest food in town, North Hollywood, California.

The night before our opening, my mother was trying to comb the red and white paint out of my hair with a mild solution of turpentine and laundry detergent. At the same time she was trying to convince Connie Lupino, the mother of movie star Ida Lupino, that she should purchase a half interest in the Lodge for $500. We were $500 away from our liquor license, and without that all-important piece of paper, our opening would be a disaster. Connie had made out the check, but at the moment, was reluctant to let us get it in our hot little hands. Finally, with tears flowing out of her pretty blue eyes, she tore up the check and sobbed, "Hazy, dear Hazy, I just can't afford to take the risk." Hazy's response to this tragic news was simply to yank two handfuls of hair out of my scalp.

"My God, Peter, what are we going to do?"

I waited patiently for her to replace the divots and then suggested a collect phone call to Uncle Harry Lind back in Cairo, Illinois.

Everyone should have an Uncle Harry. If you can't have one, you don't know what you're missing. Good old Uncle Harry. He telegraphed us a $500 loan, no strings attached. We dutifully turned the money over to the state liquor board and prepared for our big opening night.

I was putting a film together as an opening for the Lodge. I asked Bing Crosby if I could film him out on the golf course for it.

Peter Lind Hayes performing with his mother at the Grace Hayes Lodge in North Hollywood

"Of course," he said. "When?"

"Thursday," I answered, holding my breath.

"Fine, I'll be there."

I had hired an expensive camera crew but when Thursday came and so did the wind. I had to call Bing to cancel and tell him we would try for Monday.

"No. Monday is no good for me. I'll be working all day for Paramount."

I thanked him for the gesture and said good-bye.

Monday showed up and so did Bing. I was dazzled. As he rounded the corner, I asked, "What happened to Paramount?"

Bing winked and said, "I called in sick. Where's your camera?"

Ventura Boulevard today is a luxurious highway, but in 1938 it was a simple black-topped, two-lane road. This, along with our distance from Hollywood, prompted all the wiseacres to predict our complete failure within six weeks. What the wiseacres couldn't predict was the affectionate response from the Hollywood luminaries.

Practically all show people have a humble beginning, and when the chips are down, and the "Hey, Rube" yell goes up, there is a curious camaraderie that seemingly comes from nowhere.

Hollywood knew that Grace Hayes and her "kid" were starting a desperate project in the Valley, and Hollywood graciously decided to attend. At 7 P.M. our first customer warily entered the Grace Hayes Lodge. Seeing the place completely empty, he nervously ordered a scotch and soda and threw a $20 bill on the bar. The bartender furtively sneaked the $20 to me and I ran rapidly to the motel next door for change as there wasn't a penny in the cash register.

At around 8 P.M. the heavens opened and the stars

came down. Impressive big, black limousines, one after another, drove into our parking lot. Star after star gave us warm greetings—Clark Gable, Myrna Loy, Hedy Lamarr, Jack Benny, William Powell, Groucho Marx, Louella Parsons, Hedda Hopper, Jimmy Starr and many local columnists.

The stars and the newspaper people made the Grace Hayes Lodge the most talked about place in Hollywood for the next three years. Forrest Tucker and Johnny Weissmuller became our unofficial bouncers. The show at this point consisted of Hazy, myself and a four piece orchestra, but the real show, of course, was the machinations of my mother persuading Hedy Lamarr that she should sing "When Irish Eyes are Smiling," or Groucho Marx having his arms twisted until he agreed to play Rhett Butler with two tourists playing Scarlett and Mr. O'Hara.

These little playlets were recorded and a copy was given to the tourists so that they could brag back home about the time they acted with Groucho in the Grace Hayes Lodge. Another famous routine—"Who's On First?"—was introduced by two neighbors of the Lodge, Abbott and Costello.

Hazy was in full swing now, mistress of all she surveyed. New waiters were added. Night after night, drinks were being served in our parking lot from 8:30 P.M. on, and irate customers were always rapping on the windows to indicate that those on the inside should get out and give those on the outside a chance to get in. We recovered our entire investment after only nine weeks of "frolicking" 16 to 18 hours a day.

The work was beginning to fray our nerves and it was obvious that mother and son were going to need some help soon. Help sometimes comes in odd packages. The two odd packages that showed up one evening turned out to be Charlie Foy and Joe Frisco.

Friday night was a big fight night at the American Legion auditorium. It was also a big night for the Grace Hayes Lodge. It was the beginning of our weekend and Hazy was forever reminding Frisco and Foy to leave the fights in time for our first show. On several occasions they had been late, but this particular Friday was to be a memorable one. The great Metropolitan baritone Lawrence Tibbett was in the audience.

Mr. Tibbett sent for me before show time and asked me not to call on him, I reassured him that we never embarrassed our guests. I made a mental note that Mr. Tibbett was sporting at least a three-day's growth of beard, a hole in the seat of his pants, and plaid eyeballs. Mr. Tibbett drank.

Hazy meantime was parading back and forth like a polar bear looking for two lost cubs. It was show time and our two stars were nowhere in sight. We decided to improvise the first show in order to get that all-important turnover in customers. We ad-libbed material we hadn't thought of in months. Then, in sheer desperation, Hazy started a community sing. Since the war years were imminent, she finished on a strong patriotic note with Irving Berlin's "God Bless America."

Midway through the first chorus, the rest of the audience was eclipsed by the booming voice of Lawrence Tibbett. Mr. Tibbett, completely uninhibited now, was bawling out the lyrics like a disenchanted bull. Presently, even Hazy stopped singing and Mr. Tibbett finished on his own. As the last sound of that gifted voice echoed through our little saloon, the entire audience stood as one and gave him a heartwarming ovation.

Mr. Tibbett was visibly moved by this demonstration

and boldly marched to the microphone. My mother gingerly handed it to him, whereupon he looked at it disdainfully, turned to the audience and asked, "Do I need this gadget?" The answer in unison was an overwhelming "NO!" Tibbett dispensed with the microphone and launched a brilliant attack on "The Road to Mandalay."

Our pianist went right along with him and the first chorus was robust and very loud. The second chorus, however, dropped down to a mere whisper—a sotto voce delineation that was superb. You could almost hear the audience thinking, "Look, Maw, Lawrence Tibbett. No cover, no minimum. Lawrence Tibbett!"

Naturally, Frisco picked this particular quiet moment to make his entrance, and naturally being a little conscience stricken, he burst upon the scene singing at the top of his lungs, *"They called her frivolous Sal, a peculiar sort of . . ."* That's as far as he got. The bartender clamped a big hand over Frisco's mouth and wrestled him to the corner of the bar. Frisco listened to the singer for a few moments, turned to the bartender and said, "This k-k-kid's g-g-got a g-g-good voice. Hazy ought to sign him up."

"Shut up you bum, that's Lawrence Tibbett!"

"Aw, t-t-to hell with that, you can ch-ch-change his name!"

One night Bing Crosby was sitting at a corner table and a rather inebriated woman kept maneuvering her date around the dance floor in order to get a better look at "der Bingle." At one point her dancing partner stepped aside, and she slipped and fell right at Bing's feet. He looked over the edge of the table and said, "Get up, kid, and I'll get you a draw."

Life and the Lodge were rolling merrily along, but the long hours were beginning to tell on Hazy. A consultation with a doctor led her to her decision to spend two weeks at the Cottage Hospital in Santa Barbara. Business was brisk and things went along as usual, but all hell broke loose when Hazy returned from Santa Barbara.

It seems Foy and Frisco had gotten their fingers caught in the till and several bookmakers were threatening to take inventory on the Lodge. Hazy settled all bets by striking Charlie with a chair. This ploy severely injured Charlie's pride and also broke two of his ribs.

Charlie didn't have an Uncle Harry, but he did have a successful brother named Brynie Foy. Brynie loaned Charlie enough money to open his own cabaret at Cold Water Canyon and Ventura Boulevard. Within six weeks we at long last had strenuous competition for the Valley trade. The feud was on between the Hayses and the Foys, which prompted me to write a parody on the famous hillbilly feud between The Hatfields and the McCoys:

Oh, the Hayeses and the Foys
They were reckless Valley boys
And they took up family feudin' when they'd meet.
Charlie Foy has lost his hair
Hazy struck him with a chair
So he opened up a sewer down the street.
All their fightin' started one bright Sunday mornin'
When Ol' Charlie Foy confessed what he had did.

He had lost the family money on a horse called "Happy Honey"
So she grabbed that chair and struck him on the lid.
All the people came to Foys with great big bundles
And all this it seems he couldn't figure out
For what put him in a quandary,

All the people brought their laundry—
They thought that Foy was Chinese without doubt.

Due to the spectacular success of the Lodge, my career in films was rollicking along. I was under stock contract to Paramount and the college I had missed in real life I was enjoying in "reel" life— in one B picture after another, practically every one about life on campus. The movies starred such marquee values as Jeanne Cagney, Jackie Coogan, Jackie Cooper and last, but not least, Betty Grable. Meanwhile because the studio already had a starlet named Linda Hayes under contract, when I signed my contract, they decided to give me a Peter. Alas! From then on, it was Peter Lind Hayes.

My biggest thrill, of course, happened when Paramount loaned me to MGM to dance with Lana Turner. The picture was *These Glamour Girls* and also starred Lew Ayres, Anita Louise, Jane Bryan, Tom Brown, Richard Carlson and Owen Davis, Jr.

Outside of my dance with Lana in a rented set of tails, every single line I had in the script was taken away from me and given to Tom Brown, Richard Carlson or Billy Bakewell. The director permitted me to remain in all the scenes, and I nursed my injured pride with the conviction that my silent responses to what the others were saying would eventually force the audience to ask, "Who the hell is that kid?" They didn't.

My romantic life at this time was pretty flighty. I had an occasional date with a struggling young actress at Paramount named Susan Hayward (a Scarlett O'Hara hopeful), a few sessions with the "oomph" girl, Anne Sheridan, a pursuit and ultimate failure with Jane Bryan (my favorite actress at the time) and finally a friendly four or five weeks with Judy Garland.

Hazy was in a movie with Judy. She played Mickey Rooney's mother in *Babes in Arms*. This was the same year Judy played Dorothy in *The Wizard of Oz*. She was rapidly becoming the biggest star at MGM and was very kind to me. She tried to involve me in every publicity stunt the studio arranged for her, and it was damned embarrassing to constantly hear an angry photographer snarl, "You there, whoever the hell you are, will you step OUT of the picture?"

One evening I played a record for Judy composed and conducted by a brilliant musician named David Rose. I permanently stepped out of that picture.

It was just about this time that Darryl F. Zanuck had sent a bullish looking talent scout by the name of Ivan Kahn (no relation to Genghis) on the prowl to find some new talent in the Deep South. He took a look at a beautiful singer named Mary Healy. Kahn liked what he saw. It wasn't long before New Orleans—with all the fanfare that Queen City could muster—sent an unsuspecting Mary off on a train ride to Tinsel Town and to me.

Bob Hope, left, sits with Judy Garland and Peter Lind Hayes

Nine

"Star Dust"

**Sometimes I wonder why I spend the lonely nights
Dreaming of a song**

*—Music by Hoagy Carmichael,
 Lyrics by Mitchell Parish*

M:

I certainly had no stardust in my eyes, even at 18, and no great hopes of becoming a movie actress when I arrived in Hollywood. I certainly had no idea I would soon fall in love and be married. I already had handsome beaus back home, though they soon faded into pleasant memories.

During the whirlwind year I had in California before I met Peter, I enjoyed meeting different people. Twentieth Century-Fox actually encouraged it. They wanted their contract players to be seen about town. It was another part of being a Hollywood starlet. There was a call each morning from Harry Brand's publicity office to ask my roomie Dorris and me what we'd done the night before and with whom! I rarely had anything racy to report. The voice of my straitlaced Southern discipline saw to that!

My busy social life included Washington Senator Magnuson, a friend of Harry and Sybil Brand, Bob Sterling, Randolph Scott, Art Lewis (a young producer on the lot) and Edgar Bergen, whom I had met earlier when he played the Roosevelt Hotel in New Orleans. When Edgar introduced me to Charlie McCarthy, Charlie leaned forward and whispered, "Tell me Bergen, just what are you doing with this young girl?" By the way, that was before he became the father of a beautiful baby girl named "Candy."

I'm amused when I remember that Artie Shaw called one evening.

"Hey Mary, have dinner with me." He was an attractive man and a fine musician and I would have gone out with him, but I already had a date. The very next morning I read in Louella Parson's column that he had married Lana Turner that very night! That was Hollywood. Gee, if I'd gone out with him, maybe he would have married me (joke)!

I went out with several handsome actors, but certainly no one I could imagine spending my life with. Good looks alone do not hold my attention long. I've always been much more attracted to men with brains, humor, and talent. One night, a "pretty boy" whose name I won't mention—he's still around—took me to Ciro's, "the place to be seen." While we were dancing, he suddenly stopped and tousled his hair. Zanuck had just walked in! Another time, an actor had his arm around me at a party. When he saw a famous producer walk in, he smoothed his hair and flexed his muscle! It was hilarious.

There was, however, one actor I liked very much, Franchot Tone. He was separated from Joan Crawford. Joan was a much bigger star than Franchot when they met, but by 1938 he was one of the Top 10 most popular

The glamorous Mary Healy

Mary Healy, a 20th Century Fox starlet

stars in Hollywood and she was considered "Box Office Poison." (Years later when a movie based on her life was produced, our daughter Cathy Lind Hayes had a part in it!) Joan's career was soon on the mend, but her marriage to Franchot wasn't and they divorced. That was about the time we met.

Franchot was frequently cast in movies as the rich playboy and actually he did come from a wealthy Eastern family. He was a Phi Beta Kappa scholar at Cornell, so he was not only attractive, witty, intelligent and charming, he was also very knowledgeable about literature, music, and especially the theater—his greatest love.

On our first date I remember he took me to an exotic Russian restaurant. While we listened to the beautiful music strains of the balalaika, he looked deep into my eyes and called me "dushka." Remember, I was a very naive teenager—politically and every other way. I was pretty dazzled by him. He seemed to know everybody. Jimmy Stewart and Henry Fonda were his friends—they were all young and handsome "boys around town" at that time.

Dorris Bowden and I couldn't have picked a more exciting time to be in Hollywood. It was at the peak of its Golden Years. I believe, and it is generally agreed, that 1939 was one of the best years in the history of movies—*Gone With the Wind, Grapes of Wrath, Wizard of Oz, Mr. Smith Goes to Washington.* My roomie was lucky enough to appear in three great films, all directed by the legendary John Ford, *Drums Along the Mohawk, Young Mr. Lincoln* and *Grapes of Wrath,* in which she was given the important role of Rosesharn.

The writer of that masterpiece was the brilliant Nunnally Johnson. He was witty and talented, just oozing with Southern charm and the top screenwriter in the movies at that time. No wonder Dorris fell desperately in love with him. He was John Ford's favorite writer and Zanuck considered him the best this side of Hemingway. It was Nunnally's idea to film *Grapes of Wrath,* which was considered dangerously radical then. The book had even been banned in California.

I was included on most of Dorris' dates with Nunnally. My roomie and I looked out for each other, especially on dinner dates. Dorris and I were both supporting some of the folks back home "way down South." Dorris, Nunnally and I were together so much that Nunnally referred to us as a "menage a trois" in his Georgia drawl, of course. So I got to hobnob with interesting and famous people, including Steinbeck, whom I remember as a charming and attractive man. He put his own stamp of approval on Nunnally's screenplay for *Grapes of Wrath.*

"Nunnally," he told him, "this is first-rate." And indeed it was.

Dorris was falling more and more in love with Nunnally. However, she was still seeing other people and if I had a date, I'd make sure there was another man for her. We were "glamorous starlets," but our pay was less than stellar. In fact, we were quite poor! If we could get a couple of nice fellas to take us out to dinner, that was a high point. Nunnally usually took us to Chasen's, which was where all the big stars and producers dined. Harold Ross of *The New Yorker* and Dave Chasen were friends from Nunnally's "New York days" when he was a member of the famous Round Table at the Algonquin Hotel.

Dorris and I went out one evening with Franchot Tone and his friend, Burgess Meredith. All during dinner Dorris talked about Nunnally Johnson. "Nunnally said this and Nunnally did that." When our dates left at the end of the evening, Burgess said, "Dorris, get thee to a Nunnally." Which of course she did.

When the studio sent them to New York for the premiere of *Grapes of Wrath,* she and Nunnally saw a lot of each other. Nunnally had been married before, so he was a bit more cautious, "We shouldn't get married. You're too young." Dorris was heartbroken. She flew back to Hollywood and wept buckets all over our little apartment on Roxbury Drive. However, it was romantic and had a happy ending because Nunnally called from New York and begged her, "Please come back to me." The next thing you know, she flew off to be married. The ceremony took place in the home of their dear friends, Helen Hayes and Charles MacArthur.

I lost my roomie, although we continued our friendship. Dorris and Nunnally moved into a beautiful home in Beverly Hills and I telephoned my mom in New Orleans. "Mama, it's about time you retired, Come live with me!" Happily, she agreed and we moved into a comfortable house in Cheviot Hills, near the studio.

Once Dorris was married to Nunnally, she reluctantly gave up acting. She had so much talent. But when you start having a family your priorities change, especially having Christie, Roxie and Scott to look after. Nunnally was a much sought after producer. Dorris was hostess to parties with the biggest stars and writers of Hollywood in attendance—Bogart, Mason, Marilyn Monroe, you name it. Peter and I were usually invited.

Dorris's movie career was over, but mine was just beginning. When Jule Styne, my vocal coach, was working with me in his rehearsal bungalow, he was always pressing me to sing louder, louder, LOUDER. I think he liked the way I sang, though he didn't ever tell me. One reason he wanted me to sing louder was because he thought maybe I could fill Ethel Merman's shoes. He had the word that she walked away from a major part in a forthcoming million-dollar Fox musical. No one thought to ask me if I wanted to be another Merman. Of course there could only be ONE. Ethel and I later became good friends. I don't suppose it's surprising I could do a pretty fair imitation of her in our nightclub act! Later, when Peter and I did our act at the Waldorf, Merman came to see us often and after being introduced with much applause, stood up in front of the microphone moving her mouth and hands while I stood behind her and did my "Merman singing."

I guess you could say I did my first public Merman impression for Irving Berlin, who took a hand in my fate. Of course I had heard the studio buzz that he was coming to Twentieth Century-Fox. I certainly didn't know he was coming to hear me! Even Jule was nervous about the arrival of the Great Man. It's funny—I wasn't, but I should have been. It was one of the turning points of my life.

I remember thinking he was friendly and soft spoken. (The comedian Joe Frisco said, "You had to h-h-h-hug him to h-h-h-hear him.") Irving Berlin sat at the piano himself and played for me while I sang my audition for the film *Second Fiddle*. What a joy! The songs were "Back to Back" and "I'm Sorry for Myself," which I eventually performed in the film with the King Sisters. Apparently Mr. Berlin approved, but I knew I could never have been given the role without Zanuck's personal stamp of approval. My audition tape was sent to the upper office and Zanuck agreed to give the part to an unknown. Me! The publicity office build-up began. I was on my way!

The title *Second Fiddle* refers to the character played by Tyrone Power, a Hollywood press agent working for an eccentric memo-writing movie mogul and trying to find the perfect heroine for the movie version of a popular novel. It was an inside spoof of David O. Selznick's *Gone with the Wind* search.

The mogul hires a naive ice-skating schoolteacher from Minnesota (Sonja Henie). To get more publicity, the press agent cooks up a phony romance between the teacher and the studio's pompous male star (Rudy Vallee). The teacher naively believes the romance is for real. Meanwhile, the press agent falls in love with the teacher himself. Are you still with me?

I played the heavy (thanks to all my dieting, a much lighter heavy), a singer/actress who was Rudy's real girlfriend and not crazy about her beau pretending to woo Sonja. For years after that, Nunnally Johnson would make fun of my awful dialogue. Mostly, I was to be angry. I frowned a lot and said, "I don't like it." And, for variety, "I still don't like it."

Sonja's character's story was a bit like my own. When David O. Selznick searched far and wide for Scarlett, Darryl F. Zanuck also scoured the hinterlands for talent. The scriptwriters also borrowed from Sonja Henie's personal life. There were rumors over the years that Sonja and Tyrone Power's romance in 1936 was cooked up for publicity but that she believed it was genuine. I have read that Ty was the great love of Sonja's life and that she hoped to marry him.

Unfortunately for her, Tyrone was the great love of several other people's lives too. During the filming of *Second Fiddle,* he was in love with the French star Annabella, whom he married in April of 1939 while we were still filming. Sonja was very cool to Ty—icy, if you'll pardon the expression. I didn't get to know her well, but one could see she was a very strong lady. She also was the world's highest paid movie star at that time.

The director of the film was Sidney Lanfield. I got off to a brilliant start with him by oversleeping, arriving very late for my first day of filming. I was mortified. He seemed to take a particular pleasure in mistreating people with no power—like nervous little me. Luckily, I had a formidable Power on my side. Dear Tyrone took me under his wing. Lanfield had directed him before in *Thin Ice*. They already disliked each other intensely.

Ty was the king at Twentieth Century-Fox when I arrived in Hollywood in 1938 and one of the country's most popular stars. The critics dismissed him as the new Valentino. When I look back at his work now, it's clear he was a fine actor. At the time, I was just so grateful for his kindness to me.

He was breathtakingly handsome, with the biggest softest brown eyes I had ever seen. I suppose it's surprising I wasn't physically attracted to him—nor he to me. I adored him like an older brother. In fact, I often wished we might make a movie together playing brother and sister. I have heard of course that he had a tumultuous private life. He was full of fun and boyish charm and was a truly kind and gentle soul.

The Twentieth Century-Fox press agents decided not only to let art imitate life, but to let life imitate art. They cooked up a studio romance between Rudy Vallee and me to help publicize the movie. Of course the Vagabond Lover didn't need any help from the studio with his love life. His dance card was always full. However, he invited me to the Coconut Grove where he was the orchestra leader at the time. I sang on his national radio show.

Rudy also wined and dined me—at the studio's request, of course. He was always very professional, but we didn't click romantically. Maybe because he asked me to wear a black satin dress when I went out with him!

There were photos of us together and column items all over the country—including New Orleans. The hometown folks were horrified! Little Mary with a known womanizer, so much older, DIVORCED! I could truthfully reassure them there was really nothing between us. Besides, I never wore a black satin dress!

What the studio and newspapers didn't know was that I had a crush on someone I met on the *Second Fiddle* set who was 13 years older than I, the brilliant composer and conductor Alfred Newman. He was intelligent and talented, a true Renaissance man. He was extremely well read and also appreciated good classical music. Schoenburg was his teacher and friend. One of the high moments of my life was recording those Berlin songs with Alfred conducting the 50-piece studio orchestra. Whenever I heard his music, I was enthralled. Over the years, Alfred was the musical director for more than 200 movies and won nine Oscars for his wonderful musical scores.

About that time, I went to New York for the premiere of *Second Fiddle.* Twentieth Century-Fox first promoted this film internationally a four-way radio hook up. Nothing like that had ever been done before. Sonja was in Norway, Tyrone in Hollywood, Rudy Vallee in Chicago and I was in the Big Apple for the first time. At the New York premiere, a little girl ran up to me and asked, "Are you anybody?" Well, I certainly wasn't "anybody," but not because the publicity department wasn't trying. Zanuck had Harry Brand, head of publicity, give me the big buildup and pictures of me were run in newspapers and magazines all over the country.

I then took another fateful train ride, this one from New York to New Orleans for our next *Second Fiddle* premiere. I sometimes wonder how my life might have changed if I had taken some other train. While sitting alone in the dining car, I was joined by an attractive gray-haired couple. During our conversation, they brought out family photos and I was told one of their five handsome sons, Frank, would be in Hollywood soon. Naturally, I gave them my telephone number. Frank was going to Hollywood to visit his old friend and school roommate—Peter Lind Hayes.

The New Orleans premiere of *Second Fiddle* wasn't quite as exciting as the Atlanta premiere of *Gone with the Wind* that year, but it was pretty thrilling for my family. All 72 of them met the train. What a homecoming! They literally rolled out the red carpet for their native daughter's movie at the Saenger Theater on July 12. I was whisked from the train station in a big black limousine to the Roosevelt Hotel. I never dreamed I would return in such grand style to New Orleans to the same hotel where I used to sing on the local radio station not so long ago. I was given the huge and elegant celebrity suite on the 19th floor! Wow!

My family saw the movie many times. During the entire run of *Second Fiddle,* Ma Mere went to the movie theater every morning and stayed all day long until she was practically asked to leave. She saw the show over and over. Also, there was a huge cut-out cardboard figure of me in the white fringed dress I wore when I sang Berlin's "Back to Back" in the movie. My sweet old grandmother took that life-sized picture and put it in her old house on Esplanade Avenue with her beautiful antiques, where I used to sit on the floor as a small girl, playing dolls. Though my Mama was proud and happy for me, Ma Mere was the real stage mother in the family.

But I found all this success scary. I felt like I was in a whirlwind and it wasn't much fun having people clamor over you. I also found the big crowds exhausting and frightening. I was beginning to realize success hadn't brought anyone I'd seen in Hollywood much happiness either, at least that was my teenage observation. Alice Faye was the queen of Fox at that time. She didn't look happy and indeed she walked away from her very successful movie career in 1945. She later did national radio with her husband, Phil Harris, and devoted herself to her family. I had liked Alice on the screen. She had an unusual and endearing quality and seemed like a good-hearted person off the screen. I know she went out of her way to help Tyrone Power. The press often painted me as a threat to Alice and rivaled our careers. Ridiculous! But of course that was just publicity. They said the same thing about Betty Grable, who actually did take Alice's place eventually. Then Marilyn Monroe arrived on the scene!

I made two other movies for Fox—*20,000 Men A Year* with that gallant Virginia gentleman Randolph Scott. I had dates with Randy but once again, they were publicity for the movie. I also made *He Married His Wife* with the handsome and charming Joel McCrea, who was married to beautiful Frances Dee (until his death). That was another show business couple, married even longer than Peter and I—more than half a century or approximately forever! By the way, I'll confess I had a big crush on Joel. He was tall and gorgeous!

My next movie, *Star Dust,* was written by the wife of Ivan Kahn, the Twentieth Century-Fox talent scout who discovered Linda Darnell, Dorris Bowden and me. In my part as a hopeful young singer, I got to sing the title song, "Star Dust." It was the first time Hoagy Carmichael's classic tune was ever performed on film.

Dorris' character was dropped from the script (not unusual) because she was on another assignment and

Linda's character was being developed more. In the movie, she fell in love with the football star, played by John Payne. But in real life, this sad young girl fell in love with our *Star Dust* cameraman Peverall Marley, 20 years her senior. Linda and I didn't see much of each other outside of work, which wasn't unusual, so I didn't know about her private life. But I gather it wasn't too happy. She became a big movie star. I read she died in a tragic fire in 1963. Ironically, it was while she was watching an old rerun of *Star Dust* on television.

One of the great heartbreaks of her life was her later romance with Howard Hughes. She fell deeply in love with him, but apparently he wasn't serious enough to marry her. Howard Hughes passed through my life a few times too, but luckily for me, he didn't linger.

I met him at a very glamorous party given at the Clover Club for Hollywood's most eligible bachelors—Jimmy Stewart, Henry Fonda and Cary Grant. The Clover Club was a private nightclub on Sunset Boulevard. Very swank. I went with Dorris and Nunnally and Billy Bakewell, an attractive bachelor and actor friend who was in many movies. He was friends with Lew Ayres and Franchot Tone and well liked in Hollywood.

During dinner, Billy introduced us to this tall, dark man. I barely heard him when he asked me for a dance. However, it wasn't long before I discovered he wasn't a swinger on the dance floor—in fact, we barely moved. Frankly, I was really into the jitterbug at the time and he certainly wasn't my type. I kept thinking, "WHO IS THIS?"

Nunnally asked me, with his mischievous smile, when I got back to our table "Do you know who you just danced with Mary?"

"He sure can't dance," I answered.

"That's Howard Hughes, the famous aviator and billionaire. He just flew around the world in record-breaking time."

I wasn't aware of his public image. Nunnally also told me Hughes had just bought the RKO movie studio and was "looking." But looking for what, I wondered?

I was a little more interested when Howard called soon after and asked me out to dinner. I'll never forget our first date. By now, Dorris and I were very excited about this famous visitor. We had spiffed up our little apartment, expecting his arrival with chauffeur and all the trimmings. Just before Howard was due, he called long distance from San Diego.

"Mary," he seemed to be yelling over the roar of planes, "I'll be late but I'll be there tonight." Looking back, I believe he had lost some of his hearing already, probably from test flights in open cockpits during his early years.

He didn't seem to hear my reply, "O.K., Howard. I'll wait."

Finally, when Dorris answered the door, she was amazed to see Howard himself standing there wearing a typical JC Penney suit with a black necktie and tennis shoes. As "roomie" looked out the window, we got into his old broken-down Nash car and went to a diner nearby. He ordered burned lamb chops! After that he drove me around town and pointed out some houses he'd bought for his "girlfriends." Then we went to his studio and he ran a movie starring Jean Harlow. He soon drove me back to Roxbury Drive. I tried unsuccessfully to get him in a conversation about planes. He told me he loved traveling by train! He also told me he was in love with Katharine Hepburn. That was it!

On another evening I had a date with Franchot Tone,

who was a friend of Howard's. This time, Howard was dating Gene Tierney, another newcomer to Fox. We were out with a group at the famous Trocadero. While we were on the dance floor, Franchot laughed and said, "Watch Howard when the check comes. He only hears what he wants to hear." Sure enough, Howard let Leland Hayward, the famous actors' agent, pay the bill, which I imagine was enormous. Leland was with Margaret Sullivan and those two seemed very much in love and later married.

Howard advised me paternally. "You're a nice girl. You ought to get married and have a family." Before the year was over, that's just what I did.

About that time I was called by the front office one morning and asked to be at Darryl F. Zanuck's office at 4 P.M. to sing "Your Kiss," a song written by Alfred Newman's brother Lionel.

Zanuck was just over five feet tall, slightly built and there was usually a large Cuban cigar jutting out from under his thin mustache. I understand he actually played polo, but at the time I wondered if he didn't use the riding crop he always carried on the yes-men and flunkies who seemed to follow him everywhere.

Lionel Newman and I arrived at Zanuck's office at 4 P.M. sharp to perform. It was my first visit to that famous office. It was miles long and we sank into the carpets when we walked toward his desk. Nervously, I sang my best. Lionel was soon dismissed and I assumed the boss and I were going to discuss my career, various ways to increase my "exposure." But when he walked around the desk toward me, it was Zanuck who was "exposed!"

I was dumbfounded! I ran away in shock and went right to my friend Alfred. He was angry, but didn't seem surprised. He had heard Zanuck was famous for his afternoon trysts. There was even a side door to his office, so the girl of the day could exit discreetly. Zanuck liked everyone to think he was a great success with the ladies. I believe the whole episode turned me off being a movie star.

I'm grateful to Darryl F. Zanuck for the part he played in helping launch my career. I've often wondered if he didn't also bring about its abrupt demise. Maybe he did me two favors. When he didn't renew my contract, I left the movies which I never really enjoyed and ventured onto new avenues—first Broadway which I loved, and later nightclubs and television where I had so much fun working with my husband. Yes, not only did I reject Zanuck's advances, I also committed the ultimate sin for a starlet. I got married.

Ten

"Jam Jumpin' "

**The Jim Jam Jumpin' is the jumpin' jive
Makes you get your kicks on the mellow side**

*—Words and Music by Cab Calloway, Fred Froeba and
Jack Palmer*

M:

When I returned to Hollywood after the *Second Fiddle* premiere, I got that call from Frank Donahue, whose parents I had met on the train ride to New Orleans.

Frank asked me out to dinner to a new place, the hottest spot in town. The Grace Hayes Lodge was in North Hollywood, out on Ventura Boulevard in the San Fernando Valley. Off we went to a little brown log cabin building with red and white awnings. It was nothing fancy, but famous Hollywood movie stars had moved out to the "Valley" and thought it was a great place to go because of its terrific floorshow. It was not unusual for members of the audience to get up unannounced—Judy Garland, Johnny Mercer, Bing Crosby, Bob Hope and many others to sing or "do their thing!"

The Grace Hayes Lodge was a show in itself. The atmosphere was intimate and warm, almost like being in someone's living room. Charlie Foy and Joe Frisco were in and out. Frisco's "horse race routine" was a classic and later became the inspiration for Frank Loesser's song, in *Guys and Dolls,* "The Horse Can Do." Grace Hayes was the M.C. and if the audience wasn't receptive when Peter was doing his act, she often said in her deep voice, "Shut up. My son is on." And they loved it.

My future husband was one of the first ever to do satirical impressions, which he wrote himself. He made quite an impression on me that night, to say the least.

His vignettes were filled with drama and pathos, then when he had the audience near tears, he would zing them with a joke or a funny song. He was Ronald Coleman in *A Tale of Two Cities,* doing a "fah fah bettah thing" than he had ever done before. He was the tyrannical Charles Laughton browbeating "Mistah Christian" in *Mutiny on the Bounty* with just a slight swish at the finish. (Years later we went backstage after seeing Tyrone Power and Mr. Laughton doing *Don Juan.* When Tyrone introduced Peter to Charles, Laughton said with great amusement, "Oh yes, I know Mr. Hayes, he does a scurrilous impression of me.")

Peter was John Barrymore's Hamlet, trying to figure out whether "to be or not to be." As Lionel Barrymore, he sang a popular song of the day, "Peckin.' " Of course while he was singing, "Lionel's" head looked just like he was "peckin' ". You may not remember the 1937 movie *Night Must Fall,* based on a gruesome Emylyn Williams play. Peter mimicked Robert Montgomery (who carried his victim's head around in a hat box). He spoke hypnotically in a thick Welsh accent about the victim's eyes, "Eyes with no look in 'em." Dramatically, he covered his own eyes, then burst into a rousing chorus of the hit song of the day,

"I'se a Muggin' " (*I'se a muggin', boom doddy doddy!*) He had a wonderful three-octave or more range singing voice and did a hilarious impression of Nelson Eddy pondering the "Sweet Mystery of Life."

Peter made me laugh out loud at his impression of my *Second Fiddle* co-star Rudy Vallee's nasal twang. He was a big hit with the audience and with me that night. For his finish, he sounded just like Ethel Waters singing "Cabin in the Sky!" I remember thinking, "Wow, that young man really has talent."

When the show was over, Peter came to our table to say hello to his old school chum. He was a little withdrawn and shy when we met. That intrigued me too. It happened that we arrived just in time to help celebrate Peter's birthday. Bob Hope, already famous for his benefit work, was heard to say, "This is the first time I've ever done a benefit for a piece of cake!"

The Grace Hayes Lodge was so much like someone's living room, people often seemed shocked when they received a check at the end of the evening. Peter was allowed to pick up a check now and then, but he always had to explain to Hazy why. For instance, Hazy wanted to know why he had signed a check for a certain Frank Donahue.

"Well Hazy, he's an old friend of mine. We went to school together back in New Rochelle. Besides, he's just introduced me to a lovely girl named Mary Healy."

When I wonder what my life my life might have been like if I hadn't met Frank Donahue's parents and he hadn't taken me to the Grace Hayes Lodge to see Peter, I only become more convinced we were destined to meet one way or another.

Because our paths soon crossed again.

Gossip columnist Louella Parsons started a trend

when she took out a group of young Warner Brothers stars on a tour of movie theaters around the country. First the movie would run, then the players would put on a live vaudeville show. The studios did this type of tour to promote their films. The theme song "Movies Are Better Than Ever" was used to make this point.

Jimmy Fidler, another Hollywood columnist, was preparing to emulate Louella. Fidler also had the power of the press and radio. Naturally, the studios bowed to his every whim. His group was going to tour the key cities.

"Since Mary Healy is a musical performer and Peter Lind Hayes is a nightclub entertainer, they'll do a song and dance act together," he announced. Paramount (who held Peter's contract) and Fox (who held mine) of course agreed with Fidler.

The rest of the group consisted of Helen Mack (MGM), who had great acclaim for her performance in the movie of the Charles MacArthur/Ben Hecht play *Front Page,* Edith Fellows (Columbia) and Michael Whalen (Fox). We were kept on studio salary ($75 a week for me) and Fidler paid our transportation and living expenses. Since Peter was the only one with experience in a vaudeville presentation, Jimmie gave him an extra $125 on the side.

Fox's great choreographer Nick Castle was given the chore of teaching Peter and Mary a chorus and a half of Cab Calloway's popular song, "The Jim Jam Jump is the Jumpin' Jive." Peter had been in vaudeville since he was six years old and was a total pro. But let me clearly state, I was no dancer. Peter had his work cut out for him trying to turn me into one. We rehearsed and rehearsed. I didn't take this nearly as seriously as Peter did, plus, he made me laugh a lot, which is probably why he married me. I'd get to the part of the number where we sang the double-talk lyrics, "FOO-RE-AK-ASAKY," forget a step, and start laughing. I never found out what the words meant. Our rehearsals were lengthy.

The day of departure finally arrived, and we all boarded the Santa Fe Chief. Trains back then were first-rate, "The only way to go." I found trains very romantic.

Two days out of Los Angeles we ran into a blinding snowstorm. I sat looking wistfully out of the window and Peter came and sat beside me. I was pleased. He kept our group happy with his great humor.

"I've never seen snow before!" I told him. Suddenly, he kissed me. Because I was so surprised, I stood up gave him a little slap on the cheek and left him standing there. But I think he already knew he had me. He followed me to my roomette. That was the beginning of our romance.

Our opening night at the Fox Theater in Detroit was complete chaos. None of the cast had ever been on a stage before, including Mr. Fidler. Peter's vaudeville training was a blessing and his solo act was a smash.

Now let me tell you about "Jumpin' Jive." I was introduced and sang my songs, then Peter met me center stage for our number. Midway through the first chorus, I forgot the lyrics after the first few steps into the routine. I started giggling, just a little at first, with Peter trying to get my attention, but by then I was convulsed with laughter, holding my sides and grasping the curtain.

I committed the cardinal sin of breaking up during a performance. Peter had been trained by his mother when he was a little boy that that was the worst "no no!"

"My Gawd girl," he lectured me sternly. "Don't you realize these people paid 40 cents of their hard earned money to come in and see you make a fool of yourself?" This statement only brought on more hysterical laughter.

We were on the road together for months, laughed a lot and fell in love. When the show closed on the road we went back to Hollywood, and spent a lot of time at the Grace Hayes Lodge.

Peter says he had to compete with Franchot Tone, Alfred Newman and Senator Magnuson for my hand. I had some competition too. He dated glamour girls like Lana Turner, Ann Sheridan and Susan Hayward. One night when Peter and I were together at the lodge, Susan Hayward came in. When she saw me sitting with Peter, she turned and expectorated. In other words, she spat at me, that little vixen! Peter just laughed.

P:

Because of the good notices I had received out on tour in *Variety*, bookers were clamoring for my services. I played Washington and Philadelphia without Hazy at the grand salary of $750 a week. I soon became lonely in Washington and spent most of my time at the Variety Club in the old Willard Hotel.

One evening I aimlessly stuck a quarter in the slot machine and hit the jackpot. I stared at $26 worth of quarters and mumbled, "This is an omen." I'm only half Irish, so I used half of the quarters to call Miss Healy in Hollywood.

"Hello Mary? This is Peter. Will you marry me?"

"Peter! You're drunk!"

"Mary, I've never had a drink in my life and I must know. I open at the Earle Theater tomorrow in Philadelphia."

"Well, you call me tomorrow after your first show and I'll give you my answer."

I spent the rest of the quarters calling Hazy to give her the news. I ran out of quarters. The last thing she shrieked into the telephone was, "You son of a bitch! You can't do this to me."

But I did call Mary back the next day for her answer.

M:

"Peter, you're not serious," I said.

I really thought he was kidding when he proposed, but he finally convinced me and I accepted. Peter's mother got very depressed over our news and took to her bed. He was her only son and she didn't want to lose him. My mother, however, was very happy about the announcement. I had the invitations printed. We were going to be married on December 25 in the little Church of the Good Shepherd on Santa Monica Boulevard in Beverly Hills.

Dorris Johnson, my former roomie, was having a very special gown made for my wedding party and Nunnally, who was to be Best Man, said in his inimitable style, "I can't find the black tie that goes with my tails." Meanwhile, down in New Orleans, Aunt Ollie, who designed the most beautiful wedding parties in the New Orleans social world, was working away on my wedding gown.

The wedding announcement was on the front page of the *Los Angeles Times* on December 12. My photograph ran next to a picture of the gangster Bugsy Siegel. That December day, Bugsy had beaten a murder rap in Los Angeles because of a legal technicality. The *Times*' banner headline also predicted that the war in Europe could be over by 1942 if the United States helped Britain. I didn't dream how much the distant war in Europe would soon change our fate—Peter's and mine.

I also didn't dream that Peter would set off a little bomb of his own a couple of weeks before the wedding. Just as Nunnally had called off his wedding to Dorris, Peter called me and said, "I can't do it." I was stunned but I said very calmly, "Okay, if that's the way you feel about it."

P:

My last two days in Philadelphia were very frustrating. Being an only child, I was concerned about my mother's reaction to our impending marriage. Hazy was struggling to make a living and I also worried about her attitude toward Mary. She could be and probably would be very difficult. When I finished my engagement, I boarded a TWA plane.

Halfway across the country we ran into a snowstorm and were forced down in Kansas City. Another omen, I thought. Frustrated, I walked around the airport for over an hour. Finally I made up my mind and called Mary to call off the wedding. Without a word she hung up the telephone.

I believe I cried all the way home.

Now if you think you've seen people cry, let me tell you about my mother. I had not told her that the marriage was off. When I arrived at the Lodge, she had taken to her bed. She was propped up by two pillows and surrounded with Kleenex boxes. A river of mascara and tears had flooded the floor and she was still bawling and moaning.

"Hazy stop all that. I'm home and the marriage has been called off."

She dramatically wailed like a stricken banshee.

"My God. Now you'll blame me for destroying your marriage. How could you do this to me, leaving me with this place around my neck, while you were out having a good time in Washington and Philadelphia?"

Logic was never Hazy's major suit. I spent hours trying to convince her that nobody has a good time in Washington or Philadelphia. Especially doing five shows a day! We wailed and railed throughout the night. Twice I sent out for more Kleenex and mascara.

I usually admired my mother's timing, but that December morning, it was off. She had cried just 38 seconds too long. In her presence I called Mary.

"Mary, this is Peter. I'm terribly embarrassed, but if you are still willing, let's drive to Yuma and get married tonight."

M:

Why Yuma? I never did know and I don't think Peter did either. He picked me up at 6 P.M. in his red second-hand Buick convertible. You've heard of the expression "driving rain." That's what we had all the way to Arizona. We drove all night—singing songs and laughing all the way. Later, we were married at 4 A.M. by a very sleepy justice.

When we called our mothers to let them know we had eloped, Hazy swooned but my mother said, "Wait just a minute. You're getting married in the church." The invitations had been printed for December 25, 1940. Instead we were married a week earlier, December 19, at the now

Jim Jam Jumpin', December 7, 1941

famous Church of the Good Shepherd on Santa Monica Boulevard by Father Gilbert V. Hartke.

I felt strongly that Peter and I were doing the right thing. It wasn't until years later that I realized how disappointed my roomie Dorris, my mother, Aunt Ollie, and all my family were about our decision to elope. Aunt Ollie had designed the utmost in a wedding dress and my family was busily gathering all the trimmings for a beautiful wedding. On our honeymoon, we stamped "VOID" on our wedding invitations and sent them out as Christmas cards.

"Merry Christmas anyway!" we wrote.

P:

You know what it is to deprive a lady of a church wedding, but by now you must know, Mary is exceptional.

A honeymoon was in order so Mary and I decided that Carmel, California, would be a delightful place. We looked at our bank balances and decided that we couldn't afford the famous Del Monte Lodge at Pebble Beach.

We were so carefree and happy and decided that we could spend at least 10 days in a motel in that very beautiful part of Northern California. We moved into the "Lobos Lodge," and the first three days were heavenly. After the third day, the telephone started ringing. It was my mother.

"Okay, you're married now, Okay? But what am I supposed to do with this white elephant called the Grace Hayes Lodge? People keep asking about you. What the hell do you want me to do, starve to death?"

Reluctantly, we cut the honeymoon short by four days and drove back to Hollywood.

Mary and I rented a small apartment in the Villa Italia. It was down the street from Schwab's Drug Store, where they discovered Lana Turner, just off Sunset Boulevard. I immediately went back to work at the Lodge, and Mary became a housewife. The Hollywood studios didn't like it when their fledglings ran off and got married. Soon Mary was dropped by Fox, and I was dismissed by Paramount.

The hours at the Lodge were becoming very depressing. Hazy sensed that I was dejected and suggested that I build a small house for Mary and myself on the back end of a piece of property she owned on Valley Heart Drive in North Hollywood. The property was a commercial acre, the front half was on Ventura Boulevard but the back half overlooked the slumbering Los Angeles River. I thought that was a Jim Dandy idea, so mother and son set up a conspiracy to surprise my new bride. The architect was a man named Charley Atwater, an old friend of Hazy's.

He promised to build the house at cost. It was to be a very simple frame house—one bath, one bedroom with a fireplace running through to the living room, a kitchenette and dinette. The overall cost was not to exceed $7,600.

Our house at 12946 Valley Heart Drive was finished in five weeks. I very slyly suggested to Mary that we take a drive out in the Valley. I kept making smaller circles, until presently we were in front of the house. "Say, this one looks brand new, let's take a look at it." We walked up the two steps to the front door. I tried the door and it was unlocked. I pushed it open, swept Mary up in my arms and carried her over the threshold screaming, "Hallelujah! Mary, it's ours."

Before her feet hit the floor she asked, "Who owns the property?" (I told you she was exceptional.) The thought had never occurred to me that we were building our house on someone else's property. I guess I never thought of Hazy as someone else.

We moved into the house, and I continued working at the Lodge. I finally persuaded Mary to join me. She would sit in a corner and I would have someone to talk to between shows.

Hazy would simply nod in our direction occasionally and that was all. The tenseness was beginning to annoy me so I made a little plan. I explained my scheme to Mary and she agreed. For the next few nights Mary stayed home. I gave no explanation to Hazy for her absence. After the fourth night, curiosity was killing the cat. As I was preparing to go home, she called me over to the checkout counter. She was huffing and puffing on a cigarette. She put the cigarette down and asked, "Where's the kid?"

I sobbed a little and blurted out, "Hazy, you were right. I never should have gotten married. I was too young. She's a lousy housekeeper and the other day she washed out my favorite briar pipe with soap and water."

There was a long pause, she lit another cigarette, inhaled deeply and said, "You know, you're no bargain either!" (My plan was working.) For the next half hour she told me how sloppy and indolent I was, how grateful I should be to have such a beautiful girl give me the time of day and that I had destroyed her career by marrying her. This tirade went on and on and, when I left, I promised to try and make it up to Mary.

The next night, Mary and I bloomed all over the Lodge; I even invited her up to sing a song with me, and it went very well. Hazy was sitting with a large party, as I passed the table, I heard one lady say, "Aren't they a lovely couple?" I overheard my mother reply, "Yes, I saved their marriage, you know."

My theatrical agent at the time was practically part of our family. His name was Lou Irwin, and I loved him. He came into the Lodge one night with another agent, Charles Yates. They were proposing that Mary and I take out a unit on the road. The show would be called "Sweater Girls," a remake of the Jimmy Fidler tour, and if we stayed with it for 10 weeks we would make quite a bit of money.

We needed the money to pay off the mortgage on the house. After a tearful conference with Hazy, we took to the road again. The tour was what allowed us to pay off the mortgage and hide a little mad money. We had to scramble for our keep.

M:

Peter decided to tell Hazy he would continue to perform at the Lodge only if I could work with him. She paid us very little. As Peter joked, the deal was we'd get our meals half price!

Under Peter's influence, I used to do numbers with a little drama, like "A Nightingale Sang in Barkley Square," in sympathy for the British, who were bravely fighting Hitler all alone at this point of World War II. I'd tighten my fist and say in my best British accent, "You blasted murderers!" We were a big, big hit with the customers.

In May 1941, Peter and I were signed to play in the musical *Rio Rita* with the delightful Joe E. Brown as part of the Los Angeles Civic Light Opera Festival. We doubled at the Grace Hayes Lodge.

Over the next few months, we also toured the country in Elsa Maxwell's *Sweater Girl Revue*. (Sweaters were considered very daring then, by the way. Will Hayes, the infamous Hollywood censor, banned them from the movies.) Peter did his impressions, was the master of ceremonies, and was always the hit of the show. The Chinese Kim Loo Sisters were a very good trio on the bill. I had great fun with my fellow Hollywood glamour girls—Grace McDonald, June Preisser (another New Orleans girl who was in many musicals during the 1930s and 1940s, including some Andy Hardy movies), Cecelia Parker (Andy Hardy's sister Marion), Barbara Pepper (Lucille Ball's good friend who later appeared in dozens of *I Love Lucy* episodes in various guises).

My big spot was "A Nightingale Sang in Berkeley Square" with all the "rockets' red glare and bombs bursting in air" special effects by Peter. I sang standing in front of a lamppost. We also performed our "Jumpin' Jive" dance.

I rarely got our number together quite right until one fateful day in December. It was Sunday morning December 7th, 1941, and I was barely awake. We wondered why there were so very few people in the audience. It was an early show and we hadn't heard the news. The Japanese had attacked Pearl Harbor. America was at war!

P:

Mary and I returned to Hollywood despondent and dejected. I wanted to work as much as I could before the inevitable "Greetings" from Uncle Sam arrived.

We returned to Valley Heart and continued helping Hazy with the Lodge. Neville Fleeson, whose song "Apple Blossom Time" was a big hit for the Andrew Sisters, was now at the piano. He had worked with Hazy years before

The photo to announce a wedding that almost didn't happen

in vaudeville and he was an expert at special material. He wrote a special satirical piece for Mary on *Rain*. Mary was a smashing Sadie Thompson (who had starred in the play on Broadway) and she stopped the show every night. Frank Fay, once married to Barbara Stanwyck, the star of the big Broadway hit *Harvey* and my favorite comedian, was in the audience one night. After the first show, I asked him to take a bow. He was gracious but also very caustic.

He addressed the audience and said, "You know this Grace Hayes is a shrewd woman. She married Charlie Foy, who came with Joe Frisco the comedian, song and dance man. She discovered she needed a piano player and married Newell Chase to beat the union scale. She told her son to learn how to impersonate the movie stars so that his flattery would draw those egocentric people to her saloon. Then one day she looked at Peter and said, 'Son, we need a girl singer.' " Then, Fay turned and looked at Mary. When the audience laughed and applauded, I let Hazy take the bows.

Two of our most loyal customers at the Lodge were Ronald Reagan and his then wife, Jane Wyman. My first speaking part in a movie was at Warner Brothers's studio. I was a bandleader and the "new kid" on the lot was "Dutch Reagan." We were both from Illinois and became good friends.

The Hollywood columnist Louella Parsons announced that she was going on the road with a variety show, the kind of review Mary and I were doing when we fell in love. Louella selected Jane Wyman and Ronald Reagan from the Brothers Warner.

Since Jane and Ronnie had never been on a stage before, Mary and I set about helping them with a corny straw hat and cane routine. ("We just got back from

Frisco town. We just got back today. In fact, we wrote this little song while speeding on our way.")

The legendary John Barrymore, the Great Profile, was in the audience of the Grace Hayes Lodge one night and also the popular comedian Milton Berle. At the end of our second show I introduced Mr. Barrymore. He was at the peak of his radio success with Rudy Vallee and received a wild round of applause. He strutted onto the floor, relieved me of the microphone and proceeded, in his most articulate fashion, to praise the comedic talents of Milton Berle.

He spoke for about five minutes and then said, "Ladies and gentlemen, I give you America's greatest young comedian, Mr. Milton Berle!" Barrymore handed the microphone to Berle and returned to his table.

Milton's forte has always been his brashness. Instead of thanking Barrymore for the praise, he began to attack him. He ridiculed his performance on the Vallee show, called him an unpredictable ham, referred to him as the terror of the censors and then proceeded to plug his upcoming radio show.

"Incidentally folks, I'm not having a broken down actor on with me. I'm having the eminent English star with me, Mr. Charles Laughton. You know Mr. Laughton, don't you Barrymore?" A hush fell over the audience and from out of the darkness Barrymore bellowed, "Kiss my ass!"

It was one of the loudest laughs I had ever heard. Milton was so pleased, he tried to get Barrymore to follow him down to Charlie Foy's nightclub and repeat the performance.

I remember as an usher at the old Gem Theater back in Cairo, Illinois, I had always idolized John Barrymore. I used to pull my nose every day at noon recess. The other students were awestruck. They didn't know that I was trying to create the classic Barrymore profile. (Of course I overdid it until I looked like an anteater.)

Luckily for me, a charming light comedian named Dennis O'Keefe was reluctant to do a film at RKO. It was a musical entitled *Playmates.* The stars were Kay Kyser and his band, my idol John Barrymore, Mae Robeson, Lupe Velez, and Patsy Kelly. David Butler, the director, offered me the part one day on the golf course.

I fairly drooled my acceptance. At last I was going to actually work with the Great Profile. Barrymore had promised the director that he would be on his "good behavior" and proved it the morning the picture started.

A large black limousine delivered him an hour late to the sound stage. He gingerly stepped out of the car and promptly threw up all over Mr. Butler.

The plot was a fragile little thing—Barrymore had been asked to help Kay Kyser get rid of his Southern accent. At one point Kay asked Barrymore to "demonstrate one of them Shakespeare speeches."

Barrymore settled back into an overstuffed chair and said, "Well, Kay, it's been a long time, let me see."

The director called "action" and the great actor wet his lips. "To be or not to be, that is the question. Whether 'tis nobler in the mind to suffer the slings and arrows of outrageous fortune . . ."

On and on he went. Everyone was enraptured at the sound of the great man. Suddenly, in the middle of the soliloquy he started to weep. Tears were cascading down that now dissipated face. He expected the director to yell, "Cut," but the director wanted to capture all of this moment on film and the camera kept rolling. Barrymore stuck his tongue out and started licking his own tears. After a few seconds he looked straight into the camera lens and said, "That's the Goddamndest gin I've ever tasted."

We became very good friends, I am happy to report, and I was with him night and day for six hilarious weeks.

The nights were spent at my mother's saloon. It was beneath Barrymore's dignity to pay a check so naturally he became a permanent guest of the Grace Hayes Lodge. John Carradine, another Barrymore idolator, approached him one evening and said, "Mr. Barrymore, friends tell me that I look quite a bit like you when you were a younger man." Barrymore snarled, "That's quite possible, my dear fellow. My father was an indiscreet man in his youth."

On another occasion an elderly character actor approached him stating that he had appeared on the stage with Lionel and John in *The Jest*. Oh, said John, "What are you doing now?"

"I'm appearing on Broadway with Maurice Evans in *Richard the Second*."

"How about next season?"

"I'm going back to New York with Maurice. He's doing *MacBeth*."

"What?" roared Barrymore. "That cockney faggot is going to play MacBeth? Man, when MacBeth walks on the stage his balls should clank!"

Barrymore used obscenities I had never heard, but his words lost their shock value for me because he had such an eloquent way of using them.

I recall we were having dinner at the Brown Derby one evening and he was regaling me with some of his very bawdy stories. His voice was echoing around the Derby and the four letter words were annoying a man seated nearby. The man had his wife and two small children with him and the offensive language was more than he could bear. He summoned a waiter and complained. The waiter shrugged his shoulders and said, "I'm sorry, but that's Mr. Barrymore."

The man turned purple with rage and said, "If you don't stop him I will." With that he flew at our booth but was intercepted by two more waiters. He was dangling in mid-air by his lapels, fuming and fussing. Barrymore rose majestically, looked at him and said, "What is this? A peasant with a petition?"

We were in Sak's department store one day. He had picked out a half dozen neckties and handkerchiefs and was asking that they be charged. The sales clerk asked for the address and then the last name. John winced and said, "Barrymore."

The young girl said, "First name please?"

He arched his eyebrows and said, "Ethel, you bitch."

At that time Nunnally Johnson had never met John Barrymore in spite of the fact that he and Charles MacArthur co-authored a play about John entitled *A Stag At Bay*. Since Mary and Dorris Johnson were former roommates and very good friends, I arranged a small dinner party. John was delighted at the prospect of meeting Nunnally. I suggested he not be late and "For God's sake, please watch your language."

He showed up at our little house in North Hollywood way too early, at four in the afternoon, much to the embarrassment of my nervous bride who arrived from shopping, carrying bags of groceries for the evening's big dinner. Barrymore was looking very dapper in a dark suit, white shirt and a black tie with a pearl stickpin. I sensed he'd had some of his "daytime medicine." It was vermouth. After six he would switch to anything. Lacquer, paint remover, rubbing alcohol—anything that wouldn't set fire to his teeth.

The Johnsons were not expected until 7 P.M., so I spent a great deal of time pleading with him to "cool" it with the naughty words. He promised to be a good boy and I saw Mary heave a sigh of relief. I had asked him for a photograph when we were working on the movie. He brought it to the house inscribed "To Peter, my bastard son from your loving Father, John."

Promptly at 7 P.M. the doorbell rang. As I opened the door, Barrymore grabbed Nunnally by the hand and said, "Well you old horse's cock, I'm glad to know you."

Dorris Johnson paled and she and Mary disappeared into the powder room. Nunnally was not drinking at the time and was there to find out if there was any sanity left in John—enough, to be certain he could trust him with a play. As the evening wore on, the girls wore out and it was then that Barrymore started on his story about the 74 hours he had spent in an Indian whorehouse.

"After I had humped everyone in the establishment, including the madam, I retired to the kitchen to partake of a midnight snack. The pimp was in the kitchen and, curiously enough, he was a Greek. What the hell he was doing in India I will never know. He was a magnificent brute of a man wearing nothing but a burly bathrobe. As he reached for a cracker, the robe opened and I saw the biggest horse's dong I had ever seen. I grabbed it and shook it and said, 'I'm glad to know you'."

At this juncture, Nunnally said, "Peter, I think I will have a drink." Nunnally had some sort of condition that was not appeased by alcohol and after two drinks his face usually turned into silly putty and his mind went wandering. The evening was not turning out the way I had planned. It was also time for Mary and me to report to the Grace Hayes Lodge for the first show. I gathered everyone together as best I could and led them to our supper club. I placed John, Nunnally and Dorris at a small table just inside the door. A very large woman spotted John and was leaning all over him trying to give him a big wet kiss. John recoiled in horror and shouted, "Madam, you look tired. What have you been doing? Fucking?"

I was on stage now but kept a wary eye on Nunnally. He was weaving from side to side and suddenly let go with a loud sneeze. The sneeze propelled his head forward and the bridge of his nose shattered the glass he was holding. I was panic stricken and rushed off the floor to aid him but he would have none of it. He pushed me away and grabbed his wallet. We finally got him into his car and dear little Dorris drove him home.

The next day I called him to see how he was feeling. "Nunnally, are you all right?"

"Yes, Peter. I'm fine, but your friend Barrymore, that son of a bitch, tried to roll me."

On another night at the lodge a pretty young girl with her GI boyfriend was badgering John for his autograph. She embraced her date and begged, "Please Mr. Barrymore. He's going tomorrow." John studied her for a moment and said, "If he's going tomorrow, make sure he comes tonight."

The stories about Barrymore are legend.

When his daughter Diana was very young, he was invited to address the girls at her school. After his speech, he announced that he would accept a question and answer period. The girls were a little shy in the presence of the great man. After awhile a young student teenager stood up, adjusted her glasses and inquired, "Mr. Barrymore, in spite of their tender age, in your considered opinion, do you think Romeo and Juliet were physically intimate with each other?"

Barrymore cocked that left eyebrow into a fishhook and snorted, "In the Chicago company they were!"

Indelicate? Yes, but by today's standards, Mr. Barrymore would be considered a "poisoned choir boy." In spite of the shocking vocabulary, there were other facets to this brilliant man.

I think John Barrymore overdid everything in life two or three times. Of course he was sated and jaded and most of all bored. When his intellect discovered this, it immediately sent out an order to self-destruct.

I loved the story about the night he called Winston Churchill—collect—from a telephone booth. The call went through incredibly fast and the two laughed and giggled for at least a half hour. Remember, this was while Churchill faced Britain's "darkest hour."

Playmates was to be the last appearance for Lupe Velez, Mae Robeson and John Barrymore. I think they all died deliberately rather than face the reviews.

There were many rumors about his final deathbed scene. This is the one I would like to believe. He stirred briefly from a deep coma to find an extremely ugly and ancient nurse hovering over his bedside. He stared at her for a moment and sighed, "Oh well, jump in bed anyway!"

Lucille Ball and Desi Arnaz were courting each other at the same time we were and often came to the Grace Hayes Lodge. They were married in November of 1940, a month before we were and built their first house nearby in Northridge. Our paths were getting ready to cross again.

Eleven
"Why Do They Call a Private a Private?"

**Why do they call a private a private
When his life is a public event?**

—Music by Frank Loesser, Lyrics by Peter Lind Hayes

P:

The familiar "Greetings from your Draft Board" started nailing a lot of my companions and I knew that if they looked in my right ear and couldn't see daylight through my left one, I would soon be in the army. The army did not appeal to me, but the Air Force did, so I decided to enlist.

I asked Bing Crosby for a letter of recommendation.

"You write it. I'll sign it," Bing said.

I was given an extra week to finish a film. Ironically enough, the film was entitled *Seven Days Leave*. The stars were Lucille Ball and Victor Mature. At that time, Victor and Lucy had a better war going for them. In spite of the fact that they were playing two sweethearts, the chemistry wasn't working and she had slapped him several times during their love scenes.

I was told to report to the Cadet Training School at

Santa Ana as soon as I had finished my last scene. I became involved with several re-takes but finally was released by the director. In my Army uniform costume and seven inches of Max Factor's makeup, I jumped into Mary's 1937 Ford and raced madly to Santa Ana.

My new life was beginning. My logic was firm, the war would be over in a few months, but in the meantime, the Air Force would teach me how to fly. When I showed up to be sworn in, my military career almost came to an abrupt finish.

With all that make-up the sergeant thought I was gay!

My estimate about the length of the war was also a little off. Not much though, only four years to the day. I checked into a motel at Santa Ana after being told to appear in front of the obstacle course at 5:30 the next morning. I was three months short of being 27 at the time and had never faced an obstacle course in my life. Physically I had never been very strong. Healthy, yes, but strong? NO!

The sergeant started putting me through the paces and his derisive laughter offended my male hormones. I had fallen off or tripped over every obstacle in my path. I was finally pulled to my feet and told to "Go wait in the jeep!" After several phone calls, I was told that I was being transferred to the R.P.U. unit in Santa Ana. "Oh, really? And what, may I ask is the R.P.U. unit?"

"It's the Air Force Radio Production Unit, and you'll be with a lot of them other rat fink actors."

I was ordered to report to Col. James Higgs and Col. Edward Dunstetter the next morning. I moaned all the way back to the motel. My dream of becoming an American ace had vanished.

Private Hayes reported to the two colonels and was

assigned to be a radio actor. Colonel Dunstetter was the conductor of a 65-piece orchestra that included the names of every great musician he could recruit from the Hollywood sound stages. Colonel Higgs was in charge of the writers and the actors.

Each Saturday we would do a live network broadcast for 5,000 privileged cadets. The radio broadcast was a musical comedy show and Hollywood always supplied us with very big movie stars. During the week we would do legitimate dramas exhorting the greatness of the Air Force. We would shout brave words into a defenseless microphone. These words were written by some of the fanciest captains and majors the Screen Writers Guild had ever turned out. We actually had a soundman finally crack under the strain. After 700 missions over Europe, the noise from his turntable unnerved him and he went into shock. One of the majors decorated him with our highest award—a typewriter ribbon.

Saturday became my favorite show of the week. After all, we were hobnobbing with the bigwigs of the era: Bing Crosby, Al Jolson, Bob Hope, Clark Gable, Spencer Tracy, Charlie Ruggles, Pat O'Brien, Danny Kaye, Milton Berle and many, many others. Our comedy writers and entertainers consisted of names like Tom D'Andre, Bob Hope's funny brother, George, Bill McCauley, William T. Orr, Ben Gage (then married to Esther Williams), Lou Busch (who became "Joe Fingers Carr") and First Class Private Frank Loesser who became—Frank Loesser.

We had Lee J. Cobb for a while but one damp and cold morning he refused to run around the track of an outdoor arena. The PT sergeant threatened to have him court martialed for insubordination, so Lee went AWOL. When they found him, Lee was doing Chekov with a small repertory company in the back of Schwab's Drug Store on

Sunset Boulevard. The government surprised him in the middle of "The Evils of Tobacco."

I was finally invited to help write the comedy sketches for the Hollywood stars. Joy to the world, my favorite American icon was coming to town—Gary Cooper. I had never met the tall laconic actor, but to me he simply was "Mr. America." I envisioned Gary Cooper in every town from Maine to California. I pictured him leaning against a gas pump, sucking on a blade of grass, and the townspeople calling him "Slim." I had mastered an impression of his clenched-teeth-delivery and immediately set about teaching Bill Orr how to emulate Cooper's faltering enunciation of each and every word.

Bill was a quick mimic and so I wrote a brief sketch for the three of us. Cooper was painfully late for our "live" broadcast and I was worried about my sketch. I had no idea whether or not he was a good sight reader. I handed it to him and pleaded with him to read it through with us before airtime. He agreed and very slowly began to read, "Thank you very much, it is a great pleasure to be a guest of the United States Air Force."

Bill Orr walked up to Cooper and through clenched teeth said, "Hi, Coop, how are you?" Cooper turned back to the written work and responded, "I am fine corporal, and how are you?" I moved in to him and with my best "Cooper" voice said, "Hey Coop, we do pretty good with the girls, don't we?" Cooper looked warily back at the script and said, "Yes, Soldier, I guess we do."

Suddenly he dropped the script, looked down at me and whispered, "What the hell, sergeant, do I really sound like that?" He was a wonderful, sweet, shy man and I could never resist staring at the boob tube if he was on the late, late, late show.

Because of gas, meat and butter rationing, the Grace

Hayes Lodge had started to flounder and Mary decided to try her wings on Broadway. Father Gilbert Hartke, the Holy Ham of Catholic University, had decided that Walter Kerr had created a musical that deserved a Broadway outing. Since Father Hartke had married us two years earlier and had become a fan of Mary's, he recommended her for one of the feminine leads. Walter was amenable, so Mary took off for New York to sing and dance in *Count Me In*.

M:

Those early months of 1942 were so frightening because we didn't know what would happen to Peter or to me—or to the world, for that matter. I found myself on yet another long train ride to New York, this time taking me away from Peter and from all my friends in Hollywood. I was overwhelmed by the loneliness and fear of going into a strange city by myself. I went into the ladies room and began to cry. A kind lady followed me. Through my sobs, I explained my predicament. She comforted me and encouraged me with words I've never forgotten. "When an opportunity presents itself, you must take advantage of it," she told me and patted me on the back. "This could be a turning point in your life." As it turned out, she was right.

Count Me In was first presented at Catholic University in 1942 and was a big hit. It was written by Leo Brady and Walter Kerr, who was teaching drama at C.U. Walter would be known one day as the famous drama critic for *The New York Times*. In later years, he and his talented wife Jean Kerr, the author of *Mary, Mary* and many other successful books and Broadway plays, would become our neighbors and lifelong friends.

The Shuberts bought *Count Me In* and brought it to New York. The play was a hit at Catholic University precisely because it had a small and intimate feeling. But when the Shuberts produced it on Broadway, they kept trying to make it bigger and grander with changes that weren't necessarily for the good of the show.

I remember being in the theater for the first reading, sitting around a worklight, meeting the new people and getting acquainted with the different roles. Then endless rehearsals, struggling to learn lines, creating the characters, then props, lights, and with musicals that great moment when the conductor gives the downbeat and the music is heard for the first time. What a thrill! Live theater is unique and so different from film in many ways. When music is involved it's always a joy for me, especially the first time it all comes together.

New York! New York! I'll never forget the thrill of my first Broadway show at the Barrymore Theater with Hal LeRoy, the super tap dancer, June Preisser, comedienne Louella Geer—music, music, music. I would stand in the wings and watch Gower Champion practice and practice, as all great dancers must. There was no doubt he was destined for success. When he later teamed with Marge, who became his wife, they did very special work on stage and in films, including the legendary MGM film version of *Show Boat*.

Another dancer, Jack Cassidy, who was a teenage chorus boy, was given his first Broadway experience in the play too. He married Shirley Jones and they became parents of David Cassidy of *Partridge Family* fame.

Most of all, I admired the brilliant choreographer Bob Alton. In fact, if Bob Alton had directed *Count Me In*, it might still be running. He had a fine sense of humor that made him fun to work with and also helped calm the nerves of this Broadway novice.

I remember for the big finale we all came out and sang "The Star Spangled Banner." This was during the war, remember, and patriotism was running high. In my anxiety, I started the song three beats before the group. Everybody in the audience laughed and I was humiliated. Backstage after the show Bob snapped his fingers and shouted, "Everybody on stage please." All assembled. "We're going to have a special rehearsal tonight so that Mary Healy can learn to sing 'The Star Spangled Banner' on cue." Everyone laughed and it eased my embarrassment.

It was also great to work with Charlie Butterworth, the stuttering comedian. Actually, he was an intelligent man with a law degree from Notre Dame. He had to support his acting habit by working as a journalist until he became one of the country's most popular actors on stage and in films.

Irene Sharaff designed the unique sets. An outstanding one that I particularly recall used a variety of shades of red in an unforgettable motif. I never saw so much red and it turned out fine!

I played the ingenue and rehearsals kept me busy. But I still missed my new husband, so I had mixed feelings when the play closed. I was sad, but I was also happy to be given a chance to spend some time in California with Peter.

P:

When Mary left for New York, I was really alone and

miserable. To console my lonely heart, I began to stuff my lonely stomach. I became a nervous eater. Each morning's roll call became a "sweet roll call" to me. Immediately after I was present and accounted for, I skipped around the corner to the pastry shop and pursued my study of the intricate art of doughnut dunking. I was a past master. I knew just how long to hold a chocolate covered doughnut under coffee before the point of disintegration was reached. I had also become a slob!

One night after I finished a banana split at my favorite Owl Drugstore, I decided to invest a penny toward finding out just how much of a slob I had become. I held my breath, stepped gingerly on the scale and dropped a coin into the slot. After a shriek that sounded like the cry of a frightened peacock, the scale released a card which told me that I should be ashamed of myself and that I weighed 183 pounds. My first inclination was to laugh my weight off, but then I turned the card over. I was expecting to see a smiling picture of Caesar Romero or Tyrone Power. But no, the picture was of beautiful Mary Healy! I sobbed a little as I blurted out, "Everyone loves a fat man, unless they're married to one!"

The sudden realization that I had become a fat man prodded me into a diet that lasted 26 hours. At the end of this ordeal I crawled deliriously back to the pastry shop and devoured everything in sight. I was actually on my seventh doughnut when lightning struck. A tall, lean sergeant had tracked me to my hideaway and was telling me that the Colonel wanted to see me. I had glorious delusions as I struggled toward the administration building. "The Colonel," I mused, "has chosen me to be the first to know that the war will be over in 20 minutes and will *I* be able to get *him* a job when we all return to civilian life?"

I was wrong. The Colonel wanted me to be the first to

know that he was sick of me and was lending me out to the First Motion Picture Unit in Culver City for a training film called, *Crash Landings in Unfavorable Terrain*. I saluted smartly and asked if the "part" was any good just before I was thrown out of his office.

I had heard of the First Motion Picture Unit. I remember one night Fred Allen very wryly stated that America had nothing to fear because that afternoon the First Motion Picture Unit had advanced three frames. My orders were in perfect shape so I had no trouble passing the Santa Ana border. I had one day's delay en route and was told to report at Fort Roach (as in Hal Roach) on a Thursday at 7:15 A.M. This was a little early for an actor of my stature, so naturally I was trembling with indignation as I approached the ominous gates of Fort Roach.

As I passed through the gates, I spotted a coffee stand and rushed madly toward the solace I knew I would find there. The attendant was kindly and smiled knowingly as I asked for "hot coffee, two of those chocolate covered ones and one of those with the coconut on it!" I had submerged one of the doughnuts and was drooling in eager anticipation of that moment when it would be ready.

Suddenly from nowhere, a hand shot out and encircled my wrist in a vice-like grip. My eyes traveled slowly up the arm until I saw a corporal's stripes. Being a sergeant, I felt confident. I looked further and found that my antagonist was the Montana cowboy actor George Montgomery, who was married to Dinah Shore.

"Hi-ya, George, ol' boy." I said. He tightened his grip on my wrist and sneered, "Have you looked at yourself lately?"

"No, I haven't, George, and let go of my doughnut!" His piercing cowboy eyes glared into mine.

"Get with it man. Jump out of bed in the morning and take a cold shower. Get to work with those barbells!"

"George!" I hollered. "Let go of my wrist, you're ruining my doughnut!" At this point I bit him on the arm. His agonized scream brought us to the attention of a passing lieutenant. The lieutenant quickly brought us to attention and bellowed, "What is the meaning of this, men?"

"Nothing sir," I said. "This corporal won't let me have my doughnut!"

The lieutenant studied the situation for a moment and then in a God-given voice, said, "Corporal, let the Sergeant have his doughnut!"

Montgomery released my wrist, but it was too late. The doughnut was done for. This tragic incident happened many years ago, but I was never able to sit through a George Montgomery movie.

After finishing *Crash Landings in Unfavorable Terrain,* I was ordered back to the R.P.U. unit in Santa Ana. There was bad news and good news waiting. The bad news was for Walter Kerr and Leo Brady. One critic had summed up their Broadway venture *Count Me In* by saying, "Count me out!"

The good news was that my lovely Mary was returning to me. At the time, I was living in two rented rooms with Bill Orr, Tommy D'Andre and George Hope—no place for a lady. Pvt. Frank Loesser was in the same dilemma; his wife Lynn was expected soon. We put our heads together and pooled our resources with Hal Bourne (pianist) and Harry Bluestone (violinist). The six of us moved into an ancient house in Costa Mesa.

The major problem with the house was that it had only one bathroom. Hal Bourne was a mild hypochondriac, Frank Loesser was a full fledged one and Lynn Loesser had to have the bathroom when the magic moment arrived—which was most of the time. Consequently, Harry Bluestone and I spent an awful lot of time in the orange grove next door. Because of the bathroom, hostility started raising its ugly head. Frank and I set a little ploy in motion to rid ourselves of the two musicians and finally it worked. They became disgruntled and moved out. Oh joy, the two couples now had the house to themselves and the toilet was put on a schedule.

M:

Peter and I lived with the Loessers because housing was so short in California. A lot of the guys stationed there were musicians, including some great ones right out of the studios. We'd all play poker till the wee hours and life was lots of fun. Since I was trying to find a job, I only came down from our little house in North Hollywood on weekends, but I made good coffee and they liked my cooking.

Frank bought a small pump organ on which he frequently composed his songs. One night he surprised us with a new song, "Once In Love With Mary." Later on he changed it to "Once In Love With Amy," which became a big hit for Ray Bolger in *Where's Charley*? He had to change the name, he told me, because that was the character's name in the play, but I couldn't help feeling that it was my song. That's also when Peter and Frank wrote the wonderfully funny song, "Why Do They Call a Private a Private? (When His Life is a Public Event)."

P:

Frank and I were both bored with our activities at the R.P.U. One evening I suggested that we write a GI show and travel it throughout the entire West Coast training command. I had written a lyric that intrigued him:

Why Do They Call a Private a Private (When His Life Is a Public Event)?

I know why they call a corporal a corporal,
Because he's got two stripes.
I know why they call a sergeant a sergeant,
Because he always gripes.
Yes, I know almost all military types, but
Why do they call a private a private
When his life is a public event.
The Pennsylvania station, that crossroads of the nation
Has nothing on a regular Army tent.
They snore and snore and snore all night,
They drop their shoes and light the light,
It's hell to have to smell a regiment,
(Have you been marching?)
Why do they call a private a private,
When his life is a public EVENT.

Frank sat down and put a gay little patter tune to the lyric. This is how *On the Beam* was born.

We spent weeks assembling our little revue and even put The General Orders to music and finally we were ready to audition. The two Colonels liked what they saw and assigned the project to the new man in town. The "new man in town" turned out to be Fredrick Brisson. It seems Mr. Brisson, along with his lovely wife Rosalind Russell, had attended President Roosevelt's birthday ball and now Captain Brisson had been assigned to the R.P.U. unit in Santa Ana.

Captain Brisson decided that the first thing we should do was to fly the West Coast command and check out the facilities. I had been flying commercially since 1933 and had no fear of airplanes. Frank was moderately calm until Thunderbird AFB in Tucson, Arizona. We were not aware of Captain Brisson's sense of humor. You see, he was Danish.

He had set us up with two hotshot pilots in an Air Force pursuit plane. We had all the flying gear including a parachute and were placed in the back seat of two very fast airplanes. Following the Captain's orders, the two pilots turned the crank on us—barrel rolls, stalls, upside down, hedgehopping, figures of eight and power dives. After 20 minutes of this, we taxied to a safe landing. I was the first to emerge. Frank was ashen when he boarded the aircraft, but now when he stepped out, he looked like a jolly green midget. He leaned against the wing of the plane and said, "This is too much adventure for a Jew!"

The next order of the day was to line up at the commissary and purchase as many Schick blades as they would sell us. Schick blades were hard to come by during the war years, and Captain Brisson just loved Schick blades.

The project had been approved, and back at Santa Ana I set about putting my GI troopers together. We were assigned three con buses and three drivers. Matt Dennis was in charge of our five-piece band composed of Ran Wencil (a mad comedian), Jerry Adler (with brother

Larry's leftover harmonicas), Ray MacDonald (great dancer), Bill Willard (*Variety's* man in Las Vegas), and various and sundry others. We all doubled as singers, dancers and comics. The morning our caravan was scheduled to leave Santa Ana, I asked Frank which bus he wanted to ride in. He replied, "Oh? I'm not going!" That was the morning I dubbed him "The Loesser of two evils." He went on to write oh so many hits.

On the Beam had been my original idea, so naturally I felt like General MacArthur as we rolled out of Santa Ana. Our mission was very successful in Southern and Northern California, but what I hadn't realized was that most of the West Coast training command was located in isolated plague spots in New Mexico, Arizona and a state called Texas.

By the time we reached Texas, little "cliques" had been formed and everybody's nerves were on edge. By now we had covered more than 5,500 miles in those hard-assed buses and had survived mainly on hot dogs, hamburgers and chili. I don't think I have to remind you that this particular menu would not be conducive to the good life in a non-air conditioned-re-con bus.

We pressed on. Finally we reached the asshole of all creation. They called it Marfa, Texas.

The PR man for the Air Force snapped me to attention and said, "Sergeant, you may have a tough time out there today. You are appearing before 700 cadets who have just been washed out as pilots. They don't like it, but perhaps you can cheer them up."

Well, let me tell you there was no way of cheering those kids up. In the middle of some of our best material audible sobs were heard. I would look down at the front row, and the tears were threatening to inundate the stage.

On The Beam was a disaster. I was very upset. As we were packing up, a private invaded my dressing room and said, "Sergeant Hayes, there are two GIs out here who would like to talk to you."

Having just failed miserably in my life's work, I was willing to talk to anyone. In came a replica of Abbott and Costello. I studied them for a moment and said, "Yeah, what do you want?"

"Well, Sergeant, you had a rather tough time out there tonight, and we would love to join your show."

"Yeah, what do you do?"

"Well, my name is Johnny Silver, and my friend's name is Mario Coccoza. We both sing. I'm a baritone, and he's a tenor."

"Well, shit! What am I going to do with two singers? You know this is a GI show, and who the hell needs two more singers?"

Mario then took over the conversation and said, "Well, if you don't want singers, let's go to the mess hall and have an early breakfast." We went to the mess hall and I watched him devour a dozen eggs and a half side of bacon. I was amazed, and suddenly asked, "What do you weigh?"

"Well, weight has always been my problem. I weigh 276 pounds, but I'm a barbell nut and tomorrow I'm going on a diet."

"Well, what in the hell do you want from me?"

"I'm from South Philadelphia, and just before I was inducted into the Air Force, I made a record with Koussevitsky and I want you to hear it."

We wandered over to the rec hall and suddenly I heard the greatest tenor I had ever heard.

"Now look, it's tough to get anyone transferred in the

Air Force, but I'll call my commanding officer and see if I can have you two clowns transferred to our unit."

"Captain Brisson, this is Sergeant Hayes, and I have found two live people in Marfa, Texas, that I think would work wonderfully well in *On the Beam*."

"Oh really, Sergeant? What do they do?"

"Well, sir, they are both opera singers, and I have an idea. The boys are cleaning up the barracks with mops and pails and suddenly, Mario, the tenor, forms the ugly bars of a jail with the mop sticks and does the aria from *Aida*. Of course, sir, Johnny Silver could reverse his overseas cap and become the "femme fatale" of the opera, and suddenly, Mario would break down the mop sticks and triumphantly carry off the baritone. I think it would work, sir."

"Well, Sergeant Hayes, you know it is terribly difficult to get a pair of GIs transferred from one unit to another."

"Yes, I know that sir, but would you try?"

"Yes, I will Sergeant." When we left Marfa, Texas, Mario Coccoza and Johnny Silver were on the bus.

Our next stop was Sedalia, New Mexico. We had done our show to another dejected group of "washed out cadets." After the show, the commanding officer said, "There is a man out here who would like to talk to you."

I jumped to attention and asked, "Oh sir, what is the man's name?"

"Moss Hart," he replied. I had heard of Moss Hart and was eagerly awaiting his appearance. Mr. Hart invited me to join him in a dark corner of the rec hall as he wanted to talk privately. Moss was a tall, dark, soft-spoken man who kept reminding me of Edgar Allen Poe's "The Raven."

"Sergeant, I understand you are in charge of this show."

"Yes sir, I am."

"I'm doing a show for the Air Force. We are calling it *Winged Victory*. It will be a serious show about cadets, but I also need some entertainment. By the way, what is the fat tenor's name?"

"His real name is Coccoza, but since joining us, he has changed it to Mario Lanza. Coccoza means melon in Italian, and he got tired of me calling him 'melon head'."

Mr. Hart made a list of the entertainers he wanted from *On the Beam* and his last words were, "I have total priority, and the group I have named will be sent for in a few weeks."

The last stop for *On the Beam* was at the Gunnery School in Las Vegas, Nevada, the future Nellis Air Force Base. A family reunion was in order.

Hazy was now the hostess at El Rancho Vegas, the first hotel on the future Las Vegas Strip. She had sold the Grace Hayes Lodge in North Hollywood after a disastrous fire. While I was on the road, she had thrown in the towel and leased the place to Bill Miller and an old vaudevillian named "Think-a-drink Hoffman." Charlie Foy and Joe Frisco were doing very well and Miller and Hoffman were doing well also.

Hazy was an avid poker player and this one particular evening, she was wheeling and dealing at Hugh (Woo Woo) Herbert's house. She was "bumping" and "raising" all over the place, and at 4 A.M. she received a phone call from the owner of the motel next to the Lodge. The message was direct and to the point. "The Lodge is afire!" Frantically she raced to protect her meal ticket. When she arrived, smoldering black smoke had engulfed the entire front of the place and no firemen were to be seen. She borrowed a large bucket from the motel and frantically tried to douse the flames.

In California, 4 A.M. was the ideal time to move houses. In 1942 there was very little traffic at that early hour. Sure enough, as she peered over her bucket, here came a single frame house on wheels. Two men were waving red lanterns and directing the truck driver.

Foy and Frisco had apparently heard about the fire, and had driven down to watch the old Hour-Glass-Girl's club go up in flames. Frisco was within earshot when he suddenly noticed the house waddling around the corner of Ventura Boulevard. He turned to Foy and said, "She must have expected the f-f-fire, h-h-here c-c-comes the n-n-new club!" That wasn't the nicest thing to say to a Lady Bug when her house was on fire. She hit him with the bucket and when last seen they were both running down the middle of Ventura Boulevard. Even in her high heels, she almost caught them.

The firemen finally showed up, but the Lodge was a total disaster. It was also woefully underinsured and within a week, she had sold it at a tremendous loss. It was then she had decided to accept the job at the El Rancho.

As the Hostess with the Mostest, she was determined to show *On the Beam* a good time in Las Vegas. We were scheduled to spend three days at the Gunnery School and then return to Santa Ana. In those three days, we took the town. At that time, Las Vegas had a population of 26,000 people, and they all came replete with bowlegs and cowboy boots.

Hazy "put us on" every night at the El Rancho and it was the first time I had ever seen cowboy boots give a standing ovation to an opera singer. Mario Lanza was a riot every night and I was so proud that we had rescued him from an incinerator called Marfa, Texas.

Our mission had been accomplished, and we returned to home base. We had traveled 8,600 miles in those three re-con buses, and I was elated. Mary welcomed me back to our estate in Costa Mesa and I slept for two days with clenched eyes. At our first roll call, I was told that orders had been cut for me. Jerry Adler, Ray MacDonald and Mario Lanza were also to report to Mr. Moss Hart at the Forty-Fourth Street Theater in New York City.

Mary was coming to New York with me. Our life's savings at this point amounted to very little, so we decided that Mary would take a train and I would go by troop train, at Uncle Sam's expense.

Mary arrived ten days before I did and rented a two-room flat on East Forty Fifth Street. Another new life was beginning. The new life turned out to be newer than the apartment. It was so small, as Fred Allen used to say, "Even the mice were hunch-backed," when you closed the bedroom door, "the knob got into bed with you." The price was right for a sublease—$145 a month, furnished.

The next morning, all of the GI Gypsies assembled at the old Forty-Fourth Street Theater to audition for Moss Hart's *Winged Victory*. Actors, singers, dancers and comedians are a furtive lot. Most of them are emotionally unstable, so you can imagine how intense the auditions became. It was no longer a question of your professional career; the audition was also for your Army career. If you failed, chances are your ass would be shipped overseas on the next boat.

We knew Mr. Hart sat in the dark abyss of the otherwise empty theater, and one by one, we were called out to do our thing—sing, dance, tell a joke. I must admit I felt confident and reasonably safe. I had written and perfected a GI drunk routine. With my fatigue hat and an obnoxious set of false teeth, I auditioned.

I was right, the drunk convulsed Mr. Hart and, during future rehearsals, I was called on many times to entertain Mr. Hart's illustrious friends—George S. Kaufman, Gertrude Lawrence, Noel Coward, Bennett Cerf. I felt a certain security, but the endless rehearsals and auditions became boring.

Claude Stroud was one of the Stroud Twins. I never missed their funny radio shows with Edgar Bergen, Charlie McCarthy and W.C. Fields. He became my new Air Force buddy. His brother Clarence had been drafted into the Army so I became the alter ego twin. The Strouds had also been in vaudeville. Claude and I had a lot in common.

Everything went well until opening night in Boston. *Winged Victory* was a very "heavy" show and Mr. Hart had invited George S. Kaufman to Boston for the premiere performance. The show was an hour and a half too long.

Naturally, the next morning we were called to the theater very early for some judicious cutting. Three hundred of us were lined up in the bleacher set and my name was the first to be called. Mr. Hart took me by the elbow and in his best Ronald Coleman voice, started walking me in circles. I was strutting now because the accolades were incredible. "Peter, you were magnificent last night. I haven't heard an audience howl like that in years, it's the funniest routine I have ever seen. It was hilarious. It stopped the show. But it's out!"

I went into a state of shock and after picking up the pieces, I retired to a phone booth and called Hazy.

"He did what?" she asked.

"He took my routine out," I replied.

"You son of a bitch, I told you never to be good out of town."

After the war, Moss gave me an autographed copy of the book of the play. The inscription reads, "To Peter Lind Hayes, who took the biggest cut since the Panama Canal and like a perfect gentleman."

It was suggested by Mr. Kaufman that Mr. Hart's play could not gather in the audience after the clowns had left in the South Pacific scene. Lee J. Cobb complained that he could not play his big dramatic scene as a doctor cursing his lack of supplies and challenging the gods while he wept over the mangled bodies of airmen with broken wings. "What the hell are they laughing at?" he was heard to mumble.

There were so many actors in *Winged Victory*—Edmund O'Brien, John Forsythe, Don Taylor and several hundred others too numerous to mention. Naturally some had good scenes and some had none.

In two world wars our Commanding Officer, Colonel Dunham, had never ventured as far overseas as Catalina Island. His show business background consisted of playing the organ in a Baptist Church in San Antonio, Texas. When pressed, he would also admit that he had taught the Siamese twins, Daisy and Violet Hilton, how to play the saxophone. Wasn't it logical then, for the Air Force to put him in charge of all these actors, singers, dancers, communists and homosexuals? OOP's! I almost forgot to mention that Colonel Dunham was also General Hap Arnold's brother-in-law. Nepotism in the Air Force. Tsk! Tsk!

Winged Victory lingered for months at the old Forty-Fourth Street Theater. It was sort of a patriotic duty to see it. Finally we ran out of patriots and were given orders to take to the road. We were to travel from city to city by troop trains. At the close of each engagement we would assemble in full battle dress and march smartly to the railroad station. We all had "rhythm" so naturally we marched quite well. It was rather embarrassing to see emotional women sobbing in the streets and throwing flowers at our feet. Didn't they realize that our gas masks had been removed long ago and replaced by a container filled with peanut shells, orange peelings, candy wrappers and half empty gin bottles?

Twentieth Century-Fox had decided to produce the film of *Winged Victory* and George Cukor, who was famous as a director of women, naturally was given the assignment. The entire cast was camped in luxurious tents on a sandy beach at Santa Monica. (WAR IS HELL.)

Twelve
"Once in Love with Mary"

Once in love with Mary
Always in love with Mary

—*Music and lyrics by Frank Loesser*

P:

Soon the film was finished, and so for that matter, was *Winged Victory*. We had one last week to play in Richmond, Virginia, and then we were to be given our new assignments. We troop trained it all the way back to Richmond and finally, *Winged Victory* folded its tent and slowly faded away.

We were given a 14-day delay en route. Claude and I and some other entertainers were given orders to report to Kearns, Utah. I returned to New York to visit Mary who was then in a Choderov play called *Common Ground*. Mary knew I was tired of "play acting" the part of a soldier and that I relished the thought of finding out what it really was like "over there." Not brave, mind you, just curious.

Mary had been working in small supper clubs to keep from digging into the money we had put aside for a really

A handsome man in uniform

rainy day. Fortunately my "delay en route" did not conflict with her schedule, so we enjoyed ourselves completely.

We went to an Actor's Benefit of a play entitled *The Hasty Heart*. Seated two rows in front of us were—guess who? Johnny Silver and Mario Lanza. They were both nattily garbed in snappy civilian sport clothes.

During intermission I cornered Mario and hissed, "You barbell bum. I'm going overseas and you could break me in half with one arm. How the hell did you get out?" Mario gave me his famous cherubic grin and said, "I told you, Pete, my post nasal drip!"

After I had stopped grinding my teeth, he added, "By the way, Pete, since you are going overseas and you may not come back, I want a clear conscience. That record I played for you back in Marfa, Texas, was the great Italian tenor Beniamino Gigli. It wasn't me at all."

That revelation made me laugh out loud and I complimented Cocozza on his cleverness. But all through the second act Mary had to ask me to stop grinding my teeth. (Well at least the son of a gun really could sing.)

M:

When we saw him in New York just before Peter went overseas, none of us dreamed Mario was on the brink of superstardom. Mario always gave credit to Peter for discovering him. Just before he died in 1959, we were invited to a grand dinner in his Italian villa in Rome—actually it looked more like a castle. I remember the Gettys were part of their elegant dinner party and the champagne was flowing. Mario seated Peter right next to him.

"Pete, if it weren't for you, I'd never be here," he said

again and again. Peter interviewed him for our national radio show. It was Mario's last interview and aired twelve days after he died. Peter also played Mario's recording of "Voce e notte" in tribute to his friend.

P:

Inevitably dates have a habit of showing up. My time to go overseas was at hand and after a tearful farewell with Mary, I took off for Kearns, Utah, for training. Kearns is just 14 miles from Salt Lake City. I have no idea what Brigham Young had in mind when he turned to his followers and said, "This is the place." I realize the Mormons were persecuted because of their religious beliefs, but at that time I felt that Kearns, Utah, was as close as I could get to hell without going there directly.

The next day was spent on the firing line. Despite the fact that I had little or no basic training I had always been pretty good with a rifle and my carbine was an excellent weapon. I was relieved to make marksman with a score of 156. The M3 submachine gun was a different matter. Seventeen out of a possible 25 and it scared the hell out of me. I'll not elaborate on my last minute overseas training except to mention that it was strenuous, healthy and body-building. I really enjoyed it and slept like a baby.

Before leaving *Winged Victory*, secret orders had been issued to me under the code name Zebra. I had no clue what they meant, but was told to present them to my commanding officer when I arrived at my destination. Since we were confined to post at Kearns, I decided to take inventory and find out if I could put a show together.

The cast will not overwhelm you, but here it is, the roll call: Claude Stroud, Jerry Adler (harmonica), Danny

Scholl (tenor), Walter Long (dancer), Julian Stockdale (guitar), John Tyers (baritone) and Joseph Gant Gaither, our stage manager.

Since I was the ranking non-com. I became the boss man. At night we clowned and danced and sang all over the post. There were thousands of men so we never ran out of audiences, and by God, we were good.

There must be some sort of ESP for lonely soldiers on any Army base. We were never told anything, but suddenly the air became electric with anticipation we knew the hour was at hand. Two days before our orders were cut to entrain for Seattle and that "boat ride," Stroud came running into the barracks shouting. "Peter, Peter, have you seen the bulletin board?"

"No, Stroudy I haven't. Why?" Stroud clicked his heels and trumpeted, "Any man 38 or older doesn't have to go overseas."

Stroud was 38 and I was heart broken. I was about to lose my GI buddy.

In retrospect it was a selfish thought. Claude and Gloria had a baby daughter, and the government, in its wisdom, was giving the man back to his family. As a Tech Sergeant, my rank was beginning to rankle me. Simply because of my rating I was put in charge of 50 men, three of whom had jumped ship twice before.

The long march to the train was exhausting, especially since I was trying to manage my theatrical props, my GI equipment and to safeguard a precious bottle of Chivas Regal Scotch that Stroud had given me as a going away present.

There was a sign in front of the railroad station at Kearns that stated: "Through these portals pass the best damn soldiers in the world."

I fell down three times trying to reach that goal.

Meantime Stroud rode alongside of us in a jeep tossing Red Dot cigars from a helmet liner in my path. During the train ride to Seattle, my main preoccupation was keeping a wary eye on the three "ship jumpers." Because of these men, our reputation preceded us to the Seattle port. As soon as we boarded ship we were stuffed down a hatch and found ourselves in the "hold."

If you're not "yar," the "hold" is below the water line and by now our group had blossomed to around 300 men. Our ship lay at dockside for more than two hours and since most of the men were from Arkansas, Texas, Oklahoma, Indiana, Kansas, Nebraska and Illinois, the gentle notion of the S.S. *Lyon* bobbing about in its slip did not appeal to their landlubber stomachs.

In about four minutes all 300 started throwing up. An idiot corporal was guarding the hatch. When I pressed my face to the hatch and mouthed the words, "Give us some air," he smiled and thumbed his nose at me.

After we were two hours at sea the hatch was finally opened and we were allowed to come topside. Who the hell could swim back to Seattle now?

We had mess after this, and not being too hungry, I went aft to gaze at our convoy of seagulls. They are glorious in flight! How expertly the sea gulls handle themselves as they glide in and out of our backwash of air! They're pretty aggressive and fearless. You could almost reach out and grab them as they taunt you to throw something overboard. I watched the seagulls for quite some time but was wondering what was in store for me.

I was destined to have a restless night on the briny. If you have never been on a troop ship let me explain that you sleep in one of five canvas slings that are arranged like dresser drawers. The headspace between your nose and someone else's ass is about four and a half inches.

The guy above me coughed and farted so much I thought I had a cold.

Up on deck at 5 A.M. to sweat out a two-hour line for breakfast. The eggs were scrambled and tasted like putty. Even the oatmeal had forgotten its ancestry and refused to taste like anything but sawdust. I went to confession in a barber chair and was given a penance of five Hail Marys. I really didn't expect more. When in the hell did I have the time to commit a sin?

I gathered the Pigeons together and asked for permission to do a show. Permission granted. We racked them up. The Pigeons were a huge success. I reminded myself not to be carried away because these guys were ready to enjoy a funeral. Two thousand men packed into this tub, lonely and homesick—including me.

M:

Meantime in the big city I had been so glad to be given a chance to do another Broadway play, this time in the provocative Edward Choderov play *Common Ground*. Frightened at first because it was my first straight play, I soon found I loved working as a dramatic actress. Choderov was a fine New York writer and I got to work with quality actors.

It was a drama about the tragedies going on in Europe at the time. In its plot, American entertainers flying over Italy were shot down, captured and held prisoners by an Italian Fascist played by the excellent Luther Adler. The other passengers were a Groucho Marx-type jokester played by Philip Lobe, a singer/pianist played by popular Nancy Nolan, and a Hollywood starlet played by yours truly. George Jenkins designed the set, which won the Tony that year.

The entire play took place in a bombed-out Italian palace with a balcony and staircase stage left, which was perfect for Lord HaHa's anti-American speeches to the captives. Luther Adler made us entertain him—and we knew if we didn't do the songs right, he'd shoot us! Luther gave a powerful performance. He did a tirade in Italian, which he had learned phonetically and delivered so brilliantly that people who knew Italian understood every word. Nancy Nolan always brought down the house when she sang for him, "It's a Big Wide Wonderful World." Once again I sang "Star Dust." That song kept coming into my life!

Luther Adler came from a well-known New York theatrical family. His sister Stella Adler was a famous acting teacher. He saw how nervous I was opening night and he gave me some good advice, "Remember," he told me, "this will be the first and last time you will give THIS performance. So pull it all together and give it all your energy."

That advice has served me well many times over my life, and not just for my work in show business. It applies to any endeavor you undertake. The play had a good run and was considered a success. I was even nominated for a Tony Award. I didn't win, but I didn't mind losing to Anne Bancroft in *The Miracle Worker*. She was just beginning her acting career then too and she was superb.

There was a camaraderie in New York theater that you didn't have in movies. So I wasn't lonely long, although of course I missed my fella overseas. Two of my close friends were Shirley Eder, the columnist, and comedienne Nancy Walker. You might remember Nancy from many years later when she stole the show as Rhoda's mother on the television series *Rhoda*. We'd go to Sardi's for lunch and dinner and sitting there would be Mary Martin, Helen Hayes, Ethel Merman and other great Broadway stars. It was another world for me, and just as much fun as meeting all the Hollywood royalty the year before.

Don Murphy, Nancy Nolan and I loved to go after the show to hear Mabel Mercer sing at Tony's, a club down the street from "21." Mabel always had first-rate pianists. She found songs, mostly show tunes that other people weren't singing, and presented them in a most theatrical way. I have special admiration for people who can tell a story with a song lyric. One reason Frank Sinatra is so great is that you believe his stories. He touches your heart because he believes the lyrics every time he sings them. This is real artistry, real creativity. Mabel was a very special singer too. I guess I heard every great jazz singer in New York at that time.

After *Common Ground* closed, I worked in New York as a nightclub singer myself. It was always hard to find a place to live during those years. I often stayed with our good friends, Frank and Lynn Loesser. Frank was turning out one hit song after another. John Steinbeck was their friend too so I got to see him and many other interesting people.

Then I was booked in *Springtime in Brazil,* a play in Chicago starring Milton Berle. I replaced Rose Marie. Milton, like Peter, had been in vaudeville as a boy and was a total pro. Milton's path—and ours—would soon lead us to a brand new medium called television. Television? We'd barely heard of it. But working with Milton was fun and another learning experience for me.

But I missed my Pedro. . . .

P:

It was June of 1945 when the Pigeons winged their way into the South Pacific. Our transport boat was rumored to be carrying hundreds of cases of nitroglycerine. We were dogged by a Japanese sub and had to zigzag across the ocean. One spark and Davy Jones would have had to build a larger locker. I filled my mind with my lovely Mary, worlds away in New York.

While we were waiting for permission to land in Honolulu, we watched the gun crews from our S.S. *Lyon* open up on navy planes buzzing overhead. They virtually blew the hell out of the sky. The crossfire was actually stunningly beautiful to watch. It looked so real and my God! It was!

It was great to plant the dogs on terra firma once more, though Honolulu was less than a tropical paradise at the time. What a dump! Every jukebox played nothing but Bob Wills and His Texas Playboys. We hitchhiked to our depot, changing vehicles six times. It rained every 13 minutes and I was soon mildewed.

A high spot was a bottle of milk I happened to find along the way. It tasted so-o-o good. I guzzled it like the swells back home guzzled champagne while they watched Mary singing in the New York clubs. It was my last milk for many months to come.

The next morning, we started taking jungle training with the infantry. From all the heckling, you'd think we were fighting on different sides. The infantry didn't like the Air Force and the Air Force wasn't too fond of being their guests.

That night I was sitting next to a 30-year master sergeant at the show. While drinking our coffee, I asked him how long the Air Force boys usually stayed at the Replacement Depot. He looked at my stripes and smirked, "Well the last batch was here about two weeks. One morning around 4 A.M. we got 'em all out of bed and welcomed them to the Army." That statement helped me get rid of a pretty rotten dinner and also frightened me into promoting a 12-hour pass.

Bright and early the next morning I took a bus to Hickam Field. I was not on familiar ground but a corporal pointed me in the general direction of the special services building. I presented myself to a surly captain who asked me to state my business.

"Well sir, I was shipped over here with secret orders called Zebra. Apparently they are so secret no one has ever heard of them."

The captain glared at me for what seemed a lifetime and then barked, "Stand at attention when you're addressing me!" I snapped to and waited for my heart to start beating.

"Now get one thing straight, Sergeant. There are channels in this man's army and the proper way to do things is through channels and through channels only!"

"Oh my God," I thought, "this man has seen too many movies." He was about to continue his attack with wild threats about a court martial when suddenly a kindly voice was heard. The kindly voice was wearing a full colonel's wings and there was an immediate transition in the captain's manner.

The colonel squashed the captain and I heard him say, "You come in here, son, and we'll see if we can find out what the trouble is."

Well, when he called me son, I knew this Andy Hardy had found a friend. I explained our predicament. It was true there were no such orders as Zebra.

"How many are you?"

I answered, "We are seven, sir, and are called the Winged Pigeons."

The colonel asked, "Are you any good?"

"Oh, yes sir, we are, and, sir, we are all professionals."

"Okay, Sergeant, I'll call the General at the Replacement Depot and have you all transferred to Hickam tomorrow."

I had a sudden impulse to kiss his hand but I fought it off. I whistled and sang all the way back to camp. The Pigeons were pleased as punch when I told them about almost getting my ass in a sling, but that the mission was accomplished. It was a thrill to be back in the Air Force again. Hickam was lovely. No signs of the pasting it had taken on that tragic December 7, 1941. Great country, America!

We were confined to the base for the length of time it took to process us. Colonel Stansbury was to be our new boss. He was primarily interested in athletes and was a little curious about seven hams. Our big test took place June 23 in Hickam's famous Starlight Bowl.

The permanent company of Hickam was a little smug when it came to entertainment. After all, they had been exposed to practically every big star in show business through the auspices of the USO. When seven USA clowns came on in fatigues, they weren't too thrilled. Whispers of "goldbricking" were overheard. However, the fatigues seemed to work well psychologically! When they realized there was some talent under those sloppy clothes, the scorn turned to admiration.

After our baptism by fire, we were gathered in by three old friends, Navy Lt. Art Jarret, Bob Crosby, and Lt. Commander Marshall Duffield, a former all-American quarterback from Southern California. He had worked his way up and was doing a splendid job for the Navy. He never lost a ship nor his humble manner. We went to Bob's house and told a lot of lies until the wee small hours of the morning.

My 30th birthday was surprisingly happy. The Winged Pigeons chipped in and gave me a B-4 bag. It was quite the nicest thing that had happened since I'd joined the Air Force. That evening I had another surprise birthday present. The Pigeons did a show for 55,000 men at Bellows Field. Just think of that moment—55,000 men from all branches of the services. They were not easy in the beginning, very discerning; but once they accepted you, oh brother—absolutely sensational!

Five officers came back after the show to tell us they would start a campaign "down under" that would make the Winged Pigeons famous before we got there. "Down Under" meant the entire chain of the Mariana Islands starting with Johnson, Eniwetok, Kwajelein, Guam, Okinawa, Saipan, Tinian, Iwo Jima and Ishima.

Colonel Stansbury put the wheels in motion to send us down under in a converted B-24 Bomber. I needed one good lead instrument. One day it presented itself to me in a driving rainstorm. It turned out to be Master Sergeant Joe Bushkin, the famous jazz pianist from the Tommy Dorsey era. A traveling piano at this time was out of the question, but I knew Joe also played cornet. Joe had been in Moss Hart's *Winged Victory,* but we had traveled in different circles.

There were many musicians in the company and Joe was intolerant of anyone who wasn't musically inclined. Bushkin had not received an assignment and was desperate to join us. Again, Colonel Stansbury made the necessary arrangements and the Pigeons had a "crazy" new member.

Now we were nine and July 7 was our red-letter day. We took off in a B-24. Our first stop was Johnson Island. It was so tiny, I was surprised a B-24 could land there. We did a show for the Navy and then I met my first gooney bird. A gooney bird is twice the size of a seagull and thinks it can fly. It can't! But it keeps trying. For hours the Pigeons watched the gooney birds. They were hilarious. Time after time they would awkwardly climb a ladder to the top of the slanted roof of a Quonset hut, peer left and right to make sure no one was looking, and then, with fierce determination rush headlong down the roof. At the edge of the roof they would proudly spread their wings. Some of them managed to stay airborne for four or five seconds before plunging to the earth like a ton of bricks. This tremendous drop would stun them for a moment but slowly they would rise, shake their silly heads in disbelief and start the whole damned thing all over again.

It was also time for the Pigeons to fly. Except for a refueling stop at Eniwetok, we pressed on to Guam. Guam was similar in topography to Hickam. A very large, overpopulated, complacent permanent company of disgruntled men. We did many shows, one worth noting.

The Admiral Nimitz group invited us over to perform for CINPAC. Wow! The facilities were fabulous. We worked in a natural bowl about 100 feet below the Admiral's house. Nimitz was in conference with British liaison officers and he kept sending a sailor backstage to cut down our microphone. Every time the sailor did his job, I did mine. I turned it up again. I wanted those 5,000 people to hear every precious word.

On the way back to the air base we saw all the bombed out villages and the sight of the original beachhead, plus, naturally, the well-kept graves of the hundreds of our boys who "bought it" on that particular spot. Guam had only been secured nine months earlier and already roads and buildings were more modern than those back in Hawaii, 3,300 miles away. It really was remarkable what we had done.

July 17, we left Guam in a C-46. We bypassed Saipan and Tinian and made our way to the sands of Iwo Jima. This little island was not yet secure and there were cracked-up B-29s all over the landing strip. Only 10 days earlier, 200 well-organized Japanese had crawled out of their caves ready to die for Hirohito. They carved their way through tents and killed a lot of our guys in bed. The bloody hand-to-hand combat lasted several hours before the enemy was finally annihilated.

There were still a lot of dead Japanese soldiers on the beach and with a high wind the smell of that place sure didn't remind me of Hershey, Pennsylvania at eventide.

Mt. Surabachi sort of smiled complacently as it gazed down and counted its dead. The harbor was loaded with dead ships, twisted and broken in the middle, crawling with maggots and stinking to high heaven with the acrid perfume of the reaper. All this depressed me during the day, but at night, Mother Nature just wouldn't quit with her artistic paintbrush. She whipped up little moon and sky jobs that sent the proverbial shivers up and down my aching back.

Good God, it was hot as hell in that land of the rising sun. If I wanted a nice hot shower, all I had to do was pour some water in my helmet liner, balance it in the cinders, and come back in 10 minutes. I thought I was at the Ritz. Bushkin and I borrowed a jeep and drove to the site of our shows, a natural amphitheater. While wandering around, I picked up a Japanese shoe, but the soldier's ankle and foot were still in it, so I buried it in the sand.

By July 31 we had played every installation on Iwo Jima, including a two-day trip to the spot where Ernie Pyle had been killed by sniper fire. We had by-passed Saipan and Tinian and a Colonel Erickson informed me that a Marine Lieutenant by the name of Power was flying two airplane engines to Saipan that afternoon. I was told that he was having chow in the mess hall. I went in search of a hitch back to Saipan. Power was pointed out to me and as I drew near to his table, I was overwhelmed. It was Tyrone Power, the movie star. Having a comedic turn of mind, I made a big mistake. I approached the table and said, "Ready on the set Lieutenant!" Tyrone, not amused by my ad lib, stared at me sullenly and said, "I beg your pardon Sergeant?"

I snapped to, saluted smartly and started my pitch for a ride back to Saipan. After he heard my plea, I was told curtly to have my men and gear at his plane at 1300 hours. I gathered the Pigeons together and complained bitterly about his attitude. We scattered ourselves and our equipment in and around the two engines and waited for the C-47 to take off. After we were airborne for an hour, the co-pilot came aft and told me the Lieutenant would like to see me in the cockpit. Why the hell wouldn't he want to see me? Mary had done a picture with him and he had been in the Grace Hayes Lodge many evenings. As I entered the cockpit, he stood up, closed the door and threw his arms around me.

"Peter, I'm so glad to see you!"

I was embarrassed now and said, "Oh, really? You weren't so happy to see me in the mess hall." I added a pointed "Sir! " to that last speech.

He laughed out loud and said, "Knock it off with that Sir crap." It was then he explained the predicament of a movie star in a Marine boot camp—that simply because he was Tyrone Power, he was challenged to a fistfight every other day during his training. That reminded me of every strange kid's first day in a new school. One always had to prove oneself at first recess. Kind of foolish, but even tough Marines were once little children. Some day perhaps we will all grow up.

We arrived in Saipan and Tyrone Power became the greatest host we ever had. After every show, he would pick up us and take us back to his small officer's club. Volleyball, ice cream, beer and chow were the order of the day and we reveled in his generosity.

I became ill on Saipan and was sent to hospital with a bad case of dengue fever. Dengue is akin to dry rot. I not only ran a high fever, but my legs, ankles and feet started to look like a good prospect for a leper colony.

It was then that my mail started catching up with me. There was some disturbing news from my beautiful Mary. It seems Hazy had found out about our "rainy day" money and had slyly borrowed $5,000 from Mary to make a down payment on a piece of property in Las Vegas. The transaction had left Mary on her uppers and she was wondering when and if she would get the money back.

This knowledge started a letter writing campaign to my mother that was hysterical. After several exchanges, I threatened to write directly to President Roosevelt and enlist his aid in pushing her to return the money. The little scheme frightened her and the loan was repaid. At least I now knew that Mary wasn't starving to death.

A Quonset hut on Saipan is not the most attractive hospital one could wish for. The kid on the cot next to me was receiving a penicillin shot every hour on the hour, 24 hours a day. By now his body looked like a worn out punch board and every time he heard the footsteps of a nurse approaching his cot, he started screaming.

One morning the reflection on the ceiling of the hut convinced me that the sun had risen. Not at all. It was a B-29 that had crashed on takeoff from Tinian across the bay. It was completely loaded with bombs and continued to burn for 72 hours!

Finally, I was released from the hospital. We worked for weeks on Saipan and then Tinian and our next orders were cut for a pleasant little plague spot called Okinawa. We have since given Okinawa back to the Japanese. I'm glad.

By now the Pigeons had done more than 480 shows and had never been fired on once. On several occasions it was touch and go as far as the GIs were concerned. After one show on Okinawa, it was thrilling to hear Tokyo Rose call out our names and tell us that some of the Jungle Japanese had enjoyed us also. They were gutsy little fellows and on several occasions were known to strip a dead GI, don his uniform and silently sweat out a chow line for food.

Okinawa was more of the same, and except for a horrendous typhoon, uneventful. Little did we know that Okinawa was almost, but not quite, the end of the line for the Winged Pigeons.

The Japanese surrendered on August 15 and we waited for further orders. Three days after the surrender the Pigeons arrived in Tokyo. Wow! The older and the very young Japanese were pleased to see the Americans. They had had enough, but the military-aged men were humiliated and very angry. Their weapons had been confiscated but not their fists. Fights broke out constantly in the downtown Ginza district.

We were ensconced in a Red Cross building directly across the street from the Emperor's palace. On several occasions we had the pleasure of seeing General MacArthur, scrambled eggs, corncob pipe and all, strutting around our building. He didn't seem to recall that I had told him to "hang in there!" way back in Seattle.

We did many shows in public places that were often broken up by enraged Japanese. It's not much fun to try and entertain while the audience is involved in a massive riot. I must say, Bushkin was the most resourceful of all the Pigeons. By our third day in Tokyo he had secured his own pad, his own geisha girl and somehow managed to have all of his laundry done. We stayed 45 days in Tokyo and it was very exciting. Rumors of demobilization were flying thick and fast and my main concern was getting back to Mary, and trying to figure out how in the hell I could make a living.

We hitched a ride back to Guam and anxiously set about promoting a trip back to the States. Having received two battle stars, which was the equivalent of 10 points, it dawned on me that I, and several others in our group, were still five points short of what was needed to get a discharge.

General Spatz was now the Supreme Commander of Guam, and I had heard that he was leaving for Washington in three days. I suggested to his aide that we do a farewell show for the good general. The aide was amenable to the idea and we started preparing the most important show the Pigeons would ever do. We were all ensconced in the same tent and I called a "heavy" rehearsal. I cut everyone's performance to the bone. There was heavy whispering from our dancer, Walter Long. I cut him out altogether, but I assured him that he was very important to the operation, and to stay near me at all times.

The night arrived, and so did we. It was the largest Officer's Club we had ever seen, and the building was awash with top brass from all branches of the services.

WAVES and WACS were also in attendance and everyone seemed to be in an excellent mood. The aide, with glowing credits, introduced me, and we started our command performance for His Excellency. It was a warm night and I was having a difficult time being heard above the roar of the electric fans. I turned furtively to Lang and hissed, "Walter, kill the fans."

Walter quickly pulled a plug, and every light in the building went out. By the time he got the lights back on, Generals, Admirals, Colonels, Majors, and Lieutenants had scrambled under the tables and drawn their side arms. It's called, "Nervous in the service." I finally calmed their fears and the show was a tremendous success. As an encore, I made a tear- jerking speech and recounted graphically the adventures of the Winged Pigeons. The general was very kind and responded with his own speech. The only part of his speech that I can recall was, "If there is anything I can do for you boys . . ."

"You bet your ass" there was something you can do for us, Spatzy Baby, and I requested an appointment with him the very next day. I have never seen the Pigeons so solicitous of the Boss. They washed and ironed my suntans and knelt in prayer as I took off through the jungle for the general's office. I cooled my heels for about an hour before I was ushered into his presence. I saluted smartly, gave my name, rank and serial number, and waited with bated breath.

"What did you want to see me about, Hayes?"

"Well sir, we've done more than 600 shows for more than a million men, and we were wondering sir, if there is any way we could go home?"

"Now you see here, Sergeant, there are a lot of men in the South Pacific with more than enough points to go home. Now that the war is over, we anticipate a lowering of the morale, and entertainers such as yourself are needed to keep them in good spirits. We are also keeping cooks and musicians that are long overdue for discharges."

You may think it's impossible to vomit from within, but that is exactly what I did. I finally regained my composure long enough to say, "Thank you sir," I saluted, did an about face and marched toward the door. I was sweating profusely now and crying a little.

Suddenly General Spatz barked, "Hayes!"

"Yes sir?" I wept.

The general continued, "The Air Force is not unaware of what you and your group have done. Have your boys over here at 23:00 hours and I'll present you all with a Bronze Star!"

Yipes! A Bronze Star is worth five points, hot or cold. I was ecstatic. As I started back toward our tent, I could see the Pigeons milling around, peering at the jungle, waiting for the news from Garcia. As I approached the clearing, I started walking listlessly, head down low and kicking the earth disdainfully. I shrugged my shoulders, and threw myself face down on my cot. Not a word was said, the silence was deafening. Finally, Gant Gaither broke the hush with, "No luck, huh?"

"No, Gant, and I really tried, but the only thing I could get for us was a Bronze Star."

I never should have done it that way. The next thing I knew, me and my cot were upside down in a puddle 10 yards from the tent, the height of ingratitude.

Now that we had enough points, there was still no assurance that we could get out of Guam. Transportation was at a standstill, and flying home was out of the question. We were told that our only chance of getting to San Francisco was to bum a ride on a Coast Guard boat. There was one due in that afternoon, and its name was the "Hunter Ligett." We got our gear down to the dock and waited for the arrival of the only thing between us and home.

We were a small group, which made our chances more promising. The ship at long last arrived, and once again it was time for strategy. Two or three Chief Petty Officers were coming down the ramp toward our position. I shushed everybody, "Let me point him out," I whispered. I approached the bald headed Chief and said, "Hi there, Chief, we would sure appreciate a ride back to San Francisco. There are only 11 of us, and we are entertainers."

The Chief eyed me suspiciously and then asked, "Do you play poker?"

"Oh, yes sir, and we are all loaded. Where in the hell can you spend money out here?"

He studied us a moment and said, "Pick up your gear and follow me." I had visions of sleeping on a torture rack for 15 days, but such was not the case. He led us straight to the crew's quarters and told us to hide out for a while. His name was "Skins" Miller, and, if there is a God in Heaven, please love and protect him forever and ever. Amen!

We did shows almost every night and then would retire to the crew's quarters and play poker until 5 A.M. At five a big black chef would feed us beefsteak, followed by apple pie and coffee. The poker games were still another matter. We were completely outclassed. I played very conservatively and held my own. Bushkin, however, was inclined to go to every wedding and still owes me $250.

"Skins" was a Godsend to us and 15 days later we dropped anchor in the San Francisco Bay. We had a wonderful view of the Golden Gate Bridge, along with the twinkling lights of that majestic city. I had been born in this city, and now it looked like I was going to die here. The returning troop ships were so stacked up that we spent nine days and nights staring at my old hometown.

Finally we were next in line and I was shipped to Marysville, California. The de-processing process is a tedious bore and lengthy. Curiously enough, the day I was to get my walking papers, was December 25, 1945, and in "Marysville" yet! We were sent to a chapel to get our final papers and, lo and behold, the minister had decided to preach to us for more than two hours about this holy day.

True, it was the birthday of the Prince of Peace, but what he held in his hand would bring peace to all of us—our discharge papers! We wanted those more than anything. He kept flailing the air and accentuating every point and pounding our discharges into the palm of his left hand. Every time he mentioned "Christ" you could hear a mumbled, "For Christ's sake, give us the papers!"

Irritable parents already had started honking their automobile horns outside the chapel. Finally he finished, and we all lined up to receive the papers that would allow us to proudly wear that familiar "Ruptured Duck" in our lapels.

There was no one there to meet me, because Mary was in a play in Chicago. So two other GIs and I paid a Staff Sergeant $25 to drive us to Southern California. He had a 1941 Packard and by the time we found him he had been drinking heavily. I figured one more drink would do him in and, as we gassed up, I gave it to him. He promptly passed out, and we threw him in the back seat. I drove all the way to North Hollywood at about 35 miles an hour. After a year overseas, I didn't want to wind up as a statistic on a California freeway.

Thirteen
"Around the World"

Around the world I've searched for you
I traveled on when hope was gone to keep a
   rendezvous

—Words by Harold Adamson, Music by Victor Young

M:

In the spring of 1946 when "the war to end all wars" had ended, Peter was mustered out of the service in California. After a long separation, we met each other halfway, literally—in Chicago.

Springtime in Brazil had received mixed notices and some not so mixed—they were downright mean. Milton Berle and his producers were struggling to fix it. The "fixing" was a lost cause and it was closing night when Peter and I finally got back together. Since Peter and Milton were old friends from early vaudeville days, they cooked up a routine to commemorate closing night. Peter was seated in a box seat on the upper left side of the theatre. As the final curtain fell, Peter stood and hollered "Author! Author!"

Milton acknowledged him and said to his audience, "Do you really want to see the author?"

They said in one voice, "Yes! Yes! Yes!"

Out from the wings on stage came a man in a gorilla suit with a pipe in his mouth and a script under his arm. Peter stood up and shot him seven times! The laugh they got from the audience was a good way to mend Milton's broken heart.

Peter had given much of his talent to entertaining the boys overseas, but he had also been honing his act. As a result, his material was brilliant and his timing was perfect. It wasn't long before he was wowing the audiences in New York.

P:

After winning the war all by myself, I wanted to take a year off and relax. Foolish thought, because I needed to make a living! After watching the closing of *Springtime in Brazil* I knew that relaxing was not the order of the day. I needed a job. I called an old friend, Matty Rosen.

"Matty," I said, "I've got a good act and I've got to make some bread—fast."

"Your timing is still perfect Peter. You open at the Downtown Theater in Detroit next Thursday with Bobby Sherwood and Sugar Chile Robinson. Salary: $750 a week, five shows a day." Bobby was an old friend of mine and I felt secure.

I then played the Strand Theater in New York with Miguelito Valdez. His band entertainer was a young man named Sammy Davis, Jr. I thought he was pretty good. What an entertainer! Wow!

I was then sent to Pete Schmidt's Rendezvous Inn in

Covington, Kentucky. The night before we opened there, they shot a man in the doorway. There were still bloodstains in the lobby. The Rendezvous was an illegal gambling joint. I had been preceded the week before by Joe Frisco and I understand that after his opening night show, he rushed to the crap table, pointed at the dealer and shouted, "T-t-two hundred on th-th-the come!" The shooter crapped out and Frisco ducked under the table, came up with a phony mustache, looked at the dealer and said with an English accent, "Hi, say, w-w-what's going on here?"

The Rendezvous was to be a very important engagement for me. Monte Proser, the impresario of New York's legendary Copacabana, had flown in to "cover" me at that famed waterhole. Naturally I was nervous, not only because of Mr. Proser, but the rest of the audience consisted of three hillbilly drunks and a "B" girl. I improvised a lot and the situation was so ridiculous that even Monte started to laugh. He hired me to join my old chum Desi Arnaz at the Copa.

Desi had already been at the Copa for two weeks with his Latin band and I had to fit into that Latin atmosphere somehow. Lucille Ball would hang out at the Copa just to be near her Latin Lover. They both were very kind to me and the opening was a smash.

The next morning I received rave reviews. Here's a sample from *Time* magazine, June 24, 1946:

> Broadway columnists were busy as swizzle sticks, mixing a fresh batch of superlatives. The comedian they sweated to honor was a young (31) ex-GI named Peter Lind Hayes. The hub of this hubbub has a soft speaking voice, crew-cut brown hair, a shy smile and stands 5 ft. 10 in. in a Brooks Brothers suit. He traces his comic ancestry to Frank Fay

Peter Lind Hayes gets rave notices at the Copa

(for sharpness and restraint) and Bing Crosby (for relaxation and affability). But his thoughtful, economical comedy style is probably more aptly compared with Chaplin's. Hayes thinks his comedy ideas are best expressed in his characterization of "Punchy Callahan"—a hilarious but touching portrait of an ex-pug, as shapeless, scuffed and unwanted as a worn-out boxing glove. Even after three weeks, busy Copacabana waiters still stop, look & listen to Punchy.

M:

Peter's success after the war was wonderful and I was having an exciting episode myself. One night after Peter's show at the Strand, Orson Welles visited us backstage. He asked if I would audition for the part of Madam Aouda in his Broadway production of *Around the World in Eighty Days*. Only someone with Orson's amazing imagination could have pictured me, a Southern blonde, in the role of an East Indian princess.

To work with Orson Welles and the legendary Cole Porter, who was doing the score, was a dazzling prospect!

Cole and Orson auditioned me at Cole's elegant suite at the Waldorf Towers. I can read musical notes, but I learn popular songs quicker by ear. When I was auditioning, I kept singing one particular note wrong. After a while, Cole stopped playing, took his eraser, looked up at me, smiled and said, "If you insist." He changed the note to the way I was singing it!

I got the part. Madam Aouda was an East Indian princess who spoke with a "veddy" English accent, because she had been educated in Calcutta. My hair was to be jet black. This of course meant I had to either wear

Orson Welles, left, with Mary Healy and Peter Lind Hayes

A scene from *Around the World in Eighty Days*

Mary Healy in *Around the World in Eighty Days*

long black wigs or dye my own hair. First we tried wigs, which were a disaster. They looked like, well, *wigs*! After many tries it was decided I would dye my own hair jet black. That was no easy task!

Alvin Colt, our brilliant costume designer, did a first-rate job creating beautiful long silk saris East Indian Hindu women principally wore draped around their bodies, plus elegant European costumes for traveling, complete with high-button shoes.

Orson had done a Mercury Theatre on the Air radio production of Jules Verne's *Around the World* a few years earlier. It was his dream to put it into production for the stage. He had already triumphed with his thinly veiled portrait of William Randolph Hearst in the film *Citizen Kane,* though the Hearst papers hated him for it. He had very successfully starred as the romantic lead Mr. Rochester in the film version of *Jane Eyre.* Orson's stormy marriage to Rita Hayworth was definitely on the rocks by then. She was in Hollywood making *Gilda,* while Orson spent her money on *Around the World.*

He was very handsome back then and had that golden voice and an almost childlike enthusiasm that was impossible to resist. We all loved him. Both my dressing roommate, Julie Warren (married to John Forsythe) and I were both crazy about him. He was truly awesome, but quite wonderful. When his financial troubles mounted, we were all eager to help by cutting our salaries, which were minimal in the first place.

The equally forceful promoter Mike Todd was then a successful Broadway producer. He had agreed to back Orson's production, unfortunately giving him carte blanche authority. When Orson's extravagance eventually caused Todd to withdraw from the project, he frantically borrowed money from Harry Cohn, Alexander

Korda, Cole Porter, Rita Hayworth, and anyone else he could find to finance what he called his "damned behemoth of a spectacle."

He knew what he wanted, but it was impossible to get it on that stage. We had lot of laughs and lots of tears trying to put on that extravaganza. There's no doubt that Orson was a genius, but he could not learn to discipline his creativity.

The plot is well-known: the British adventurer Phileas Fogg bets he can go around the world in 80 days and in so doing he meets with many adventures. Orson wanted to put a real circus on the stage, complete with acrobats, tightrope walkers, and a flight-for-life trapezist who slid on a platform from the balcony onto the stage.

After the first act, Orson did magic tricks with rabbits, ducks and geese. With all those birds and animals, it was difficult to avoid slipping and doing a pratfall on the stage! Peter used to visit me backstage and he'd give Orson jokes and stories to tell during intermission. Unfortunately, the magic and jokes undermined the momentum of the play and threw it off kilter.

Orson just wanted too much. As an Indian widow, Madam Aouda was to be burned on her husband's funeral pyre. In fact, I was burning when Fogg captured me and carried me away. When we were on the high seas, I was tied to the mast, with buckets of water thrown to simulate a storm. I almost drowned.

He wanted to have a train speeding across the American West and an Indian massacre. A huge eagle whisked Phileas Fogg up high in a tree. I went to the rescue and eventually led the Marines down the aisle of the theater to save him from the big bird. I took a gun from the Marines and bravely shot the bird—with real feathers floating down all over the audience. They cheered. It was always triumphant.

My song was the beautiful "Should I Tell You I Love You?" Cole Porter used to sing it in a Southern accent, making fun of me. Sadly, Orson and Cole had a disagreement, which prompted Cole to withdraw all his songs from circulation. "Shall Tell You I Love You?" was only recorded once, by Dick Haymes. It's too bad, because it was a beautiful song. It could and should have been a big hit. In spite of all their problems, Orson remained an ardent admirer of Cole's and the feeling was very mutual.

Cole was always a delight. He'd come every day to the rehearsals with his chauffeur, who would bring a little lunch basket. He always asked me to come and sit with him to share his sandwiches and tea. He'd already had his terrible riding accident and both of his legs were crippled for the remainder of his life. One of the great joys of my life was spending time with him.

I'll never forget our disastrous opening night in Boston. It was one o'clock in the morning and the first act curtain had not come down. The second act never saw the light of day. The critics naturally gave Orson a bad time. All the Hearst papers were very much against him with anything he did, because of *Citizen Kane*.

The *Variety* critic wrote that without benefit of rehearsal, the show became an uproarious shambles of faulty scene changes. Confused stagehands sometimes outnumbered the actors on the stage.

I remember another critic complained that the play had everything in it "but the kitchen sink." So naturally Orson brought out a kitchen sink for his farewell speech. Each performance got longer.

Orson wrote, produced and directed the play. He didn't plan to appear in it originally. His contribution was to only do his magic act in the circus scene. However, almost everybody in the play got sick at one performance or another. With our tight budget, Orson became the understudy for practically every part. Besides, I think he secretly loved being on the stage. Orson played Phileas Fogg. Then he played Passepartout. And he played Inspector Fix. Julie Warren said, "Next he'll be playing your role!"

Orson, I'm sorry to say, was very sloppy about his performances. He improvised these roles brilliantly of course, but he would never give the proper cues to the other actors. He thought everyone should be able to improvise.

Fogg was played by Arthur Margetson, a well-known English actor who was very meticulous about his performance. I was pretty meticulous myself. Arthur and I would be on stage and Orson would make an outrageous remark or do something we weren't expecting—totally out of character. Arthur would give me a look like, "He's DOING it again!"

Actually, Arthur was quite an eccentric character too. Peter and Desi were dazzling the crowds at the Copa. One night when Peter was between shows at the Copa, he and Lucy came backstage to see me and invited Arthur to come along to the Copa with us for the three o'clock show. Arthur said, "I'd love to, old chaps, but I just can't tolerate an evening of that crazy Cuban beating on his drums." It was then that Peter introduced him to Mrs. Desi Arnaz. Lucy took it with good humor and we left—without Arthur!

After New Haven and Philadelphia, we opened at the Adelphi Theatre in New York in June 1946. The play developed a cult following. People like Helen Hayes—of course there was nobody like Helen Hayes—but I mean theatrical people, would come again and again, enchanted, seeing it four and five times. It got a little out of hand, yes, but everything was extraordinary in that show. Unfortunately, the general public never did get around to spending any money on it and it closed after only 75 performances.

Orson overwhelmed himself with this play. He gambled everything he had on it and he lost. Its ultimate failure broke his bank account—and his heart.

Peter had opened with Desi at the Copacabana the same night I opened in *Around the World* but our play didn't last as long as their run at the Copa.

P:

The sultry, sweet smell of success was throbbing away at the Copa. Three shows a night and night after night, we did turn-away business. The old Roxy Theater approached the Copa about doubling the entire show in their theater. Desi and I talked it over and we both decided we were hungry enough to risk it.

For two weeks we were to do five shows a day at the Roxy and three shows at the Copa. My salary at the Copa was $2,000 a week, and I was to receive another $2,000 from the Roxy. Four-thousand dollars a week—almost as much money in one week as I had made in almost four years in the Air Force!

Desi and I had both seen Warner Baxter survive on brandy and aspirin in an early war movie, so that became our survival kit. The night watchman at the Roxy was instructed to let us into our dressing rooms every morning at 5:00 A.M., where we would sleep on a cot until the 11:30 show. We would do four shows at the Roxy, rush over to the Copa, do the dinner show and then rush madly back to the Roxy for the fifth show, which would release us just in time for the midnight show at the Copa.

News of my salary had been dutifully reported by *Look, Time* and *Life* magazines. The dollar signs had caught the eye of Father Gilbert Hartke, the Holy Ham of Catholic University who had married us. He had taken vow of poverty. His telegram message to me was terse and to the point. "Margaret Webster embarking on truck and bus tour of Shakespeare, need $35,000 immediately." My answer was also terse and to the point, "Sorry, did not receive your telegram." In retrospect, it sounds unkind, but I had given up my vow of poverty along with spam and olive-drab clothing.

One night at the Copacabana, the late Sid Grauman was seated auspiciously at ringside. I was doing a very quiet impression of Gary Cooper. Suddenly I heard a rather faint but nevertheless ominous mumbling from the audience. I raised my eyes just in time to see a giant waterbug approaching the microphone stand. It was at least three inches long, and by now every eye in the place was focused on the lowly heckler.

I turned to the great showman and with an apologetic air said, "Mr. Grauman, I usually work alone but tonight I would like you to meet my new partner—Hal Roach!" Ah! If only I could find someone to train a roach to do that every night.

The eight shows a day had been exhausting. Desi moved on, but I stayed at the Copa for 14 more weeks. *Around the World* had folded its tent and Mary and I were together again. Lucy and Desi's path took a different direction, but soon we would all wind up in Hollywood—together again.

M:

When I was in *Around the World* and Peter at the Copa, we realized we were going separate ways. I think we feared that if we didn't work together, there was very little chance of our marriage making it. Our motto became, "The family that PLAYS together STAYS together."

Fourteen
"There's No Business Like Show Business"

There's no business like show business, like no business I know
Everything about it is appealing, everything the traffic will allow. . . .

—*Words and Music by Irving Berlin*

P:

Mary and I migrated back to our little house in North Hollywood. I was signed by Universal to do a picture for our old friend, Nunnally Johnson, *The Senator Was Indiscreet*. I also had my choice of two radio shows. One was with Ginny Simms, the other to co-star with Dinah Shore. The fact that Abe Burrows was writing the Shore program swayed me in that direction. Little did I know that when Dinah Shore did a show, she wrote, directed, and produced everything—not well, but pugnaciously.

Dinah was then married to the Western star George Montgomery. Our first meeting was to be held at their beautiful ranch in Encino. Bobby Dolan was in charge of the large orchestra and Abe was the head writer. Montgomery sat silently throughout the entire dinner and it wasn't until the coffee arrived that he spoke his first words. He spread his big cowboy hands across the table, stood up and said, "I think I'll go out and measure the barn!" (Too many cold shoulders will do that to a man.)

The evening progressed with a rap session about the format of the show, and finally we were given our cookies and milk and sent home by the lady of the house. By the end of the six weeks, Dinah had cut so much of my stuff out of the show that I thought of calling Montgomery to ask him if he needed anyone to help him measure the barn. We did 39 weeks of radio, for the last 13 of which I had been reduced to the chore of an announcer.

My other project, the movie at Universal, was working out very nicely. Nunnally Johnson was producing *The Senator Was Indiscreet*. Helen Hayes' husband Charles MacArthur was writing, and George S. Kaufman was directing. It turned out to be the only film ever directed by Mr. Kaufman.

Our star was William Powell and I played the light comedy love interest of Ella Raines. Bill Powell knew how important this was for my career and bent over backwards to help the fledgling try his wings.

George S. Kaufman, being a "theater" person, was the strangest motion picture director I had ever encountered. He left the camera work to his cutter, Gene Fowler, Jr. He never faced his actors when we were doing a scene. He sat with his back to us and kept a strange sort of rhythm with his head. Apparently, he wasn't interested in what we were doing physically; he simply wanted to hear the cadence of the words. He would invariably turn to Gene and ask, "How was that for camera?" If Gene said, "Fine," Kaufman would say, "Good for me too," and we would move on to the next scene.

The Ford Company had decided to drop the Dinah Shore program, so naturally this left more time for our social life. By now halfway through our movie, Ella Raines decided to give a black tie party in the middle of August at the Coldwater retreat. George confessed that he didn't own a white or black tie, so we hustled him over to the costuming department and fitted him out. Ella's house was one of those cliffhangers with a large flagstone patio for gracious outdoor living.

Most of the cast showed up, along with half a hundred others whom we all know and love. Ella, from experience I assume, was a Hollywood hostess. The accordion player was still strolling and playing at 10:45 P.M. No food, mind you. Ella obviously hated people who would eat and run. Her director thought this was outrageous, however, and at 10:46 P.M. announced, "Miss Raines! You are either going to feed me now or I am calling a cab and going to a diner."

Ella's quick response to this was to call off the accordion player and invite us all to sit down to dinner. There were no place cards and, as luck would have it, my dinner partner was George S. Kaufman. We gathered around one of those typical redwood tables with about 10 other Hollywood creatures. George was on my right and, gloriously, Hedda Hopper was on my left. To the left of Hedda was her legman and confidant, Travis Banton. Travis had an unfortunate condition. If you remember W.C. Field's nose, Mr. Banton's entire face was as florid as Field's nose and looked constantly like it was about to break out in Toll House cookies.

Also, Travis was a nervous talker. He sensed that the evening was not going down too well, which sent him off in a torrential spew of small talk, "Oh Hedda, remember this?" and "Oh Hedda, remember that?" He performed a solo concert of inanities that allowed everyone else at the table to pursue their long awaited din-din.

Midway through his twelfth anecdote, I felt a strange pressure on my right knee. George was nudging me. I leaned over and quietly asked, "Are you all right?"

"Oh I'm fine," he replied, "but would you like to make a contribution?"

"A contribution? George, what in the hell are you talking about?"

"I'm taking up a collection to have Travis Banton's face boarded up for the summer!" I wet Miss Hopper's dress.

The Senator Was Indiscreet was not too well received by the critics, although President Harry S. Truman declared it to be the finest political satire he had ever seen. He added that it was ill-timed: "Politicians just ain't funny anymore." Of course, Kaufman said it better: "Satire is something that closes Saturday night."

The radio show had been a failure and Universal did not exercise my option for a second movie. The whole flurry started to look like a soap bubble that was about to burst.

Meanwhile, Mary and I had become the "Fun Couple" of Hollywood. We were often invited to famous homes, probably because we were entertaining. One evening at Frank Loesser's house, Mary improvised her wildly funny impression of Ethel Merman. Gawd, it was piercing. Marlon Brando was on bongos, as I recall. Our friend Abe Burrows was also there and suggested that Mary and I should work together. On the way back to the valley, I asked Mary how she felt about it. She thought it might be fun.

But we knew it would also be a lot of work. Valley Heart Drive soon looked like a rehearsal hall. Costumers, musicians, arrangers and a choreographer were scattered hither, thither and yon. I used every device known to incorporate Mary's singing, dancing and impressions into a mini musical revue. After two weeks of strenuous effort, I felt we were ready.

M:

Peter invited his agent Lou Irwin and a whole group of friends and peers to critique our new act. Gordon and Sheila MacRae, Bill and Joy Orr (Jack Warner's daughter), Judy Holiday, Betty Comden and Adolph Green, Frank and Lynn Loesser, Desi and Lucille Arnaz, and Mr. and Mrs. Abe Burrows.

Peter rented a spotlight and public address system and hired three musicians. All we needed was a liquor license and that warm little house could have become an instant cabaret. All our guests were given a pad and pencil for notes. We did vignettes of Broadway shows and Peter did his comedy routine, which he wrote himself.

The evening was a smashing success. Of course, with a room full of show business professionals, there were hundreds of suggestions, all warmly received. We shall forever be grateful to those wonderful people who subjected themselves to being our first audience.

The first booking of "Hayes and Healy" was the Cal Neva Lodge in beautiful Lake Tahoe. The lodge got its name from the fact that half the building was in Nevada and the other half was in California. As Peter said, you could gamble in the deep end of the swimming pool, but it was illegal in the shallow end.

P:

The boniface of the Lodge was a mountain of a man named "Bones" Remmer. "Bones" kept himself jolly by consuming a case-and-a-half of beer every 24 hours. After we were established as a hit and drawing card, I became friendly with "Bones." I rambled off a few Frisco stories for him. After the second one the beer belly started to quake.

"Where is the son of a bitch? Let's send for him."

"Well, Bones, he is just closing at the Blackstone Hotel in Chicago. He won't fly and you can't send him a railroad ticket. He'll cash it in for a bet on a horse."

"Bones" called an unemployed "hit" man in Chicago, and before he knew it, Joe Frisco was on his way to join us at the Cal Neva Lodge. Our new co-star was happy to be back in the gambling atmosphere.

"Bones" didn't quibble about his salary, I assured him that Joe would leave it at the tables anyway. We opened the show together and saved Miss Healy for the big finish. The decor of the lodge was quite rustic. Immediately in back of the stage was a tremendous moose head, spreading its antlers proudly. After my introduction, Frisco walked on the stage, pointed at the moose and said, "I wonder how f-f-fast t-t-that thing was going to g-g-get that f-f-far through the wall!" "Bones" spewed beer all over the tablecloth. Frisco was in!

Frisco's legendary finish to his act was always the "Frisco Dance." He strutted with his derby and cigar to the familiar strains of "The Dark-Town Strutter's Ball." What he didn't realize was that we were now nearly 9,000 feet above sea level. Midway through the dance he suddenly looked at me and said, "G-g-get me the hell out of here, I'm h-h-having a h-h-heart attack!" It wasn't a heart attack, but for the next 10 days, "Dark-Town Strutters Ball" became a waltz.

M:

The local press wrote that Cal Neva had a very successful premiere in the new husband and wife team, Peter Lind Hayes and Mary Healy. Peter always insisted that I keep my maiden name professionally. He said in case anything happened to him, he wanted me to be established as an individual. News of our success at Lake Tahoe filtered down to a slumbering little desert town called Las Vegas.

Peter and I had first visited Las Vegas in early 1940 not long before the war when we had been invited to fly there from Los Angeles for the grand opening of Tommy Hull's plush El Rancho Hotel. It was quite grand, the first hotel built on the old Los Angeles highway, which would become the Las Vegas Strip. Sadly, that old wooden landmark burned to the ground 20 years later.

When Peter went off to war in 1942, his mother had to close down the Grace Hayes Lodge in North Hollywood. Las Vegas pioneers Wilbur and Toni Clark offered her a job singing at El Cortez. She came and fell in love with the town and soon opened another lively saloon, this one called the Red Rooster.

Hazy saw the town's potential from the beginning. Californians loved to "get away" there, including movie stars who naturally gravitated to Hazy's saloon, no more than an adobe hut at first.

It was not unusual for Howard Hughes to fly in and out of Las Vegas during the early 1940s, nor to stop in and see Grace Hayes at the Red Rooster.

One such visit was on a sweltering hot day—even for Las Vegas. Air conditioning was scarce in those days and Hazy cooled her saloon with big electric fans. Howard came in, took off his shirt and disappeared into the Men's Room.

After a few moments Howard reappeared and said, "How do you like it?"

"Like what?"

"My shirt," he said. "I just washed and dried it in three minutes. . . ."

"So?"

"It's Drip Dry. I just bought the company."

In 1945, the famous mobster "Bugsy" Siegel was building the fabulous Flamingo Hotel across the street from Hazy's Red Rooster. The hotel was named after his girlfriend Virginia Hill, whose nickname was "Flamingo" because of her flaming red hair and long slim legs.

Bugsy and Virginia spent many evenings in the seclusion of a dark booth in the Red Rooster. Bugsy was a big fan of the place and liked Hazy's cooking. We still have some Flamingo mementos he gave her as tokens of his esteem. Virginia used to tell Hazy all her secrets and Hazy kept them—until she was too old to remember what they were!

Bugsy was not around for the Flamingo's success, because he was murdered in California. His story was well told in Warren Beatty's film *Bugsy*.

Our opening show at the Flamingo in 1948 was a traumatic experience. In spite of the garishness of the Flamingo decor, the clientele were still mostly cowboys. Peter opened the act with his comedy routine, then I joined him. That night, an intoxicated miner from Salt Lake City started throwing silver dollars on the stage. The noise of silver hitting a hardwood floor was deafening. Peter had been practically raised in saloons and he could cope with the shower of silver, but I could not—and would not.

As I was taking my first bow, I slipped on a silver dollar. The slip merely encouraged the miner and he threw another handful of silver dollars at us. I walked up to the microphone and announced, "Either that man leaves, or I'm leaving." His reply was to throw more silver dollars at us. I threw my nose in the air and walked off the floor leaving Peter to carry on alone. He said, "The customer was always right." I didn't agree.

P:

We were scheduled to do another 45 minutes together. I can't remember what I did to fill the time, but I'm sure it was someone else's act. The estimate was 138 pieces of silver and what crushed me was that the bus boys got 'em all!

One had to work under many conditions and circumstances. We were trying to make it! Hecklers have always been the bane of nightclub comics. There are stock lines that have found their way down through the years:

"The next time you have your hat blocked don't forget to take your head out of it!"
"I don't know what I'd do without you—but I'd rather!"
"Why don't you run over to the brewery and let 'em put a head on you!"
"Some guys are jerks, but you're trying to make a career out of it!"
"When snakes get drunk, they see you!"

I think my reason for not wanting to get involved with hecklers must be placed at the feet of Joe Frisco. I once asked him why he never answered a heckler. "K-k-kid, if you can't hold the stage, you d-d-don't deserve to be on it, and if you're working for a s-s-saloon keeper, don't insult a customer, he might buy a b-b-bottle of wine!"

Lou Irwin booked us into another exclusive, but illegal, gambling emporium on the outskirts of Cleveland, Ohio. The club was called "The Mounds Club" and the owner was an ex-prize fighter named Tommy McGinty. The Mounds was so exclusive that even affluent people of Shaker Heights were not permitted to bring a guest unless the proprietor was supplied in advance with the guest's Dunn and Bradstreet rating.

Three nights before we were to close, the comedy team of Olsen and Johnson were in the audience. It wasn't long before they invaded our act with all sorts of zany slapstick sight gags, prop guns, wigs, funny hats and dropping their trousers. They had a hell of a time and so did the audience.

M:

The next night, I was doing my impression of the "Incomparable Hildegard." Peter was sitting in the audience pretending to be a big lumber tycoon named Mr. Goodpile, from Des Moines, Iowa.

I was trying to coax him onto the stage to accept a dozen roses. As Peter stood up, he saw a strange sight coming through the kitchen door into the main dining room—14 masked gunmen wearing army fatigues. Their faces were covered with black stockings except for two cutout holes for their eyes. They were also carrying shotguns, machine guns and World War II burp guns.

Because the spotlight was on me and it hampered my vision, I was not aware of them yet and was getting impatient for "Mr. Goodpile" to get on with the act.

"Well, Mr. Goodpile. Are you coming up here or not?"

Peter yelled from the rear of the audience, "Miss Hildegard, I won't come up there till these clowns take off their masks!"

This unexpected ad lib stunned me. I thought Peter was being heckled by a drunk. I shielded my eyes from the glare of the spotlight and said, "If that's the way you're going to behave, you're just going to have to get out of here."

Instead of "getting out," the Number One thug marched onto the stage, took the microphone from me and hissed, "This is a stick-up lady and we're not kidding."

Now I don't care how well-armed you are, if I'm doing my act you must never try to take a microphone from me! Being a trouper, I shoved him in the face, and tried to take back the mike. In response to my defiance, he pointed his machine gun at the ceiling and squeezed the trigger.

Well, my friends, the ceiling was treated with acoustical tiling, so the short blast sounded more like a cap pistol than the sound of a real gun which I had rarely, if ever, heard. I laughed, but as I threw my head back I panicked at the sight of big holes in the ceiling. I screamed and bolted for the exit right into the musician's toilet. Hiding along with me were a frightened waiter and a piano player.

Now, remember, I had no idea what was going on in

the main room. The piano player tried to stop me from going to find out. He said, "Don't move!" After hearing the gunshot, I didn't!

P:

Now the new star of the Mounds Club took the microphone in dead earnest and issued orders. All the women were to remove their jewelry, place it in front of them between their hands, with the palms pointing up. The men were ordered to do likewise with their money and rings, but no wristwatches. Wristwatches have numbers and are traceable.

By this time, I had been told to "Shut up and sit down at a ringside table." I never realized before how much the barrel of a gun, when it is pointed at your gut, resembles the Holland Tunnel. I did as I was told. My other colleagues at ringside were Val Ernie, our bandleader, and an elderly Jewish gentleman and his wife. It suddenly dawned on me that I had cashed a check for $500 just before the show and had hidden the money under the rug in our dressing room. When I came downstairs for the performance, I had one quarter in my change pocket. I promptly deposited the quarter in a slot machine and lost it. I never carried money onto the stage with me.

I also remembered the late Al Jolson always carried a $1,000 bill in the heel of his shoe. This was his insurance in case he was abducted. Rather than disappoint his abductors, the $1,000 bill was a reward that would hopefully deter them from knocking out his teeth.

Very softly, I whispered to Val Ernie, the orchestra leader, "How in the hell am I going to explain to them that I don't have any money?" Very softly, he whispered back,

"I'm in the same boat. I don't have any either." Meanwhile, the elderly gentleman was neatly stacking about $1,400 in front of himself. He had hit the crap table pretty good before dinner and was meticulously following the orders of the day.

I nudged him with my knee and asked, "Are you going to give them all that money?"

"You bet your ass I am!" he replied.

"Well, kind sir, I don't have any cash on me, and I was wondering . . . ?" He smiled knowingly and said, "Take a little, leave a little."

Val and I took about $40 apiece. My question is, "Do I still owe him $40?"

The hold-up men were not really having an easy time of it. Most of the guests were half smashed and entirely too sophisticated to think of the entire thing as anything but a hoax. Some of them thought that Olsen and Johnson were doing their act again.

Buck Schaffner, the manager at the Mounds, was a tall, dour man with a white complexion. He had summed up the situation realistically and had very calmly melted into the crowd. Shrewdly, Buck was pretending to be a guest. But that didn't work. The fearless leader walked right over to where Buck was seated and said, "Come on, Bucky, let's go to the safe."

Buck was six inches shorter when he stood up and was trembling violently. He was so frightened that he couldn't open the safe. He finally had to scribble out the combination and the fearless leader opened it himself.

They made a pretty good haul. In the safe alone they captured $127,000. Meanwhile, back in the main room, the people were beginning to get restless and irritable.

One woman next to us was boldly refusing to remove a seven-carat diamond ring. One of the thugs wrenched her arm, took one look at the ring and said, "Don't bother to take that off. My father is a jeweler, and that's a zircon." She turned purple with rage and blurted out "It certainly is not!" Her pride had done her in.

"Well, take it off, or I'll cut your finger off!" She removed the ring and smiled smugly at her girlfriends.

The 14 men stayed at the Mounds Club for an hour and a half. The next day, in screaming headlines, the heist was estimated to be in excess of $620,000. This, of course, included insurance claims. Not a bad night's work for 14 amateurs. Actually, no one was injured.

Two days later we received a telegram from our good friend Bill Orr. The message read, "Don't you think the act is getting too elaborate?"

I don't know about our act, but the act of the holdup was a little too elaborate for the Cleveland politicians to tolerate. They were shocked, SHOCKED that such a place had been in existence for 17 years. They stomped their feet and said, "We will have no more of this sort of thing!"

Thinking it over, I have decided that it was fortunate that Tommy McGinty had been at the World Series during the night of the robbery. Tommy was very pleasant socially and I have a theory that his first thought would have been to buy the thugs off. If that hadn't worked, I'm sure his second thought would have been to hit someone. In that case the Mounds Club could have turned into a slaughterhouse.

When Tommy returned, he admitted that it was the end of an era, and the Mounds Club would have to be closed. He also mentioned that he and his Associates were thinking of moving to Las Vegas. "Oh Tommy, don't do it. It's a nickel and dime town. My mother has a place out there and she's starving to death!"

Tommy didn't listen to me and they wound up with the Desert Inn and the Stardust Hotels. If you ever need financial advice, I charge 21 cents an hour.

Two weeks in Chicago gave us a honing and sharpening up period for the new team of "Hayes and Healy." We edited, cut, replaced material, and rehearsed for hours and hours. The reason for this arduous work was simple. Our next engagement was the famous Copacabana in New York City.

When we left for New York, I was confident that all would go well. I was also looking forward to embracing my little friend, Monte Proser. During the band rehearsal, I kept expecting Monte to make an appearance. I finally asked for him. Instead of Monte I was confronted by a Boa Constrictor named Jules Podell. "Hey, kid, Proser ain't here no more. I'm da boss!" I sensed he was a Harvard man and did not argue.

Everything went well opening night. The press was very kind, and then the weather decided to get into our act. It started snowing. By the time 28 inches had fallen, New York was paralyzed. Traffic was at a standstill and Mary and I did three shows to the same 12 people. They couldn't go home. By this time Podell also was paralyzed and sent for me. "Hey, kid, youse ain't doin' no business. I tol' ya, Proser don't work here no more and I'm booking da joint 'round de clock. Now I'm willing to offer you two weeks next March."

I respected his honesty.

"Mr. Podell," I said, "I don't even know if we'll be alive next March."

He kicked a passing busboy and said, "Take it or leave it."

I thought of four years in the Air Force defending a

bum like this and said, "In that case, I think we'll move over to the Waldorf Astoria."

He kicked another busboy and our conversation ended.

Jules Podell always reminded me of a dog with a mouthful of red ants.

M:

After the Copa engagement, we returned to Hollywood for a two-week stint at the Coconut Grove. We were happy to be back in the little Valley Heart House. A very special reason for our happiness was the arrival of a bundle of joy named Peter Michael Hayes. From that time on we tried to make sure our little family would travel together.

When we performed at the Coconut Grove, it was a big affair. All our old friends in California came to see us. It was a star-studded opening night—Bing Crosby, Bob and Dolores Hope, Dorris and Nunnally Johnson, Edgar Bergen—very exciting. Among those who came was the Broadway producer Arthur Schwartz, of the song-writing team Schwartz and Dietz. Arthur was deeply involved with a show for a new medium called television. He wanted us to star in a television version of his Broadway hit, *Inside USA* to be sponsored by Chevrolet. Once again we would be working two jobs.

We were already booked within a few months to play an engagement with the Eddy Duchin Orchestra at the Waldorf Astoria in New York. We decided to risk getting our feet wet in this terrifying new gimmick television.

This was the summer of 1949. The Waldorf was a dream job—only one show a night, five nights a week, and a

Eddie Duchin time, Waldorf Astoria, New York City, circa 1949

Mary Healy and Ethel Merman

suite of rooms. Whether he remembers or not, our not-so-little son Michael was given many a bath by his proud papa Peter in a sink at the fabulous Waldorf Astoria.

The Waldorf became a feather in our cap. The show went on at 11:45 P.M.—perfect timing to catch the theater crowd. Every night we were packed. Our venue, The Wedgewood Room, was poorly laid out. We actually worked to about 10 tables in front of us and the rest of the people were on both sides. Many were even in back of us, behind the orchestra.

One evening, I was approached by a tall handsome man, a young Senator named John F. Kennedy. "Mary, we can't even see your faces. Can you help us get better seats?" he asked.

We did.

During this period, Ethel Merman became our chum. She enjoyed my shrill impression of her and never missed an opening night. During our thank you speech, Peter would introduce Ethel and the two of us would go into our act—Ethel mouthing the words while I sang behind her. LOUDER!

Eddy Duchin became another great friend. We spent almost every weekend with Eddy and his lovely wife Chiquita in their beautiful home in Long Island. We spent a lot of time with his young son Peter, who would one day be a great pianist too.

One night, Eddy told us he was flying to Boston on the weekend to see his family doctor. We were closed Mondays and the following Tuesday, he was wearing a bedroom slipper on his right foot. After the show, Peter asked him about this addition to his otherwise immaculate wardrobe.

"Well, I've had a sort of barber's itch on my right ankle. Can you imagine, my own family doctor told me it was leukemia and that I only had six months to live?"

The doctor was right and Eddy was wrong.

We visited him almost every day at Memorial Hospital and then suddenly he was gone. It was a very tragic time. Fox later did a film about Eddy's life, starring our old friend Ty Power as Eddy.

During that time, our former housemate Frank Loesser was getting a Broadway show together called *Guys and Dolls*. Frank asked me to play the Salvation Army girl on the stage. I still regret that I couldn't accept that part. The movie was later made starring Frank Sinatra and Marlon Brando, with Jean Simmons in the part I would have done on Broadway.

We set up house in the Waldorf, complete with an early version of a television set. Peter would sit at that set, as Cole Porter wrote, "Night and Day." He'd turn it on in the morning to watch the test pattern and watch until they played the "Star Spangled Banner" at night. Not many people had sets, but if you were on national television, you became a celebrity overnight, as we would soon find out first hand.

P:

The average size of a TV tube was seven inches. If you were a status seeker, you could buy a big bubble of glycerin, which would magnify the screen to 11 inches. My Gawd! With 11 inches, you could invite the neighbors over. Television was in its infancy, but if you wanted to keep up with the Joneses, you just had to have a set. A lot of people in suburbia mounted antennas on the roof long before they had the wherewithal to own one of the little devils.

Fifteen
"Getting to Know You"

**Getting to know you, getting to know all about you
Getting to like you, getting to hope you like me.**

—*Music by Richard Rodgers,
Lyrics by Oscar Hammerstein*

M:

On *Inside USA with Chevrolet,* Peter introduced various musical numbers and comedy sketches featuring top Broadway and Hollywood stars. It was on CBS every other week and was a hit. One of our very first fan letters was from Bing Crosby. Peter framed it.

Our good friend, the veteran movie producer Nunnally Johnson also wrote Peter a letter in October 1949 critiquing not so much our performances but the brand new medium of television. It was in a collection of his letters Dorris Johnson selected for publication after his death.

> Today at lunch Bill Perlberg and Jessel were full of praise and admiration for you and Bill sounded off splendidly about how beautiful Mary was and how well she sang and how much she added to the program last night. . . .

It ought to be kept in mind that the show is going to be seen on a panel not much larger than a school kid's slate and that the more you put into that little space, the less any one individual is going to stand out.

I think it is an utter waste of time to design costumes for chorus girls on television. . . . My belief is that if girls are to be used, they should be used as undressed as the law allows. Because you can't see their faces well, because the color of their garments means nothing, because they are crowded in that small stage, they seem to me a complete irritation as Arthur Schwartz used them in the show last night. There is only one excuse for production girls in a show like that and that is for legs.

How times have changed!

This was one of the very first TV variety shows, with dancing girls and boys and big production numbers. We performed before an audience and it was broadcast LIVE. No tape, mind you. When the little red light went on, you were on, ready or not.

It was a challenge to get this program on with only one camera and very limited resources. We really were pioneers! The work was exhausting. With one camera, you had to literally run from set to set.

I'll never forget the week our pal Lucille Ball was on—her very first time on TV. We were performing Arthur's song "Louisiana Purchase." Lucille finished the show and said to Peter, "This medium will kill actors. I never want to see a television camera again!"

Some of our other guests were Charles Boyer, Gloria Swanson, David Niven, Oscar Levant, Boris Karloff, Ethel Merman and Margaret O'Brien. A great character actress named Mary Wickes was a regular on the show. You might remember her more recently as the elderly nun in *Sister Act* with Whoopi Goldberg.

P:

We were living at the Waldorf, which was fine, but we needed more space. Being a home-loving Cancer the Crab, I started looking for a bigger habitat. Each weekend, we would drive through Westchester County looking at houses. We covered Pleasantville, Mount Vernon, Mamaroneck, Larchmont and Pelham. Very shrewdly I kept maneuvering Miss Healy back to the New Rochelle area. I had spent a lot of time there in the old Foy house and I felt at home. While we were still doing *Inside USA,* we bought an old Tudor house at 103 Mt. Tom Road, New Rochelle, New York.

The potential of television prompted me to assume that our future was definitely on the East Coast. At that time, New York was the center of all television activity. I was right. We stayed in that house for many happy years. The old Tudor had beautiful stained glass windows. I had even picked out an alcove for my wake. I was certain that this would be my final resting place. I had forgotten that I was married to an Aries. (They travel a lot.) We were proud of our new home and set about planning and decorating feverishly.

It took *Inside USA* 26 weeks to complete its 13-week cycle. By that time, we had established ourselves as acceptable personalities on the tube. But also by that time, Chevrolet had decided that a budget of $26,000 was outrageous and they canceled their option.

M:

The house on Mt. Tom Road was perfect for us. As we said in one of our book titles, we were just "25 minutes from Broadway." New Rochelle was not only where Peter lived when his mother was married to Charlie Foy, but also where he became a bandleader at age 16!

It was a hectic but also a memorable time for us. Our last program was in March of 1950. Just a few months later, we moved to NBC for our next TV adventure, *The Peter and Mary Show*. Later its name was changed to *The Peter Lind Hayes Show*. Mary Wickes was with us again, this time playing our housekeeper. Remember Elsie the Cow? Borden was our sponsor. One of our writers, George Axelrod, was first rate and later wrote a number of good plays for Broadway. He also wrote some very funny stuff for us. This situation comedy was another pioneer television effort—a sitcom before *I Love Lucy*. Our show lasted until March of 1951.

Desi Arnaz wrote in his autobiography that he and Lucy took a page from our book. They thought their marriage might have a chance to survive if they could perform together like we did. They formed Desilu Productions and *I Love Lucy* was born.

Believe it or not, that summer we went into yet another TV series, *Star of the Family*. As hosts, we interviewed and performed with people who were related to celebrities without revealing at first who their famous relatives were. I remember many episodes, but especially the one featuring the mother of Tony Bennett. She was the perfect Italian momma, but when the sponsor insisted that her interview be put on an early teleprompter, it lost the dear spontaneous quality of this proud Mom. Madison Avenue interfered even in the early years.

In between television shows, there were always nightclub engagements. People all over the country who had seen us on television would book us for a tidy little sum. We took Michael and our newest family member Cathy Lind Hayes on the road with us.

P:

We were determined not to be separated from our children. Our bookings called for us to spend about seven months a year on the road. God saw fit to send us a gift named Alicia Hughes. She was a tender, loving Irish lady. She stood straight as a ramrod and loved to travel. It was quite an entourage—with the kids, their nanny and our magnificent piano player, Armando Herrera, who was also with us for many years.

Soon our caravan was bouncing from supper clubs to hotels all over the country. Our little ones, Cathy and Michael, learned to swim in the famous Cal Neva pool in Lake Tahoe. By the time we went on for our first show we them tucked in bed for the night. They had lunch with us and we had afternoons free to explore the lake together.

When we were performing at Lake Tahoe, Howard Hughes often came to see our shows often. Each time he had a new glamour girl with him. I remember when he brought the ballerina Cyd Charisse.

One night he brought the very young and beautiful Elizabeth Taylor. After the show, he called our room and said he would like to come down to our cabin to say hello. To our surprise, he closed the door very carefully behind him and looked menacingly at us.

"Listen Peter," he said. "I don't want anyone to know I was here today. If this gets into Louella Parsons' column, I'm blaming you!" It was a ridiculous thing to say. He had been sitting in the audience all night long with everybody in the place looking to see the famous guests.

M:

Howard's behavior got more and more bizarre over the years, especially after he moved to Las Vegas. Yvette and Bob Mahew later became our good friends and neighbors in Las Vegas. Though they never met face to face, Bob was Howard's right hand man for years. He could certainly attest that Howard eventually became a very sick man.

Howard bought the Desert Inn because he didn't want to leave its high-roller suite on the top floor. He later bought several other hotels, including the one we always played, the Sands.

When it opened in 1952, the Sands became the playground for the rich and famous, especially after hours. The Copa Room's stars included Bing Crosby, Louis Armstrong, Nat King Cole, Milton Berle, Lena Horne, Peggy Lee, Patti Page and too many more to name. Of course Frank Sinatra and his "Rat Pack" friends—Dean Martin, Sammy Davis, Jr., Joey Bishop and Peter Lawford—made the Sands the jumpingest joint in the world.

Our engagement at the Sands was arranged by our old friend Jack Entratter. He had migrated to Las Vegas from the Copacabana in New York and was now the impresario at the "Place in the Sun." Because of Jack, the Sands was also called "The Copacabana Gone West"—complete with Copa Girls.

We were a tremendous success for the Sands, so they offered us a contract for $20,000 a week, five weeks a year for a period of three years. That astronomical salary was so newsworthy that the AP and UPI wires put it on the lines. Lounge acts make much more than that now! We eventually played at the Sands 14 times, a month each time. We spent many happy days there and always had the children with us.

One of the most dazzling Vegas openings we remember was that of Marlene Dietrich in fabulous creations designed by Jean Luis at the Desert Inn. Even the great Dietrich could be seen having breakfast at the Sands Garden Room.

Another memorable time was when Sir Noel Coward appeared at the Desert Inn while we were appearing at the Sands. Noel got a flu bug and as was the show biz custom, Peter and I doubled up and filled in for him.

P:

Noel was so grateful that he started hanging out with us at Hazy's Red Rooster. Occasionally he would sit down to the piano and play "I'll See You Again." The drunks at the bar loved it! I doubt that they knew what a genius was playing that piano.

Noel Coward was a marvelous and witty man. At one point I asked him for a picture. In the picture we already had, taken at the Copa City nightclub in Miami, Noel's fly was open, I explained.

Noel replied, "It was? Where was I going?"

"You were on your way to Jamaica."

"Oh, old boy," said Noel. "My fly is always open on my way to Jamaica."

James and Pamela Mason often came to see us perform and they also liked the Red Rooster. So did Van Heflin, Martha Raye, Phil Silvers and so many other stars.

In the early years of Vegas hotels, Nat King Cole, Sammy Davis, Jr., Lena Horne, John Bubbles and other top black performers could not sleep or eat at the hotels where they appeared for five-figure salaries. They and all the Las Vegas stars loved spending time at Hazy's Red Rooster where they were always welcome. The only color that mattered to Hazy was green—when you paid your bill.

John Sublette often appeared in our act at the Sands and traveled with us all over the country. I adored him. He was "Bubbles" of the famed vaudeville team, "Buck and Bubbles." Fred Astaire called him the greatest dancer who ever lived, and Gershwin based the character of Sportin' Life in *Porgy and Bess* on him.

Which reminds me, I remember the time I introduced the most famous Sportin' Life of all, the great Sammy Davis, Jr., for an award.

"Sammy and I had the same upbringing," I began. "We were both raised in vaudeville. Although I was often told that Al Jolson was the greatest all-round entertainer who ever lived. I disagree. I think Sammy is the greatest. After all, he is a fabulous dancer, a wonderful impersonator and a big recording star. However, there is one thing Jolson could do that Sammy never could. Occasionally Jolson would work in white face."

Sammy laughed louder than anyone.

In those days Las Vegas was still a pioneer town. Drinks were 50 cents, the food and the rooms were extremely reasonable, and a maitre d' never thought of sticking his hand out. Wednesday nights the Flamingo invited the public to be its guest—a roast beef dinner and all your drinks were on the house. Professional gamblers ran Las Vegas in those days, and they knew business.

Let me tell you a story about the Wertheimer brothers who had given up their connection with the Purple Gang back in Detroit to go "legit." Under the aegis of our old pal Darryl Zanuck, Lou had become a producer at Twentieth Century-Fox. Myrt and Al were dabbling around in the legalized sport of gambling in Nevada.

In the spirit of good fellowship, Myrt and Al had invited a dozen or so old cronies to visit them in Las Vegas. The old cronies arrived and looked like they had just escaped from an early Damon Runyon book—alligator shoes with Cuban heels, dark suits with loud ties and broad-brimmed felt hats.

What to do to entertain the "Boys?" Myrt borrowed a very elaborate yacht from one of the posh hotels to give them a day of fishing on Lake Mead. Alligator shoes with Cuban heels do not take well to teak decks, but arrive at dockside they did.

Being natural-born gamblers, their first order of the day was to ante up a hundred dollars apiece. The first one to catch a fish would win the pool. One of the boys decided to go below to sleep for a couple of hours. He surfaced after three hours of shut-eye and was amazed to find no one had caught a fish. He wiped the sleep from his eyes, threw a hundred dollar bill in the pot and asked for string. Seven minutes later he hauled in the first catch of the day. As he reached for the pot several of the other boys hurled obscenities at him and demanded to know "how he done it."

"It's very simple, you meatheads. The first two times I threw the string over with just the bait. No hook. You gotta convince 'em the game's on the square!"

Today the men in the gray flannel suits run the hotels. They want the coffee shop to show a profit. (Ho, ho, ho!)

After the Hughes organization took over the Sands, one of the pit bosses told me that a computer had spit out his name and he was on the carpet. He was asked if he sent a man in Arkansas $250 worth of frozen steaks. He admitted it. He was dressed down and told Hughes was not running an Arkansas charity. The pit boss asked if they could send for the books on the "man from Arkansas." They did. The man from Arkansas had lost more than $1.5 million to the Sands in less than 18 months. Now, if you had received those beautiful steaks, where would you return on your next visit to Las Vegas?

Our next television adventure was to co-host *The Stork Club* show with the world's most fabulous host, Sherman Billingsley. The idea of putting the Stork Club on television was the brainchild of the golden boy of CBS, Irving Mansfield. The format of the show was three 15-minute interviews a week with the celebrities that visited that famous watering hole on East 53rd Street. Our first producer was our old friend Abe Burrows.

We had become friendly with Abe while on the road. He was an original, funny and multi-talented man, a writer, a nightclub comedian and later a Broadway producer of *Guys and Dolls*. We used to play poker with him after our shows when we were on the road. (In fact, we had poker groups all over the country, including Mike Wallace and Dave Garroway in Chicago when we played the Blackstone Hotel. Little did we dream we'd end up living in Las Vegas—where we almost never gambled!)

The Stork Club television show was broadcast from the upper floor of the club where only invited guests could go. You were supposed to feel like you'd been canonized if the Stork Club's owner let you into the Cub Room. Three times a week we broadcast from Table 50—it was called "Table Hopping." The show put us on the cover of Gardner Cowles' *Look* Magazine.

David Niven, Bogart, and Violet with Peter at the Sands in Las Vegas

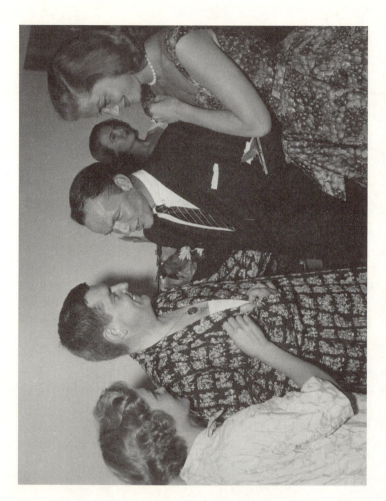

Mary and Peter with Frank Sinatra and Lauren Bacall at the Sands

M:

Our guests included the famous from Sinatra to J. Edgar Hoover—et cetera, et cetera, et cetera!

Which reminds me . . . our next director was a very attractive young man named Yul Brynner. He told us he had started his career as a circus acrobat in some obscure part of Europe. Yul played guitar and was an excellent folk singer. One day he approached us and whispered, "Wish me luck kids. I'm going to audition for Rodgers and Hammerstein in their new show." We wished him luck and the rest is history. The show was *The King and I*. He was a good friend and we loved him dearly. It was very exciting to be invited to his opening night. Peter and I knew instantly it would be a smash. We also knew, when we heard Gertrude Lawrence begin to sing, that we had found a theme song for our own act—"Getting to Know You."

Later, Yul came back to visit with us on *The Stork Club* show—but as a guest to be interviewed, in full Siamese costume. I told him how superb his character was and that when he walked onto the stage you knew immediately that he was the King. Yul told us that it was a custom of kings to send each other gifts of fabulous jewels. In finding the key to his character, Yul learned that the king of Siam would hang the "Crown Jewels" on his penis. He thereby perfected his King's walk!

P:

Yul, along with Irving Mansfield and his wife Jacqueline Susann, spent many happy weekends with us. Some would be at our Mt. Tom house, but most of the time

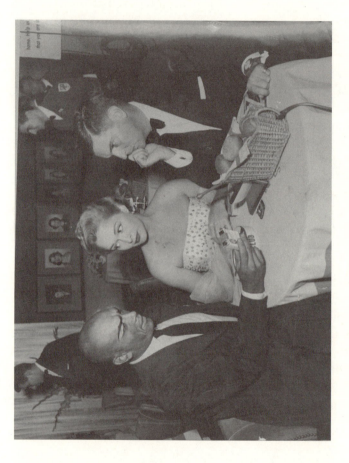

Interviewing their former director Yul Brynner at the Stork Club after his triumph in *The King and I*

Together with friend Noel Coward in Las Vegas

we would all drive to Sherman Billingsley's posh mansion in Poundridge. Sherman was trying to write off his beautiful home by growing potatoes for the Stork Club. At one point he figured out that each potato had cost him $68.

When we knew her, Jacqueline Susann had just finished her first book *Every Night Josephine.* It was a charming story about their poodle and I enjoyed it. She is more famous for her racy books, like *Valley of the Dolls.* The movie based on her novel was supposed to star one of my old girlfriends, Judy Garland, whose own sad life story was the inspiration for one of the characters. Judy, who wasn't well enough to do the movie, was replaced with another of my old girlfriends, Susan Hayward.

One Sunday evening we were driving Jacqueline and Irving Mansfield back to the Navarro Hotel. I had tuned in Walter Winchell on the car radio. Suddenly, in the middle of his broadcast he shrieked, "Flash! Irving Mansfield, the golden boy of CBS and his wife Jacqueline Susann, have decided to go their separate ways!" I switched off the radio and waited for a reaction. After about five minutes of complete silence Irving said, "This is good for us." I'm still in a quandary as to what he meant.

At that time, Irving had three shows on CBS: *This is Show Business*, *Stork Club*, and Arthur Godfrey's *Talent Scouts*. CBS decided I might be a good replacement for Arthur Godfrey, who had the country's most popular television show then.

Arthur was fiercely loyal and just as violent when that loyalty had been betrayed. His replacement on *Talent Scouts* before me was Robert Q. Lewis. One afternoon, quite by accident, Arthur heard Robert doing a radio commercial for Post Toasties. Since Kelloggs was a major sponsor for Arthur, Robert was fired on the spot. The deal for me was made and my salary was to be $2,000 per week for six months, with an option for another six months.

Arthur sent for me to sit in a corner and listen in while he dealt with the CEO of his sponsor, the Three M Company. Little Jack Horner, I sat in my corner and heard the CEO addressing the jovial redhead as Mr. Godfrey this and Mr. Godfrey that.

The problem seemed to be that "scotch tape" was about to become a generic term. They wanted Arthur to stress Scotch *Brand* tape. Just at the time Arthur was to save Scotch *Brand* tape from disaster, the Three M Company had also foisted many of their other products on his broad shoulders. I'm sure Arthur was aware of the unfairness of the situation.

I knew the option date was almost up and that they had until Monday to pick him up or drop him. The Three M contract was a very lucrative piece of change, so naturally, I was glued to the television set. Now I'll show you the absolute power and selling ability of Mr. Godfrey.

Strangely enough, he didn't mention Scotch *Brand* tape in their entire first 15-minute segment. As the trombone player picked up his instrument to lead the Godfrey Show into the next segment, Arthur majestically raised his hand and whispered, "By the way ladies, something has come up with the Three M Company. I don't care how much Scotch Brand tape you have in the house, buy another couple of packages over the weekend."

Three M picked up the option Monday.

With all that power, Arthur was always very kind and considerate with us. I once mentioned to Joe Frisco that I was earning $2,000 a week from Arthur even when I wasn't appearing. Joe removed his cigar and stammered, "You s-s-should have held out for more money!"

These were indeed halcyon days for Mary and me.

Peter Lind Hayes (left) Margaret Truman, Mary Healy and Arthur Godfrey

The contract with Arthur enabled us to pay off the mortgage on the old Tudor house we had purchased in New Rochelle and all was right with the world.

But it was indeed nerve-wracking to face Arthur's audience for two or three weeks at a time. It meant that the entire CBS TV and vast radio network would be listening to an hour and a half ad-lib show.

All the "little Godfreys" were very understanding of my plight. Tony Marvin was my good right arm and halookie. Frank Parker, Jan Davis and the McGuire sisters would go along with whatever I came up with. The first time I did the show, I did 40 minutes without remembering to do one commercial. At the break, I was screamed at by the producer, Frank Musciello, and had to do 15 minutes of "picking up" the forgotten commercials.

I only met with Arthur on rare occasions because my job was to take over when he flew off on vacations, but I always watched. I was trying to figure out how he did it. One Friday, his guest was the severe TV critic John Crosby. Near the end of the program, he suddenly said, "Well, I guess we'd better call Peter and Mary. Monday I'm going to the hospital for a serious lung operation."

Arthur beat his cancer and the network was inundated with get well cards from fans around the nation.

CBS then gave us our own radio show on Saturday morning. Our singers were Leslie Uggams, Don Cherry, John Bubbles and Jerry Vale. Andy Rooney of CBS's *Sixty Minutes* was a writer and so was a brilliant young man named Woody Allen, who made $50 a week. Abe Burrows had called us and said that Woody was his nephew and just starting out! Woody told us many years later he framed his first check.

M:

As a singer on national radio and television shows, I was privileged to work with fine musicians over the years, especially guest pianists. It was something else to get to sing with the great Teddy Wilson. He played piano with the Arthur Godfrey band, when Peter was hired by Bill Paley of CBS to replace Arthur. The band's conductor was Norman Leyden, who had been an arranger for the Glenn Miller band.

Later we worked with our dear friend, pianist Bobby Allen who wrote so many special songs, including "There's No Place Like Home for the Holidays," "To Know You is to Love You," and the beautiful "Moments to Remember." He and Peter wrote "Lilac Chiffon" together and in 1957 their song "Come to Me" became a big hit for a talented young singer named Johnny Mathis. (Royalty checks still arrive from "Come to Me.")

P:

Our agent, Lou Irwin, called and asked if we would like to play the Palladium Theater in London. "Could we do it?" You bet we could and we did.

The night before we flew to London, Mary and I co-hosted the *Ed Sullivan Show*. Ed was in Hollywood giving his daughter away in marriage. His show was then called *Toast Of The Town* and Ed always made his entrance strolling through a row of beautiful girls. I decided to capitalize on his entrance. Mary introduced me, and as I strolled through the girls, I tripped and did a slapstick fall. I doubled the fist of my right hand to break the fall and as I hit the floor I tore the cartilage away from my rib cage. Man, that really smarted! I was in a state of shock for the rest of the hour, but we managed to muddle through. It's really true—the show must go on.

Despite the pain, we took off for London in the old Boeing Monarch the next day. The Monarch was a double-decker with a spiral staircase leading to the bar. I spiraled up and down the stairway to the stars many times. My ribs were killing me. The Monarch also had sleeping bunks and all the way to London Town, I slept under Dorris Duke.

The trip from the airport to the hotel was very flattering. Enormous billboards announced our appearance in London: Peter Lind Hayes and Mary Healy, the "Life Gits Tee-jus'" couple?

"Mary, what in the hell do they mean, 'Life Gits Tee-jus?'" Mary thought for a moment and said, "Peter, didn't you make a record with that title in '47?"

"Yes, I did, for Decca, but it was a flop and I forgot all about it."

Well, it was a success in England. After being on the winning side of World War II, the British were still on coupons for candy and meat. Across the channel, France and even as far away as Italy were thriving with all the luxuries of life, while the British were still queuing up for a sweet or a piece of meat. The hillbilly homily of the song depicted their predicament precisely. The record had sold over a quarter of a million copies. I had to buy one myself to re-learn the lyrics.

The sun goes up, the sun goes down
The hands on the clock keep turnin' round
I get up and it's time to lay down
Life gits tee-jus don't it?

Jack Benny, Rochester, Phil Harris and Dennis Day were about to close a very successful engagement at the Palladium. We were to follow. The situation in London was quite different from our form of vaudeville. You did two evening performances. The first was at 6:30 in the evening for the people from the provinces, the second at 8:30 P.M. for the more sophisticated and well-traveled audience. We also did matinees on Wednesday and Saturday for the other music hall performers.

Noel Coward sent us two dozen long stemmed roses and sat in the Royal Box for our opening night. Afterward we joined him at the Café de Paree where he was appearing. He was fabulous. The next morning over breakfast at the Savoy Hotel, we were presented with a slightly heated copy of the *London Times.* As late as 1952, the newspaper consisted of four sheets. Our review was on page one.

I gulped my coffee as I read the lead. "Mary! Come quickly. I think we're in trouble!" The bold newsprint posed a simple question, "What Do They Do?" It's funny how quickly one forgets good notices but the *Times* review is engraved on my forehead. "A charming couple and a pair that the vicar would like to have around to keep his garden party going."

Noel Coward continued to be solicitous of our welfare and Douglas Fairbanks, Jr., was also very kind. We were invited to his home on the outskirts of London for a supper party honoring the Duchess of Kent. We were exhausted as we had done three shows that day. Nevertheless, before my overcoat was half off, Douglas whispered, "You will do a little for the Duchess, won't you?"

"No, Doug, we're too tired, but I see Margaret Truman sitting over there. Why don't you ask her to sing?"

He did just that. I watched as he leaned over Margaret and asked. God! She pushed him away and I would have loved to have heard what she said. She was a good friend and companion of ours in those days.

The second week we were there, Mary was singularly honored by the Variety Club. She was asked to join me on the dais at a luncheon. She was the second woman ever to be so honored. The other was Sophie Tucker.

Doug Fairbanks was also on the dais and I sensed that this British showman mildly resented an American being so "veddy, veddy British." I professed that we were thrilled with our first visit to England and that we had combed Baker Street diligently, vainly searching for some faded memory of Dr. Watson or the elusive Sherlock Holmes.

Since we had flown to London, we decided to return to America on the Queen Elizabeth. During World War II, the Queen had been used as a troop ship and her owners romantically decided to leave the hundreds of GI initials that had been carved into her beautiful mahogany handrails. What a scenario that would make, newlyweds embarking on the good Queen for their honeymoon and on a beautiful summer evening, him pointing out his initials that he had carved when he was on his way overseas to fight the war that would end all wars.

The voyage was thrilling. Mary made one mistake. She assumed that the caviar on the Veranda Grill was free. That *was* a mistake. We were not aware of her error until our steward presented us with a rather large bill the night before we landed in New York. That's a hell of a lot of caviar for a little old girl from the Irish Channel in New Orleans.

I had decided on the seven-day voyage to break in my new Dunhill pipe and grow a mustache. The pipe was a cinch, all I had to do was set fire to my tongue five or six times a day. The mustache was another matter. I have never really investigated my genes, but my mustache was red, orange, yellow and green.

As we disembarked, I was smoking my pipe and wearing my new English Bowler. Mary was carrying a cane designed by Jacque Fath. A few inches below the handle he had attached a naughty wicker basket. We looked so much like "Kansas City British." Jack Benny, who was also disembarking the ship, was prompted to say in his own inimitable style, one hand on his hip, "Oh Mary. Where did you get it? I must have one just like it!"

M:

It was during one of our early engagements in Las Vegas we were then given one of the greatest opportunities of our lives, to star in Stanley Kramer's *5,000 Fingers of Dr. T*. Peter was approached between shows by a stranger who said how much he'd enjoyed our performance. Peter was anxious to get upstairs to rest and tried to make a hasty exit, but this persistent man held onto his arm. He growled a little and said, "You don't know me, do you?"

"No sir, I don't, and if you'll forgive me, I'm a little late joining my wife." Stanley smiled and said, "I'm Stanley Kramer." Peter kissed his hand. Stanley told Peter that he thought we would be ideal for his new picture, a musical fantasy written by Theodor Seuss Geisel, otherwise known as the beloved Dr. Seuss, *The 5,000 Fingers of Dr. T*. When Peter told me later, I jumped for joy. The deal was made. We were elated at the thought of starring in a film for Stanley Kramer.

P:

Moving back into our Valley Heart house in North Hollywood was fun. The movie was to be shot at Columbia. But the transition from clubs to films was not fun. We were used to staying up all night and getting together with friends after our show. This meant there would be hours of "pub crawling." Usually we would retire about 5 o'clock in the morning. In the movie industry, Mary would have to be under the hair dryer by 6:15—in the MORNING.

Dr. Fredrick Hollander and Dr. Seuss had written a beautiful musical score for *The 5,000 Fingers of Dr. T* and there were endless hours of rehearsal before pre-recording 15 songs in front of a 65-piece orchestra. When the show was originally recorded, even the seasoned orchestra musicians would stand up and applaud. That's how good it was. We felt we were involved in a work of art, so the three months of preparing and shooting the picture flew by.

Tommy Rettig, later famous as Lassie's little boy, was playing Bart Collins, and Hans Conreid portrayed the infamous Dr. Terwilleger.

Dr. Seuss was a brilliant and warm-hearted man.

"With your talent, you must be a riot with your children," I commented.

"Oh, Peter," he replied, "I don't have any children. My motto is, you make them, and I'll amuse them."

Joe Frisco visited us on the set. When I told him the title of the picture, he was stunned. *"The Fi-fi-five T-t-Thousand Fingers of Doctor T-t-T.?* They'll never g-g-get th-th-that on a marquee. Why d-d-don't they c-c-call it *T-t-tom Th-th-thumb?"*

M:

Actually, the *5,000 Fingers* referred to one of the most elaborate sets I have ever seen in Hollywood. It was a triple-decker piano built on two complete sound stages. On the opening day of Dr. T's Institute, 500 little boys were assembled to play chopsticks on his fabulous piano. Of course, the mothers came with the 500 tykes. I was convinced it was the outbreak of World War III. Busloads of little boys, each with a five-finger beanie on his head. (People bid big bucks for those beanies on the Internet these days.)

In the film, nine-year-old Bart Collins is forced to practice the piano by his loving but misguided widowed mother (yours truly). His tyrannical teacher, Dr. Terwilleger, instructs him in the Happy Finger Method. ("The Happy Finger Method must go on!") The boy falls asleep and into a nightmarish fantasyland where he is imprisoned in Dr. T's mysterious castle. Peter played Mr. Zabladowski, the friendly plumber who also becomes trapped in Dr. T's dungeon and eventually saves the day.

The incredible sets were by the brilliant Rudolph Sternad. Choreography was by Eugene Loring, who sometimes worked with the legendary Fred Astaire. His work for *5,000 Fingers* was nominated for an Oscar. Dr. Seuss was on the set often and Peter and I admired him greatly. Ironically, he was a very quiet and reserved man.

Peter and I were disappointed when several key scenes were cut in the film's final version. For instance, in the fantasy, I am hypnotized by the evil Dr. T to do his will. That whole scene was cut. Without it, my later strange behavior must have been somewhat of a mystery to the audience.

Some excellent songs were cut too. Their lyrics were

pure Dr. Seuss and would have given the world a further glimpse into his philosophy. I particularly loved the one I sang to my little son, "Many Questions have No Answers." They also cut three of Peter's songs. One was called "Grindstone." (*When you're born into this universe, you're born without clothes. The only thing that you are born with is a grindstone for your nose.*") Another was called simply "Money." (*More people marry dollar bills than people marry people.*") Another advised, *"If you really want to worry, pick a worry worth your while, like a freckle on a pygmy on an undiscovered isle!"* They also cut our beautiful love song, "You Opened My Eyes."

There was a big press opening at the Criterion Theater in New York and there were supposed to be openings all over the country, but Stanley Kramer and the belligerent boss of Columbia, Harry Cohn, got into a fight and the studio canceled the movie's promotion budget.

Stanley was preoccupied with producing two more landmark films at the same time, Marlon Brando in *The Wild One* and *The Caine Mutiny* with Bogart as Captain Queeg. I can't help thinking if he'd been more involved with *5,000 Fingers,* the final result would have been even better than it was. After the brilliant *Caine Mutiny,* Stanley's Columbia contract was canceled.

5,000 Fingers has long been a cult favorite in Europe. It plays several times a year in Paris and is now gaining an enthusiastic following in American cities too. It was finally released in video and you can catch it on the Disney channel and Turner Classic Movies. There is also a copy of it in the Museum of Modern Art in New York.

Although, like everyone who was involved with the movie, we have regrets when we think of what might have been, Peter and I are still very proud to have been a part of such a creative venture.

Peter, Mary, and Timmy Rettig in *5,000 Fingers*

Mary Healy in a Jean Louis gown in *5,000 Fingers*

Mary Healy with Michael and Cathy Hayes in their *5,000 Fingers* beanies

When *5,000 Fingers* was completed, we were homeward bound, back to New York and the Mt. Tom house in New Rochelle. Cathy and Michael were in school and we didn't want them to be on the road anymore. We settled down to a more normal family life.

It was in our Tudor house that we were interviewed on *Person to Person* by Edward R. Murrow. It was an honor to be interviewed for this show, but it was also an ordeal. Camera crews took over the whole house days in advance, with clumsy cables and equipment all around. We treasure this film or course, particularly the footage of our children. Our little daughter Cathy sang her own version of the popular TV theme song "Davy Crockett." She sang, *"Daisy, Daisy Crockett!"* It was an early sign of her later passion for performing and promoting equal rights for women!

P:

A few months after we were in residence, Stanley Kramer came to New York. He called and said he would arrange a preview of one of his latest films at a local theater if we would assemble a group of our peers for the viewing. For such a special occasion, we spent hours casting the dinner party. Our parties and the ones we attended had pretty much the same group—Walter and Jean Kerr, Abe and Karen Burrows, Frank and Lynn Loesser, Alfred and Jean Vanderbilt, Mike and Jan Cowles, John Crosby (a columnist for the *Herald Tribune*), Rex Harrison and Lili Palmer (then married) and, of course, Stanley and Ann Kramer.

The dinner party was a huge success and everyone was excited about the preview. Stanley would not divulge the title of the movie, which added to the anticipation. Mary and I rode with Rex and Lili. New Rochelle was not accustomed to seeing a Jaguar pull up in front of RKO Proctor's theater. It was also not accustomed to seeing a tall Englishman, replete with bowler hat and a Chesterfield coat with an astrakhan collar, strut through the lobby. The movie Stanley had provided was *Member of the Wedding* with a memorable performance by Ethel Waters.

As we re-entered the Jaguar after the movie, Rex was in such a state of ecstasy about Miss Waters' performance that he was still ranting and raving as he raced his Jaguar up to a brilliantly green traffic light and jammed on the brakes. As soon as the light turned red, he sped back to our house! Soon everyone was gathered again and complimenting Stanley on his extraordinary movie.

It was then that Rex and John Crosby decided to drink in earnest. The next morning Rex was scheduled to begin directing and starring in *The Love of Four Colonels*. The "colonel" had developed four eyes by now, and Lilli was determined to get him on the road. John Crosby had been our houseguest many times, so we decided that Crosby would lead them back to the city. That was a mistake. The trip from Mt. Tom Road to New York City usually takes less than a half-hour. They left our house at two in the morning. At 4:00 A.M. they called us from the outskirts of Albany and at 5:00 A.M. they called from a gas station somewhere in Connecticut.

Finally, as the sun was rising and silhouetting the entire panorama of New York's skyline, they approached a tollbooth on the Triborough Bridge. As the astonished attendant stretched out his hand for the quarter, Harrison fixed him with that quizzical Henry Higgins stare and said, "We're seeking Manhattan!"

M:

I always loved the theater more than anything. Peter used to call me the Divine Miss Sarah—Bernhardt. We were always looking for a Broadway show we could do together.

Who Was That Lady I Saw You With opened at the Martin Beck Theater on Broadway on March 3, 1958. It was written by Norman Krasna, directed by Alex Segal and produced by the famed agent/producer Leland Hayward.

Peter played a shy Columbia chemistry professor and I was cast as his long-suffering wife. When I caught him kissing a foreign exchange student, his television writer friend concocted the elaborate excuse that he was an undercover FBI agent and the coed an enemy spy. The buddy was played by Ray Walston, who later became famous as TV's *My Favorite Martian*. Larry Storch, of *F Troop* fame, was a befuddled foreign agent. Roland Winters, who was one of the Charlie Chans in the movies, played the real FBI man admirably.

The play was a farce, heavy on the slapstick and mix-ups. The elaborate sets—including an elevator rising in the Empire State Building and a sub-basement power room with whirling machinery and gushing steam—were by talented Rouben Ter-Arutunian. The reviews were excellent, especially the one in *The New York Times*.

Al Hirschfeld, whose witty drawings of Broadway shows graced the *New York Times* for decades, did a wonderful pen-and-ink rendition of Ray Walston, Peter and me in our play *Who Was That Lady?* We still have it and love it. And Walter Kerr's review in *The Herald Tribune:*

> In a breakneck two minutes toward the end of "Who Was

That Lady I Saw You With?," Peter Lind Hayes murmurs as he uncrosses his eyes, "I'm in a submarine" . . . I think he's in a hit. Wife Mary Healy, delectable creature that she is, is steadfastly at his side, doing all the damage she can. . . . It is a comic fantasia I shall long cherish, worthy of the best of Buster Keaton, and we are all in the debt of author Norman Krasna for thinking of it.

The New York Journal-American's John McClain wrote:

Let it be admitted at the outset that I am a hopeless addict of Peter Lind Hayes and Mary Healy. I know Peter to be a monstrously funny and engaging fellow and I have been secretly in love with Mary Healy for many years. They could make me laugh and cry merely by reading the Social Register, so it is no wonder I had a fine time at the Martin Beck last night where they opened in *Who Was That Lady I Saw You With?*—a new comedy by Norman Krasna. And no condescension is implied, for the Social Register is a pretty funny book, but this new production which has happily returned Leland Hayward to Broadway as impresario is brilliantly tailored to their talents. In itself it is no masterpiece, but the mounting and the style are superb, and it should keep these kids occupied for many a moon.

The show was a hit and it might have indeed run for a long time, but fate intervened. Our contract with CBS and Arthur Godfrey was concluded at that time and we were signed for another national TV series by ABC.

P:

Norman Rockwell was commissioned by ABC to "do me" for newspaper ads while we were gainfully employed on their television network. ABC also made the mistake of presenting the original drawing to me as a gift.

My dutiful and beautiful wife grew tired of my boasting about the drawing, so I decided to even the score. I secretly sent off a half dozen pictures of Mary to Mr. Rockwell with a tear-stained letter begging him to do her portrait for our 25th anniversary.

Alas! He wrote back that he was so busy, he couldn't possibly do Mary for another two years.

Our anniversary falls on the 19th of December. We were living in North Hollywood at the time and on the 18th a large crate showed up. Sure enough, Mr. Rockwell had done a very beautiful drawing of Mary Healy.

Along with the drawing, he enclosed a handwritten letter. And I quote:

> Dear Mr. Hayes, I know I told you that I couldn't get to this picture for another two years, but after studying your wife's photographs, I decided to do it immediately. She has an inner glow and a radiance that I found irresistible. I hope she likes the drawing. P.S. May I remind you, I'm 72 years old. N. R.

Sixteen
"Many Questions Have No Answers"

**Many questions have no answers, I can't tell you why,
Now please, now please, don't keep asking why**

—*Music by Frederic Hollander,
Lyrics by Theodor Seuss Geisel (Dr. Seuss)*

M:

During the years we were under contract to CBS to replace Arthur Godfrey, we barred ourselves from doing anything but nightclubs and special appearances.

We were guesting regularly on other television shows during those years— the Danny Thomas show, the Perry Como Show. We were on a salute to Cole Porter in 1956, *You're the Top,* appearing with Cole, Bing Crosby, Louis Armstrong and our good friends Gordon and Sheila MacCrea. We also appeared on Revlon's *The Big Party,* which was hosted by Greer Garson and also featured the brilliant Mike Nichols and Elaine May and our frequent nightclub co-star, John Bubbles.

We made the rounds of early TV game shows like *Masquerade Party, To Tell the Truth,* and *Play Your*

Hunch. We also appeared in quality programs like *Studio One, Armstrong Circle Theater, Goodyear TV Playhouse, Lux Video Theater* and later, *Alcoa Theater.*

Peter starred in two *Alfred Hitchcock* episodes. In one, the wife he murdered was Lillian Gish. Peter's episode of *The Outer Limits,* "Behold Eck!" has become a cult favorite with science fiction fans. We starred in *Miracle on 34th Street* with Peter playing the John Payne role, I the Maureen O'Hara one and Ed Wynn as a wonderful Santa Claus. Technologically, TV was primitive compared to today, but I think the writing and acting were outstanding.

At some time during that busy period, I began to have strange feelings I didn't have time to share with Peter. It seemed in some curious way, I felt overwhelmed by the enormity of the audience and it was making me frightened. It drained my energy.

I went to a tennis party at the home of Nancy and Billy Talbot (the famous tennis player). It was immensely enjoyable, but suddenly I turned to Peter and said, "I've got to get out of here. I feel as if all my nerve endings have gone on tilt." I was completely baffled by it, but my overstrained nervous system was trying to tell me something, and it sure did. Slow down!

With the help of my doctor and a week or so in the hospital, I slowly recovered, but I really had experienced some kind of shock. Perhaps I should have sought professional help in addition to my family doctor, but with his help, medication, my favorite books, *Laotse, The Power of Positive Thinking, Teilhard de Chardin, Daily Word, Bridges* and my regular prayers, I gradually recovered enough to go back to work. I really needed therapy, but with these self-help books I came around and continued on with my heavy schedule.

Later on, I had another kind of problem.

"Want to hear about my operation?"

Dr. William Cahan was the young company physician for Moss Hart's play *Winged Victory* during the war. He went on to become a leading breast and chest surgeon. It was during *Winged Victory,* I had Dr. Cahan check my frequently painful breasts. In fact, I referred to myself as Miss Lumpy Breasts because I always had premenstrual swelling and pain. I started having regular exams and Dr. Cahan did drawings of the lumps he thought might cause trouble.

Breast cancer was occurring back then, of course, but you rarely heard about it. Dr. Cahan was a good friend and also in the early stages of his brilliant career at Sloan-Kettering Memorial Cancer Center. He was particularly concerned about a lump he had found in the summer of 1960. There was a black and blue mark over it and I thought I had injured myself playing golf. The bruise, however, did not go away.

In the summer of 1960, Dr. Cahan found a small cyst and promptly put me into the hospital for a biopsy. They gave me an anesthetic and as we were rolling down the hospital hallway to the operating room, the last thing I remember saying to both Peter and Dr. Cahan, was, "I love you and I love God." I was ready to meet my maker.

When I awoke after the surgery was over, my breast had been removed. I was glad it was over for I often think fear is so much worse than the actual event, but how lucky I was to know a doctor who was one of the country's most respected cancer specialists.

P:

Mary's surgery was devastating to everybody. I commuted daily from New Rochelle to the Sloan-Kettering Memorial Hospital and became more emotionally unstable after each visit. After the operation, little "Baby" Healy awoke to find her blubbering husband sobbing all over her bedside. She opened those big brown eyes and whispered, "Stiff upper lip, old boy!" I told you she was exceptional.

M:

Dr. Cahan thinks that medical traumas are often harder on the loved ones than the patient and in a way that is true. It seems strange, but somehow the operation was almost a spiritual experience for me. When I came out of it, I felt as if I were on a higher plane. Was it Demerol?

I believe my strong faith helped me through this ordeal. I also had support from my family and friends. I was hoping my operation would not be in the press, but Dorothy Kilgallen had written, "Mary Healy's friends are saying Ave's" so the word was out.

The first phone call I got in the hospital was from our friend Perry Como. We had been doing some television with him and were scheduled to do his TV show soon. I also received a very amusing letter from Arthur Godfrey, which I still have, and many, many well-wishing cards and letters. Of course, Arthur had his own bout with cancer and even talked about it on the air, a very courageous move in those days when people didn't mention such personal events. His letter, written in his gruff, honest and humorous style, carried the messages "Join the club Mary," and then, "After all, you really only need one!"

My physical recovery was rapid, but I didn't realize I was having emotional problems. It seems I am always the last to know. I was physically and psychologically shook up. Breast surgery affects a lot of women in many different ways. It can be such a blow to the ego. I remember Dr. Cahan called me, "You're doing so beautifully with your recovery. You might call Judy Holiday and try to give her a little moral support." Tragically, my old friend Judy didn't have the operation, at least not to my knowledge, and she died.

As Dr. Cahan wrote in his book, I truly was the first celebrity to "go public" about my breast cancer. I frequently worked for the American Cancer Society and have done television shows and ads trying to get the message across. In those days we didn't have mammograms, which are so important. Early detection is still the key, now more than ever.

Peter and I were also very close to a family that lived near us at that time. Dr. Irving S. Cooper was a brilliant neurosurgeon. Dr. Cahan agreed to let him stand by during my procedure. The two doctors became fast friends and later worked together on some of "Coop's" cryosurgery procedures, as Dr. Cahan later wrote in his book, *No Stranger to Tears.*

At the house on Mt. Tom one evening during the Christmas holidays, Dr. Cooper was opening a bottle of wine when Peter handed him a wine bottle opener, a gift we had just received from Hammacher Schlemmer. Cooper was always curious and he looked over the gadget with real interest. It had a needle-like extension on one end that was connected to a cartridge. Once it was pushed through the wine cork, compressed air from the cartridge forced the cork out. Cooper became fascinated by the thing.

He had been working on a new procedure for alleviation of the symptoms of crippling Parkinsonism and Dystonia and was looking for a way to treat them by inserting a tiny cannula into the brain. This could stop the tremors by destroying the diseased nerve cells without leaving any solid residue. He fashioned a hollow needle-like instrument through which he could inject frozen liquid nitrogen (196 degrees centigrade) to deaden the tremor center. This was early cryosurgery, later used by Dr. Cahan to successfully treat certain types of cancer. Dr. Cooper's important pioneering work on the alleviation of Parkinson's Disease has had worldwide success. Ironically, he was a non-smoker who died at an early age of lung cancer.

P:

Dr. Cahan advised us that the best therapy for Mary would be to get her back to work. Nineteen days after the operation, we did the *Perry Como Show* on national TV. Twenty-two days later we flew with the children to California to start a new TV series called *Peter Loves Mary*. We filmed the series on a non-air-conditioned stage at the old Republic studio. Even with her traumatic experience, the little lady from the Irish Channel was game.

M:

Looking at the kinescope of the *Perry Como Show*, where I did an impression of our friend Lena Horne, you

Peter loves Mary

can even see a bit of the bandage showing under my Don Loper evening gown. But we settled into the routine of our new series.

When we were doing *Peter Loves Mary,* I remember very fondly a handsome young actor named Steve McQueen, who was shooting his cowboy series *Wanted: Dead or Alive* on the stage set next to ours. His public image was very macho and reserved, but I remember how much he loved comedy. He had wonderful ways of expressing that side of his personality—like riding his motorcycle right through our living room set in the middle of a scene! We often had lunch together and he and Peter had a great time, sharing jokes, pranks and stories.

Steve would very soon become a superstar, largely thanks to the movie *The Magnificent Seven,* which also starred our great old friend Yul Brynner.

It was during this time we also became friendly with a young television comedian named Johnny Carson, who would soon become a legendary host of the *Tonight Show.* By the way, when Jack Paar left, before Johnny could start as host of the show, Peter and I were substitute hosts. So Joan Rivers was not really the first woman to host a nighttime talk show—I was! Can we talk, Joan? (For the record, Peter and I made our last national television appearance on Johnny Carson's show in 1977.)

P:

Lucy and Desi were still our close friends during this period too. Socially, we were still very much together. Many nights Desi, Bill Orr, Gordon MacRae, Edmund O'Brien, Dean Martin and our wives would journey to each other's homes to cook dinner and play poker.

But after the tremendous success of *I Love Lucy,* it seems business and pleasure were not mixing too well for Lucy and Desi. They had built a magnificent mansion in Beverly Hills. Desi built his own hideout directly in back of the main house. Mary and I were invited to dinner one evening. I think it was Lucille's ploy was for us to try and patch things up.

When the four of us sat down to dine, one word led to another and before one could say "Babaloo," Desi reared up from the table and, cursing in Spanish, threw his napkin across the table at Lucy. Desi then proceeded to storm out of the dining room. Lucy gave me the nod and I dutifully followed the bongo player to his nest. For over an hour we talked seriously, but Desi was adamant. He was determined to leave Lucy. I returned to the main house with the news and Lucy seemed disconsolate. There was nothing left to say, so Mary and I prepared to leave.

We whispered good night and as I was going out of the front door, I pursed my lips and made the sound of a horse neighing. Lucy grabbed me by the lapels and shouted, "Wait a minute chum. How the hell did you do that?"

We returned to the living room and presently Mary fell asleep on the couch. I spent three hours trying to teach Lucy how to sound like a horse. She used the bit many times later and I never regretted my instructions. She was a great dame and a comedic genius.

M:

Peter Loves Mary was successful at first. Unfortunately our top writers were eventually lured away to the *Dick Van Dyke Show,* which got off to its own shaky start at about the same time. Like our show, it was set in New Rochelle. *Peter Loves Mary* was canceled in 1961. I was actually greatly relieved because it meant I was able to take a break, finally!

I took a sabbatical, as they say, but Peter continued to work. I flew to London and met with my former roomie, Dorris, and her husband, Nunnally Johnson who lived abroad at that time. She and I took the Caravelle to the south of France and did a lot of resting on the Cote d'Azur. Peter and the children soon joined us in London and our little family flew to Ireland for a brief holiday, then back to New York where our pace was soon more hectic than ever.

After having traveled so much during our lives, we were so happy that at least we were able to stay put for a while doing a six-year run with a national WOR Radio show. We did five days a week with our friend and producer, Fran Hair. We even broadcast the show from our own home. When the show first started, the technician came to our house to get us on the air. But our guests had to go through our dining room and kitchen and then down into the washroom to get to our "studio."

While explaining this predicament to friends, I leaned on a wall to say, "If we only could have our guests come in the front door, then we could usher them down to our basement." It occurred to me right then to knock the wall out (with help) and let people go down to the basement directly from the entrance hall.

With a bit of doing, we set up a round poker table in the cellar and before long we were on the air five mornings a week, 9:15 to 10:00 A.M. Between covering countless Broadway show openings and with book publishers sending us all the current books—usually along with their authors—we had more than enough to discuss in our 45 minutes.

I took on a lot of the book reviews, while Peter covered many openings without me. Peter later said I must have had an inside track because whenever I decided to attend the openings with him instead of reading the book for the next day, the show often became a "hit."

We were there for some memorable theatrical events. If a show was not a hit, and the morning notices were in agreement, Peter did his critique, and I would mention the costumes and scenery that I liked and some of the celebrities that attended the opening.

The highly regarded theater critic Walter Kerr and his talented wife, Jean, became our dearest friends. They frequently joined us at Sardi's before plays. As the final curtain descended, Walter had to rush to the *Times* building so that his review would be in time for the morning edition of the *New York Times*.

It's sort of an unwritten law that critics not discuss the play with each other. NBC's Edwin Newman rushed to do his report at NBC's studio nearby, so that his was the first review to be heard on TV.

One night we took our daughter Cathy to Liza Minnelli's first Broadway opening, *Flora the Red Menace*. Liza was great, but we didn't think the show was going to make it. After the play, it was pouring rain and our driver and friend, Don Vecchio, picked us up in front of the theater. Edwin was walking to NBC, so we offered him a ride. Peter had lectured Cathy, who was very young, "Now, Cathy, when he gets in the car, you're not supposed to say anything about the show." Cathy didn't say a word on the whole drive to NBC. When Edwin was leaving he said, "Nice to meet you Cathy." And she answered, "I don't care what you say. I think it was a great show." That's what comes from life around show biz!

Oprah Winfrey was just a baby when we were doing regular book reviews on our national talk show on radio. It seems everybody who had written a book during those years wanted to be on and sometimes those interviews were hard work. Often authors were uncomfortable talking. It was live radio, yet they would just sit there and nod and say "Uh-huh!"

I tried to give myself a bit of therapy by interviewing medical and psychology authors of the day, whom I found fascinating. I honestly tried to become a conduit to our listeners for anything I found enlightening. There were so many books arriving daily that to keep up the pace, I had to take a Speed Reading class.

I remember when William F. Buckley arrived one morning (he was driving an English taxi, with his typewriter next to him). He was so articulate and erudite during the interview that Peter went looking for the dictionary as soon as he departed.

Peter always lightened the show with his humor. He had bought a Mynah bird, which we kept in the laundry room. The bird's name was "Humphrey" and his entire repertoire consisted of saying, "Hello Sam."

There was a morning when one of our steady guests (Sam Levinson) came down our steps into the studio and Peter said, "Sam, I want you to meet a new member of the show. . . ." Peter put Humphrey on the microphone he controlled so the bird could be turned on or off. At that moment, the Mynah said "Hello Sam." We laughed and laughed when Sam said, "Peter, you're a ventriloquist!"

Peter's technical ideas were also invaluable. He invented new technologies as we went along, like a "tele-fun call" where we talked for five minutes or so with stars right in their dressing rooms—Rex Harrison, Elizabeth Taylor, and so on—the minute they walked off the stage.

Guests at our parties at the Mt. Tom house were predominantly talented songwriters, including our old and dear friends Johnny Mercer, Jule Styne and Frank Loesser, who all wrote so many big hit songs. Frank gave us one of his biggest hit songs to do before anyone else when we played the Mayfair Room at the Blackstone Hotel in Chicago, "Baby It's Cold Outside." It was such a showstopper that the audience insisted we "do it again." That song went on to win an Academy Award.

At another party, Noel Coward sang with Robert Allen at the grand piano feeding him the lyrics as he played every song Noel had written. Noel kept saying, "My dear boy, you're mah-velous," much to the enjoyment of Celeste Holm and Bennett and Phyllis Cerf.

When we were on the radio daily talking to millions of people, appearing in nightclubs and on television, I began to feel very stressed again! It was at this point that our dear friends, Willie and Marge Kasso, two talented artists, encouraged me to take painting lessons for a bit of therapy. I soon found the lessons very helpful and fell in love with art, especially modern art.

Other friends, Jan and Mike Cowles (the publisher of *Look* magazine), encouraged me go to the Museum of Modern Art for lectures and painting classes. That was the turning point of my recovery.

One afternoon I was in the Whitney Museum when I saw an abstract painting by the legendary William de Kooning. To my surprise, I suddenly burst into tears. I rarely, if ever, cry at sad stories. However, the tears will flow when I see people in marvelous acts of courage—like a fireman saving a child on TV. I can also be brought to tears by beautiful music or fine art.

The use of paint comes from the soul in a great artist and de Kooning was one of the greatest. It's difficult to put it into words, but de Kooning's painting put me on another plateau of understanding myself and life. I believe it helped me begin the process of healing psychologically. I never got the opportunity to tell him how his paintings helped me over a difficult time in my life.

For our 25th anniversary, Peter drove out to de Kooning's East Hampton studio in the Springs to buy one of his paintings. The artist said he knew of us because he had heard our radio and television work. Peter told him, "My wife is a great fan of yours. She loves your paintings. Frankly, I don't understand what you're doing."

De Kooning laughed, then walked around his studio, saying "no, no, no" in front of each of his paintings. Finally, he stopped and said, "This one. There's more of me in it and that's appropriate since it's for your anniversary."

When Peter brought it home, I cried out, "Peter what have you done?"

"Mary I didn't do it. Mr. De Kooning did it."

This wonderful painting will eventually have its home at The Metropolitan Museum of Art in New York. Seeing my de Kooning painting was an exceptionally moving experience for me, but the observations from relatives and close friends were various! The one that particularly brought Peter and me to hysterical laughter was from our friend Dr. Cooper who named it "The Flight of Red Pecker." Grace Hayes said she wouldn't have that terrible thing in her house.

This reminds me of another family story. It happened when we were doing our daily WOR radio program. We attended the New Rochelle Council for the Arts Show in Westchester and were invited to a party at the

Rockefeller mansion. Greeted by a gracious Happy Rockefeller upon entering the family compound, I was stunned by a portrait over the mantel, a beautiful Gainsborough. I said, "Wow!" She said, "If you like these paintings, you must see Nelson's hideout in the basement."

I almost immediately made my way to his "hideout!" Indeed, the walls were lined with the greatest modern artists of our time in his fabulous collection. You name them and they were there. I saw one exciting painting and thought, "Oh, that's a de Kooning."

Governor Rockefeller came along just then with three of his little children.

"I see you love art," he said.

"Yes," I answered and pointed to his three children. "Each one of those is a work of art too." He smiled and noticed I was admiring the painting I thought was by de Kooning.

"I believe in spontaneity," he said. "If you like it, it's yours." He took it off the wall and gave it to me. I was speechless. As Peter and I were leaving and saying good-bye he told the security guards, who seemed to be everywhere, to put the painting in our car. The guards were all looking at us with suspicion, taking a painting from the Rockefeller estate. The Governor saved the day and saw us to our car.

It turned out the painting was not in fact a de Kooning, but clearly influenced by his work. Writing on the back of the painting revealed that it was by a young boy at Syracuse University who had won $500, the first prize at a contest the Rockefellers sponsored for creative young people. Peter and I were overwhelmed.

When we arrived home, we showed it to our children. Michael and Cathy were sitting there smiling at the excitement of Mom and Dad. Michael peered at the painting through his glasses on the end of his nose and said, "I can just see Happy saying, 'Nelson, I thought we'd *never* get rid of that one!' " So much for modern art.

Back briefly to the Rockefellers, I'm not sure they are recognized for their many contributions to the City of New York and the world. Contributions to the Museum of Modern Art and Sloan Kettering Hospital—which helped save my life and that of many others.

While we were doing our radio show, Peter did a play, *Lovers,* by first-rate Irish playwright, Brian Friel, at the Music Box Theatre on Broadway. He took over for Art Carney. His reviews were all good and Walter Kerr wrote that Peter was "thunderingly funny." How he did the radio show and the play at the same time was a mystery to me.

James Mason starred in the last movie Peter made, *The Yin And Yang of Mr. Go,* a James Bond spoof written and directed by Burgess Meredith. James and his wife Pamela were good friends for many years and visited us often. He was an intelligent man with a delicious sense of humor and was always sketching away. One of our treasures is a pen and ink study of Peter.

P:

After six years with our radio talkfest, WOR wanted us to stay on, but they suggested that we do the show from their studio in New York at 3 P.M. I suggested that "even the owners of the station weren't listening at that hour of the day and we quit." I think the reason we lasted for six years was because nobody could figure out exactly where the program was coming from. It was great fun, and to quote John Crosby, "We had a million laughs."

By this time, our children had matured enough to start making plans to abandon the nest and run off to college. Oh God, that big Tudor house was empty with just the two of us wandering around aimlessly. We sold the Mt. Tom house to the Danish government for their United Nations representative.

It wasn't long after that when we began to divide our lives between New Rochelle and the desert oasis we call the "Land of Silk and Money"—Las Vegas.

Seventeen
"Moments to Remember"

The new year's eve we did the town
The day we tore the goal posts down

—Words by Al Stillman,
  Music by Bobby Allen

M:

It is astounding to see the changes that have been made in Las Vegas—pyramids, pirates and pleasure palaces! We remember when it was the Dust Capital of the World. They didn't name the Sands the Sands for nothing! There was empty desert sand all around for miles and miles and miles when we first saw it. And I DO mean empty.

Grace Hayes was a true Las Vegas pioneer. The fabulous Las Vegas Strip sprang up all around her. She saw Caesars Palace being raised from her back yard while she raised her vegetables and her dogs. For many years, she was the only resident actually living on the Strip.

Hazy told us Las Vegas would get into our blood and it did.

P:

My mother's last husband was a colorful little man by the name of Robert E. Hopkins. "Hoppy" had been a screenwriter at MGM for more than 20 years. It was his suggestion that MGM make the great movie *San Francisco* about the famous earthquake.

Hoppy had the "quicks." He spoke so fast, I always had to play him back at thirty-three-and-a-third to find out what the hell he was talking about. Mary and I used to call Hazy and Hoppy from back East every Sunday. My day was made after a conversation with the Mighty Hop. Here are a few exchanges:

"Hi Hoppy. Is it hot out there?"

"It's so hot, yesterday our butcher fainted in his ice box."

"Hoppy, I understand the water in Lake Mead is getting dangerously low."

"If it gets any lower, Mickey Rooney can walk to Arizona."

"Do you still have that nice rosy complexion, Hoppy?"

"Yep! Your mother slaps me a lot."

"I understand you've had another bad wind storm up there Hoppy."

"Yeah! The other day a guy got out of his car to change a tire and in three minutes he was a statue."

When the Red Rooster faded, they sold part of the land to Chevron for a gas station.

Hoppy said they took the gas off of Gracie's stomach and put in a pump!

Hazy would never admit that she and Hoppy were married for fear I would cut off the $500 a month I had been sending her. As you know by now, she was a crafty lady.

Mary and I decided to pay the odd couple a visit. We arrived in the "Land of Silk and Money" where things were not looking good for Hazy. I thought my mother was dying. Just in case, I sent for Father Ryan to give her the last rites. Hoppy was a 32nd degree Mason and kept hovering over Father Ryan during his inspection tour. Father beckoned for me to follow him.

"Are those two people married?"

"No, Father, I don't think so. I believe they are living in sin."

Hoppy was already in his late 70s, so it stunned me when the good Father whispered, "You know, lad, I could make them brother and sister."

I almost fell in the pool.

Mary and I decided the situation with Hazy was dire enough to buy a house on the 12th hole of the Sahara Golf course. The plan was to babysit my ailing mother seven months a year and spend five months back at our boathouse in New Rochelle. Las Vegas becomes an incinerator during the summer months, so we would leave the heat and return to the humidity.

But Hazy was soon out of the wheelchair and up and about, just in time. Hoppy turned 80 and was becoming very fragile. My mother became his nurse. Hoppy's condition worsened and, since my mother did not trust the doctors in Las Vegas at that time, she hired an ambulance and frantically followed it in her old Cadillac all the way to Los Angeles to his special doctor. I was in New York at the time. The telephone call was quick and to the point:

"Hoppy is dying. Come as fast as you can." I caught the next "red eye" to California and arrived just in time for the funeral. His old friend George Jessel gave the eulogy.

Mother and son left California in that old 1965 Cadillac. I was reminded of our frantic drive to the Golden State oh so many years before. We stopped in Barstow for a Mexican dinner. It was another sad Christmas Eve for Hazy and me. I spent a few days consoling her and then returned to New Rochelle.

Our son and daughter were away at school, so we decided to make our move to a little gray home in the West. Try as we might, we couldn't get our lifetime of collectibles into our new house. I preceded Mary to Las Vegas and had a wall knocked out to try to make things fit. When she arrived, the house was "fit as a fiddle" and I had a broken back to prove it.

We framed several charming and amusing hand-written cards and letters from our old friend Ronald Reagan written on White House stationery. Interestingly, one was signed Ronald, one Ron, one Ronnie and one "Dutch." We hung them in our "hall of fame"—the hallway of our little house in Las Vegas.

You see, we have a proud tradition of entertaining Presidents in this family. It started when Hazy performed for FDR.

We have a framed photo from Harry Truman, signed "To two grand entertainers." Doesn't that sound just like good old Harry? We became friendly with his daughter Margaret. She later filled in as host of our WOR morning radio show when we took a much-needed vacation.

When we performed for Truman, Mary was going to do her impression of the opera singer Helen Traubel. She had a padded dress she could slip into to look as if she weighed 250 pounds instantly. I was carrying the dress in a bag to Mary backstage when I was stopped by a terse secret service agent demanding to know what was in the bag. What could I tell him? Helen Traubel? To add insult to injury, I had to lay "Helen" down on the ground and spread her out to be searched for hidden weapons.

We also have an autographed photo of President Dwight D. Eisenhower from his inauguration party, where we performed. Tennessee Ernie Ford was on the bill with us. Tennessee Ernie, bless his little pea-pickin' heart, began to do off-color material and Eisenhower got up and walked out! Ike also came to see us at the Waldorf in New York, before he was elected President, just like that young senator from Massachusetts, John Kennedy.

Richard Nixon's secretary, Rosemary Woods, was a friend of our secretary Claudia Val. That's how we got his autographed photo and how we came to wish him a Happy Birthday on our national radio show. Of course that was before poor Nixon was "Watered Down."

The two big "N's" in history
Shared a very similar fate.
Napoleon met his Waterloo
And Nixon his Watergate.

We also have autographed photos of Gerald Ford, George Bush, Sr., and Jimmy Carter.

After we retired in Las Vegas, one of our great fun times was performing together at the opening of the city's first professional theater, the Meadows Playhouse. Peter and I starred in the lovely comedy *Harvey*. We studied as hard as we did for any Broadway opening and were just as proud of our rave reviews from the hometown press. A painting of Peter as Elwood P. Dowd with his friend Harvey the Rabbit still hangs in our Las Vegas home.

Another special joy was to perform in Tennessee Williams' *Glass Menagerie* with our talented daughter Cathy at that same playhouse. When I was young, I saw

Laurette Taylor perform in that sad and beautiful play. She was a great inspiration to me.

P:

When we made our move to Las Vegas in 1971, Hazy was 76 years old. But there was life in the old girl yet, partly thanks to her consumption of homegrown vegetables and garlic. She even had her own garlic press. She read somewhere that garlic would keep her blood pressure down. She consumed six to eight pods a day. That was OK unless you happened to be in her neighborhood!

She liked to ride shotgun in the front seat of my car. When I was due to pick her up for dinner, I always gave her a warning of an hour or so. I wanted her to start chomping on Sen Sens or Tic Tacs so I could tolerate the blue flame that came from her mouth. I never lit a cigarette when she was in the car for fear of blowing us up. I suspected my mother put garlic in ice cream and I once saw a loaf of her garlic bread walk off the table. But maybe it worked. What germ in its right mind would attack a pod of garlic?

She was strong, but time began to catch up with her.

After she suffered two strokes I decided to put her in a Las Vegas convalescent home. She objected to this move, but I felt I had no choice. We had tried nurses around the clock in her home on the Strip, but with her queenly demands, they constantly gave up after a week or 10 days.

I spent three of four days a week asking my mother to look on the brighter side. But there was no brighter side. When Hazy was well enough once again we made our annual trek back to the boathouse in New Rochelle. I dutifully called her every Saturday morning.

In the summer of 1987, I received a strange call at the boathouse.

"Peter, this is Steve Wynn calling from Las Vegas."

"Just a moment, Mr. Wynn, if this is a business call, do you mind if I tape it?"

"Go right ahead, Peter. Be my guest."

Naturally I had heard of Steve Wynn. This was the golden boy who was the proud owner of the Golden Nugget in Las Vegas and the entrepreneur who had just sold the Golden Nugget in Atlantic City to the Bally Corporation for $450 million.

"Yes, Mr. Wynn. How can I help you?"

"Peter, do you get along well with your mother?"

"Yes, I believe I do. What's this all about?"

"Well, I'm planning a new project on the Strip and I simply have to have her gas station. I'm even willing to throw in two or three hundred thousand for you and Mary if you can convince her to sell it to me."

After emitting a low whistle, I responded quite curtly that I resented his suggestion that I coerce my mother on his behalf. I said I would discuss it with her and get back to him when we returned to Las Vegas. Several weeks later we returned to the desert and the "wheeling and dealing" began.

A meeting was called at the Golden Nugget. We bundled my mother up, and with a walker, we descended upon Steve Wynn in his sumptuous stall in Glitter Gulch.

Mr. Wynn is a very bright young man and had thought of everything. At his own expense, he had hired Nevada's ex-governor Grant Sawyer, to represent Grace Hayes in the transaction. "How generous," I thought. Out came my tape machine.

"Do you mind?" I asked. Everyone agreed that it would be all right for me to tape the proceedings. One word led to another and presently one of Mr. Wynn's lawyers suggested that we go have a professional appraisal.

I bristled at this, but Governor Sawyer assured me that it was the proper thing to do. I reached over and turned the machine off.

"Peter, what are you doing?" asked our attorney.

"Well, Governor, there is really no sense in continuing this conversation. I have Mr. Wynn on tape making a substantial offer for my mother's property and also suggesting that he throw in an extra two or three hundred thousand for me and Mary!"

It was the Governor's turn to emit a low whistle. Mr. Wynn took the floor and admitted the offer had come from his own two lips. The next day he paid my mother more than $2 million for her home and gas station, not bad when you think that she had paid only $22,000 for the property in 1941 (including the $5,000 nest egg she borrowed from Mary and me). Now a volcano at entrance to the Mirage goes off on the hour nightly where Hazy's Red Rooster used to stand.

Oh! But wait! Mr. Wynn had more goodies for Hazy.

He moved her from the convalescent home into a $500-a-day suite at the Golden Nugget with round-the-clock nurses, a special hospital bed and also a pencil. The pencil meant that she could sign for anything the Nugget had to offer. She was asking people off the street to come in and have lunch with her. He also retrieved her favorite dog, BoBo, from the vet. She adored BoBo and BoBo adored her. The reunion was very touching. BoBo snuggled up to his mistress in that special hospital bed and, when Mr. Wynn approached the bed to take a bow, BoBo bit him. (Talk about biting the hand that feeds you!)

She loved staying at the Golden Nugget. I believe she has always felt that she was "born to the purple." Pretty high minded for a gal who never got out of grade school.

Life has a peculiar way of passing out its slings and arrows. Here was my mother living in the lap of luxury. She had found the end of the rainbow, but it lasted only three months. Hazy had a heart attack. They rushed her to the intensive care unit at Sunrise Hospital.

The doctor said it had been a "pretty good one." Ten days later, they decided Hazy had recovered enough to return to her suite at the Golden Nugget.

I mentioned "round-the-clock nurses." The girls were kind enough but were more like babysitters than nurses. One evening Hazy fell. She tore her rib cage and fractured her left hip.

We had to face the fact that the facilities at the Nugget were not a proper place for the tender loving care of a star of stage, screen and the National Broadcasting Company. I moved her back to the Las Vegas Convalescent Home. Steve Wynn had taken on the responsibility of her welfare, so he paid about $30,000 a year for her upkeep.

Hazy was 93 in 1988—still lucid but cranky. We visited her every other day. Twenty years before, Mary and I had flown to Nevada to bury my mother. But there I was, lecturing her on January 31, 1989 to get out of bed.

"Hazy, you have always been a fighter. You haven't been out of this bed for at least four weeks. Your body will atrophy. You simply must use your arms and legs." She studied me for a moment and whispered, "I have no desire to get out of this bed."

"My mother is dying," I told Mary.

The next day, a nurse called saying, "I have bad news for you. Your mother has no pulse."

Mary and I rushed to the home, but it was all over. I stared at my mother for quite some time. I had come into this world from that body 73 years before. I always predicted that her departure from this vale of tears would be with a bang. But she had left us without a whimper.

The nurse, touching my arm gently, said, "Mr. Hayes, I'm sure your mother died peacefully."

I mumbled a "Thank you" and then added, "Would you be kind enough to close her eyes?" Those famous blue eyes were now empty.

I was determined that Hazy's funeral would not be a mournful affair. Several years earlier we had jointly purchased three plots in Las Vegas. I remember at the time asking my mother where she would like to be placed.

She smiled. "In the middle, of course!"

"Oh no dear, you've been in the middle for over 40 years."

It was a bitter, cold Saturday, but there was warmth inside the chapel. About a hundred old friends showed up to pay their respects. My old World War II buddy Bill Willard, the local critic for *Variety,* read the eulogy and Father Ward from St. Jude's Ranch for Abused Children performed the service.

Bill Willard introduced me. I thanked everyone for coming and then played a tape of the record my mother had made for RCA Victor in 1928. At the sound of her lyrical voice singing the strains of "I Can't Give You Anything but Love Baby," smiles of recognition flooded the faces of the gathering.

I stopped the tape at the end of the first chorus and explained, "She gets a little too hot in the second half for this occasion." I felt in my heart this is precisely the way

Hazy would have wanted it. Once again she was center stage. Theatrical? Yes, but after all, we are a theatrical family.

Even after Hazy was gone, we kept up our tradition of splitting our time between Las Vegas and New Rochelle for years. We packed our clothes in sheets—an old vaudeville trick—loaded up the car and had it driven to our boathouse in New Rochelle. It was a lot of trouble, but we loved sitting on the porch overlooking the water from our boathouse. It was an endless shuttle between East and West.

We have roots and many good friends in both places. We indeed have been blessed. Our boathouse in New Rochelle was only five minutes from Foy Park, which used to house the Seven Little Foys. It was near Long Island Sound, the Glen Island Casino and near the Mt. Tom house where we lived for 30 years and raised our children.

We also had some great adventures living in Las Vegas.

M:

Like the ones we had with Francis Albert Sinatra. He has always been the Chairman of the Board in Las Vegas, dating back to the days when he and his clan used to take over the Sands Hotel.

In our hallway there hangs a framed photo of Frank taken so long ago he signed it "Love, Frankie." He gave it to us when he appeared on one of our early TV shows in the early 1950s. "To Lovely Mary and Wonderful Peter," he wrote. "How much talent can one li'l ole family have?"

One very special memory was the birthday party of a

Frank Sinatra with Mary and Peter

lifetime that Ol' Blue Eyes threw for me and two of my dear friends. Peter named us the "Aries Fairies" because we shared the same birth date, April 14. My two co-celebrants were Phyllis Cerf Wagner and Jan Cowles. Before she married Bennett, Phyllis had been very involved in many activities during her marriage to New York's mayor—the late Robert F. Wagner, and Jan was the wife of *Look* publisher, Gardner Cowles.

We would take turns hosting the birthday celebration. When Peter and I were hosts, we would invite them to our home in New Rochelle. Nothing elaborate, mind you, just a simple meal and a smattering of funny gifts. The parties each year became bigger and better. The Cowles had us down to their home in Florida for Jan's celebration, with a fabulous boat trip on a memorable moonlit night.

Next it was Phyllis' turn. In addition to things like TV shows and publishing, she and Bennett were well known for their fabulous parties.

Then Frank Sinatra decided we should all rendezvous at his "digs" in Palm Springs. Upon arrival we were put up in what Frank called his Christmas Tree Cottages. He was a very sentimental individual and every night an enormous pine tree was lit up to cast a cheerful glow on his compound. Our thoughtful and gracious host had our suites ready, complete with all the comforts—wood-burning fireplace, remote-control television, two baths and a sauna. And if that wasn't enough, there was a copy of the *New York Times* and the *Los Angeles Times* waiting at our doorstep each morning.

It was announced that the uniform of the day was black tie and that we were going to Frank's favorite Mexican restaurant. Really!

One must never underestimate the largesse and

imagination of Francis Albert. He was not only a super talent, but a fine gent. After the cocktail hour, we were all bundled into big black limousines and rushed off to the Palm Springs Airport where a United Airlines 727 was warming up. There were many multi-colored balloons hanging from the stern of the jet and an accordion player and his group were pumping out "Happy Birthday."

"I'm not getting into that thing if it needs all those balloons to get it airborne!" Peter whispered.

About 45 minutes later we landed in Las Vegas. We boarded a bus and before you knew it, we were being ushered into Caesars Palace with yet another birthday band. Caesars was well prepared for the arrival of its biggest star. The Mexican restaurant turned out to be the Bacchanal Room, a gourmet bistro named after the original one in Rome, where Nero used to dine on Christians I suppose.

The room had been closed off to all but Frank and his guests: Pamela and Leland Hayward (Pamela was our Ambassador to France and the daughter-in-law of Winston Churchill), Freddie Brisson and his wife, Rosalind Russell, publisher Gardner Cowles and his wife Jan, Bennett and Phyllis Cerf, Mr. and Mrs. Jimmy Van Heusen, Mr. and Mrs. Danny Schwartz and Peter and Mary.

The three birthday girls were seated together at the center of a long table. Each of us had a sterling napkin ring with our name engraved thereon. The girls, however, had something else. There were three Gucci bags alongside three little chamois satchels.

Peter said, "What's in the bag, Mary?"

I looked inside. There were five $100 chips.

"Gimme those," Peter hissed. "I'll cash them in."

"Not on your life, Peter. This is my night to gamble!"

After dinner we adjourned to the casino, each to his or her favorite game of chance. The men mostly shot craps and Peter decided to pursue me and my $500—with no luck. And speaking of luck, what a female Aries doesn't know about gambling would fill a metropolitan phone book. It wasn't long before the three birthday girls had lost their chips. We were pouting a little, so Frank led us to the Baccarat table.

"None of you broads really knows how to gamble. Mary, if you were my lady I wouldn't know whether to give you diamonds or dolls. Now watch this." He made some very quick moves with his hand and shouted "Banko!" Each of the girls won approximately $3,000. Apparently that was the signal to "quit while you're ahead." We all reboarded the bus and headed back to the 727. We sang and giggled all the way back to Palm Springs. It was close to 6 A.M. when we arrived at the commune.

Time for breakfast. Guess who went directly to the kitchen? Yep. Francis himself. What a host. Twenty minutes later we all sat down to a marvelous breakfast. The Academy Awards ceremony was held that weekend and the friends of Sinatra who were attending came to help us celebrate the birthday—Gregory Peck and his wife, James and Gloria Stewart, Ginger Rogers and many more.

We don't celebrate the Aries birthdays anymore. Who could top Ol' Blue Eyes?

Peter and I were also invited to Frank and Barbara's wedding ceremony at the Walter Annenberg mansion in Palm Springs along with some of their close friends and family. Tina and Nancy were standing next to him. When the Justice, during the ceremony, was saying "in sickness and in health, for richer or for poorer." Frank said with exquisite timing, "Richer is better."

Barbara and Frank invited us to spend their honeymoon weekend with them and a few friends at their nearby mountain retreat. There was a helicopter flying over with newsmen taking pictures, or trying to, while their guests were playing tennis, swimming and having a fine time!

Naturally Frank's good friends, Nancy and Governor Reagan, were there too. We greeted each other warmly when Peter challenged him.

"Governor, I'm going to take you back some 30 years." Peter and I started to sing the old vaudeville routine we had taught to Dutch and Jane Wyman:

We just got back from Frisco town.
We just got back today.
In fact, we wrote this little song
while speeding on our way.

That was as far as we got. Governor Reagan picked up the tune and did his part as well as ours right through to the big finish!

Peter: I write the words to all the songs.
Ronnie: I write the melody.
Together: If not our personalities
    We're sure our jokes will please.
    Nevertheless we'll try our best
    And hope you like ours as well as the rest
    For we're a pair of entertaining boys.
    We just came out to make a lot of noise.
    George M. Cohan in his singing ways
    Can never be compared to Peter Hayes
        they say.

Ronnie: We are full of many funny jokes.
We know they're funny 'cause we told them to our folks!

Peter: Who was that lady I saw you with last night?
Ronnie: That was no lady—that was my wife!

I love remembering the many happy times Peter and I shared with each other and with our children. We have had a wonderful life, as they say, and we'd do it all over again in a minute.

It's made us happy that our daughter shares our love of the theater. Cathy is a working actress living in Beverly Hills. She got her first professional job with the director James Burrows, Abe's son, where she earned her Screen Actors Guild card. She had a role in *Chicken Soup,* a TV sitcom starring Jackie Mason and Lynn Redgrave, and has become a respected character actress in television and films.

Cathy also won the Ovation Award in 2001 in Los Angeles for her role in the stage production of *He Hunts* at the Geffen Playhouse. Our son Michael inherited his father's sense of humor and his love of electronics. Today he is a TV engineer in Springfield, Massachusetts, happily married and living with his wife Susan and her daughter, Dana. Both Cathy and Michael have made us very proud.

It's funny but the older I get the clearer the memories of my childhood seem. My journey has been a long one and it has taken me far and wide, but it has led me back to what was most important to that "little girl" in New Orleans, my family. Most of that family is gone now, mother, aunts and uncles, brothers and sister. One of the reasons I like to go to church is to visit with them spiritually.

P:

One morning I looked in the mirror and saw an old man staring back at me. I moved furtively, but he kept following me around. After all, I was retired and semi-retarded! (Remember, old actors never die, they simply lose their parts.)

My marriage to Baby Healy lasted more than half a century and it was sheer heaven. In my darkest moments, she reassured me that all was well. Her loyalty after countless years was beyond reproach. She sustained me when all about me was chaos. Time after time, she cheered me and encouraged me to face the new day with tenacity and courage. I shudder to think what life would have been without her. Every hour of every day of every month of every year, she was my staunchest supporter. Without the smile on her face, life would indeed have been a matter of gloom and doom. I wrote her this sweet little poem:

How do I love thee?
Let me count the ways.
Promise you'll stay with me
For the rest of my days.
These promises are selfish, I know.
But will you keep them, will you?
Because, if you should die before I do,
I swear to Gawd I'll kill you!

—*Henry Wadsworth Shortfellow*

Our life has been full of pitfalls and pratfalls, but mostly filled with humor and a zest for living. If you stayed with us this far, we hope you enjoyed the ride....

Peter and Mary in their "golden years"

As they say in the parlance of show biz:
"Hey! Mr. Electrician. Kill the spotlight, bring down the curtain and let's get the hell out of here!"
APPLAUSE! APPLAUSE! APPLAUSE!

M:

**The laughter we were glad to share
Will echo through the years.**